The Unmaking of a Nun

Rachel Ethier Rosenbaum

DEDICATION

To my teachers and superiors and to all my sisters in religion .

CONTENTS

ACKNOWLEDGEMENTS

Thanks are due to my editor Ellen Pinkos Cobb, to my husband and friends Avril Marin, Lydia Johnson and Susan Milmoe who read drafts of the manuscript and provided many valuable insights.

Preface

This story is a personal account. I do not claim that my experiences or inner conflicts are the same as those of others who, like me, became nuns at an early age. I do believe however that I learned something during those ten years that I would not have known otherwise, not only about monasticism and religious belief, but also about institutions and their structure. I decided to write this account partly out of a need to detach myself from the experience by placing it outside myself, the better to understand it, but also partly to record my impressions of "the making of a nun and the unmaking of a nun". The story is true but the name of the religious order as well as the names of the sisters have been changed.

.

THE DECISION

O World, I cannot hold thee close enough!
Thy winds, thy wide gray skies!
Thy mists that roll and rise!
Thy woods, this autumn day that ache and sag.
And all but cry with color! That gaunt crag
To crush! To lift the lean of that black bluff!
World, World, I cannot hold thee close enough!

Long have I known a glory in it all,
But never knew I this;
Here such a passion is
As stretcheth me apart - Lord I do fear
Thou'st made the world too beautiful this year.
My soul is all but out of me —let fall
No burning leaf; prithee, let no bird call.

Edna St. Vincent Millay

"God's World"

     I was born into a warm happy French-Canadian family, the second of two daughters. At fifteen years old, my mother Jeanne DuPont had come to the United States to work in the factory towns of Northern New Hampshire and Vermont. She was a shy, hard working, responsible girl, having inherited, nonetheless, the ribald DuPont humor that so often translated itself into practical jokes. Though possessed of a keen mind, she would always be hesitant to speak out, beaten down as she was by a sense of inferiority, the result of finding herself so young amidst the working class poor. She exhibited a supercilious politeness with the wealthy and

1

privileged, assuming as she did that breeding and intelligence belonged to them by nature.

At her cousin's house one Sunday, my mother became friendly with Henri Ethier, a handsome, young clerk. Outgoing and affectionate, Henri had worked for his own support from his thirteenth year, working in the harsh conditions of the northern lumber camps in the winter, picking up odd jobs in the summer. His father, Ulrich, a lazy irresponsible man, had married pretty Lydia Chaloux, but though he sought her out often enough to sire six children, he did not see to their support. As a result, his young wife, undernourished, over worked, and ravaged by tuberculosis, was hastened to an early death, leaving her young son Henri (then only eight months old) in the care of his maternal grandmother.

In the ensuing years, Ulrich enlisted in World War I, but neglected to include Henri in the mention of his children and no money was sent to his grandmother for Henri's support. Henri and his grandmother scrapped together what they could to survive. My father never overcame his feelings of rejection and hurt over this outrageous act of his father.

Despite his difficulties with the French language and her reticence in English, Henri and Jeanne recognized the sterling qualities of the other and in 1933, they married. My father was delighted to become a member of the large DuPont clan for, despite its division into two rival families, there existed a common bond of love for the father and a healthy camaraderie among the siblings. My mother was delighted to have captivated the heart of her ambitious young hero. She adored him and never ceased to love him, long after his death.

My father was employed at the time as a district salesman for a large mid-Western food products company. His travels took him to Northern Maine which he loved. He easily persuaded my mother to move and in 1933, the two of them came to live in Aroostook County, some 500 miles from where they had been reared.

The people of the St. John Valley were generally poor, hardworking, and industrious, with large families and a strong allegiance to the Catholic Church. The area was remote and behind the times technologically, still in the process of being electrified in the late 30's and early 40's. The crank telephone was in operation up to 1956, my junior year in High School. That same year, the area's first T.V. station was established and this only because of the Strategic Air Command Base built nearby.

For some ten years, my parents worked side by side, throughout the region, selling their products to stores and households alike. During those years, two daughters were born to them: my sister, Marietta Marguerite in 1937 and me, Rachel Alice in 1940.

When I was three, my father, then 33, fulfilled a life-long dream. He bought a store, affiliated himself with Independent Grocer's Alliance, and opened the local IGA food market. Since my mother had always worked by his side, they decided that she would operate a restaurant, Jeannette's Coffee Pot, adjoining the food market. Though we were not farmers, nor farm laborers like the majority of the population, we were similarly industrious because we served a farming community. As a result, we opened the restaurant at 5:00 AM and the store at 8:00 AM. Both my sister and I waited on tables and occasionally helped with the cooking. We also clerked in the store early on.

I was a mischievous child and a heedless tomboy, always in the midst of things. I grew up in a carefree rural fashion, spending my leisure time playing ball, exploring, sometimes bicycling ten to twenty miles with a friend. We never locked our doors at night. We read of kidnappings and murders, but these were remote happenings. We grew up without urban fears.

My sister and I resembled each other physically, both fair-skinned, brown-haired, brown-eyed girls of sturdy build. Yet no two could have been more different than we. Where Marietta walked, I ran. Where her hair was always neatly braided, mine flew with the wind. Where I went from mischief to mischief, she remained on the sidelines making snide comments. I had a bubbly, outgoing, fun-loving personality, generous and expansive. My sister was more reserved and intellectual, contained and ladylike. I always felt that she had the upper hand on me because I was gullible and eager. When we had chores to do, I got up early, did my chores and readied myself to go out to play. Somehow my sister would rook me into helping her with her share of the work; on other occasions, she would skillfully toy with my nature - like the time she told me of a huge fire on the other side of town. At once, I jumped onto my bicycle and rushed to the scene, some three or four miles away, only to find myself deceived. But I punished her. I was strong and aggressive. I pulled her hair, kicked and scratched her until my mother or some other adult broke it up. As we never resolved our sibling rivalry, we each had our own set of friends.

My father died when I was nine, a tragedy from which I suffered emotionally for many years. My father had been my buddy; I was the boy he never had. He took me to ball games and wrestling matches; he even bought me black ice skates. I was so heartbroken that through most of my school years, whenever classmates casually mentioned their own father, I walked away to hide my free flowing tears.

My father's death dealt a shattering blow to my mother. They had been very close. Furthermore, although she had run the restaurant, it was really my father who made the major decisions. Now the heavy responsibility of managing both businesses as well as the children fell on my mother. Fearful that she would not be able to keep as watchful an eye on us as she would have liked, in the fall of 1951, two years after his death, she sent us to boarding school. My sister was entering high school that year, and though I was only entering sixth grade, I went along because my mother felt we would be less lonely together. She consoled herself with the thought that it had been our father's wish to send us away for high school because of the school's excellent reputation.

I remember feeling apprehensive as we approached the remote village that housed the school. It seemed so spooky, all shrouded in pine trees. The school itself was housed in three large three-story buildings. The main building, built at the turn of the century, was of wood construction covered with a grey worked- tin facing that gave it the appearance of granite of a European look. The sisters must have imported it to make themselves feel at home as they were French immigrants. The second building of the same construction was attached and built perpendicular to the first. The third, about ten years old, was of red brick. There was a barn, potato storage house, a laundry and various sheds on the property, for, beside their involvement in teaching, the sisters operated a farm.

Le Pensionnat Notre Dame de la Sagesse was run European-style, headed as it was by an aged French Nun. Girl boarders wore the usual Catholic School uniforms, i.e., navy blue wool gabardine jumpers and white blouses. A black smock worn by all the children in French schools was required for all activities except chapel. We looked like turn-of-the-century orphans and our only consolation in our appearance was to joke about it.

We slept on white wrought iron beds arranged in rows in the large dormitory rooms. There were no curtains or partitions between the beds, so we were taught how to undress and dress under our long bathrobes, in such a manner that no one ever witnessed the other's bare limbs or body. Each morning at six, the sister in charge awakened the boarders with a religious greeting, "Our Lord Jesus Christ be praised!" while turning on the lights. At the sound of the morning greeting, each boarder was to jump up and out, flinging back the covers all in one movement, and respond, "Amen!"

We were taught how to make beds hospital style. Morning inspection by the sister on duty was rigid and unrelenting. Beds would be stripped if not to her liking and we would be required to make it over. The rule of silence which controlled the lives of the sisters extended to the boarders, and to be caught talking meant some mild punishment such as copying out the definition of silence. I copied it so many thousands of times, that to this day, I remember "silence means quiet, the absence of noise" (the shortest definition I could find in Webster).

At 6:30 AM we were rushed down to the chapel for daily Mass. The chapel was a beautiful two story high room with murals painted on the off-white walls. The stately fleur-de-lis, symbol of the French Nation, honoring the French origins of the order, was everywhere. Celebration of Mass was a festive affair. All of us, girls, boys and sisters joined together in singing the Gregorian chants. I loved these early morning liturgies. They were colorful and joyful. The sisters, especially the older French nuns, spent many hours making the priests' vestments and the altar cloths. One was more beautiful than the other, with elaborate cut-work, and embroidery. The priest was always accompanied by a large retinue of altar boys because of the many boy boarders. These young acolytes were also handsomely dressed with surplices of elaborate cutwork. The whole gave a marvelous effect and the celebrations appealed to my romantic nature.

After Mass, we filed down the long corridors to the dining room for breakfast. We sat on benches at long tables made to accommodate eight persons and ate our meals in silence every day except for Thursdays (as it was customary in France) and Sundays. The high school girls read biographies aloud while the rest of us ate and listened.

Besides learning how to make my bed, and how to be silent, it was in boarding school that I learned to clean. My first ménage (as we called the house chores) was to clean a long corridor connecting the dormitory building with the elementary school building. The sisters had no electrical appliances, no vacuum cleaners, and no electric polishers. Instead, they relied entirely on manual methods. Each sister had a jurisdiction over which she presided and for which she bore responsibility. Sister Joseph, the old nun in charge of the corridor in question, taught me how to use the long two-and-a-half inch steel pins to extricate the dirt from the cracks between the floor boards. Hallways in the new building were never really dirty as we were not allowed to wear shoes. Each boarder was provided with a numbered pair of "skates". These were made from discarded woolen blankets cut into rectangles, folding the upper corners of the rectangles and sewing the sides together in this way:

Illustration of the skate, Abbie Wanamaker

By slipping the foot under the triangle, you could hook the skate and push it along in the process. The mirror-like floors were marvelous.

The school was large, and in those first few months, there seemed to be an endless stream of light green corridors. Unlike the sisters who had taught me before, these sisters belonged to an older European order with Missions in Africa, South America, Haiti, and Madagascar. That gave them an exotic quality, appealing to my adventurous nature.

The academic curriculum was much the same as any other except that French was taught in a systematic fashion from grade one. For those transferring into the school, it meant catch up work. I was pleased that for a few years at least, I was spared the odious comparisons that teachers indulge in: "Why your sister would never have done such a thing! She was such a lady!"

Boarding school was regulated from dawn to dusk. Following the end of the school day, we had one hour of recreation, one hour of supervised study, fifteen minutes of vocal prayer (the recitation of the rosary) supper (in silence) followed by another forty-five minutes of study. The day ended with a final hour of recreation.

Initially, I hated boarding school, feeling confined by the many regulations. The town was small and I did not understand why we could not go about as we pleased. Why no bicycles were permitted. Why I was not allowed to spend my allowance money as I pleased.

I was terribly lonely. The boarding school separated high school students from those in grammar school. Except for chapel and meal time, I did not even see my sister. On Sunday mornings, a two-hour period was set aside for visiting family. My sister always acted as if my visits were a burden to her. I was her younger sister and she did not want me "tagging" along. To try to win her attention, I used my allowance money to buy her favorite Waleeco chocolate bars. She took them, briefly acknowledged my presence, criticized my appearance, and then went back to ignoring me. To be fair, I often appeared with a ripped hem held up with pins or scotch tape. But the sibling rivalry that had always existed prevented my sister from recognizing my need for the warm support from her.

Running away was a frequent topic of conversation, especially the first few months. However, because the area was remote, runaways were easily recognized, caught and returned. So, though I laid my own plans to run away with a fellow boarder from my home town, we never had the courage to carry out our schemes.

Boarding school cut me off from the social life of my home town, except for the close friendships that I was able to maintain with the kids of my immediate neighborhood. This was more significant by virtue of my lack of kinship ties with the community. The longer I remained in boarding school, the more my social circle focused on boarding school friends.

Although the school was co-educational, we were carefully separated. The boy boarders had their own stairwells, pathways, seats in chapel, and their own dining room. The town's people attended the same school as we did but they were few in number and minimally involved in school affairs. Often they were required to work on the farm before and after school. That left them with little energy and interest for school activities. Many dropped out of school after completing the eighth grade. When parents had the interest and money to do so, they sent their sons to far away prep schools, again reducing the ratio of boys to girls. In my graduating class there were eight boys out of a class of twenty eight.

In 1954, five years after the death of my father, my mother remarried our neighbor and friend, Wilfred Sirois, a prominent businessman in our small town. The marriage was a realistic arrangement between friends of long standing. I had the usual childish reaction to the news, crying and accusing my mother of defiling the memory of my father and dramatically questioned whether she had truly loved him. Even as I spoke, I knew that I did not believe my accusations. My mother patiently explained that she would always love my father, and no one would take his place in her life, but that Mr. Sirois was an older man, a friend of ours. He wanted to marry for companionship. He loved my sister and me and had loved and admired my father. His late wife and my mother had been friends. It seemed practical for them to marry.

I listened quietly, understanding as well as I could for my thirteen years. I accepted the explanation, and saw the marriage as a practical one. Characteristically, having made up my mind to accept the fact, I brought my emotions in line, forced myself to call him Dad and came to enjoy my new status of a girl with a father.

It was during these years that my decision to enter religious life took shape. I had thought of becoming a nun as early as the third grade. I was infatuated with the principal that year, an elderly nun who let me dust her desk and read off names to her, but was too young to plan my future and I put the thought aside. I thought of it again in eighth grade but dismissed it as premature. In my senior year in high school, I became actively preoccupied with the thought that God might be calling me into his service. I became so obsessed with the idea that I constantly postponed completing college applications. One cold rainy October day, when all of us in boarding school were on retreat (a day of silence and meditation), I wandered off by myself to the top of the hill behind the school. Looking down on the church, the convent school and the village, I felt anxious, uncertain what to do about my future.

Yet, as I looked at the church steeple through the mist and rain at that moment, I felt that God wanted me to become a nun. It was not a considered decision. It was not something I weighed with pros and cons. It was something I **had** to do, a powerful emotional experience. God had touched me.

I sobbed, not wanting to give up the world I loved, already feeling an incredible sense of loss. With tears rolling down my cheeks, I flung open my arms and cried out: "*Oh world, I cannot hold thee close enough*" the opening verse of Edna St. Vincent Millay's poem. Through the tears I comforted myself with the thought that, freed from particular attachments I could then truly love the whole world. The experience was very strong and over the course of the ensuing year, I often relived the experience. Though nothing was decided on the hilltop that October day, from then on, no alternative could seriously be considered. God had spoken to me.

Six weeks later, I participated in a religious retreat arranged for juniors and seniors. I welcomed this as an opportunity to discuss the matter of my vocation. I awaited the weekend with some anxiety. Students from previous years told of a priest who advised all who expressed a desire to enter convents to wait - either to go to college first, or to work for a few years. Ambivalent about my "calling", it was my hope that he would advise me in the same fashion - a sanction from God to put off my entry.

I had expected this priest to be dynamic and forceful. Instead, he seemed melancholy. He posed questions about my attitude toward men, about marriage, about whether I had ever had extraterrestrial experiences, or visions. I was amused by this, always so firmly rooted in the earth and pragmatic.

I felt relieved thinking that surely I would not qualify for the convent, if this was a criterion of admission. But from this brief discussion, he concluded that there was no reason why I should not enter the convent. I felt miserable and confused. What would I do? Should I go on with college applications, or make active plans to enter the convent? It was shortly before Thanksgiving and I looked forward to the holiday weekend. I would discuss the problem with my mother.

"Rachel, what does a sixteen year old girl know? You're much too young to enter the convent. Go to college first and after you finish there will be plenty of time to make those kinds of decisions." She cried softly as she spoke.

November turned into February. Time was growing short. If I were to attend college in the fall, I would have to do something about applications. Maybe it would help to talk the matter over with my favorite teacher. She was a sympathetic listener.

I went to her room after class one afternoon and began my story. I had thought of going to the Georgetown School of Foreign Service, I explained, but was in conflict about whether I should enter the convent instead. I tried to seem cool and detached. I had thought of applying but now time was growing short. What should I do? I had not filled out any college application forms, but now I felt pressed to make a decision.

If I went to college, she argued, I would become engrossed in other things, and would probably never again give serious consideration to a religious vocation; that really wasn't giving myself a chance to determine if God was calling me, was it? Why not enter the convent now and find out. I could leave if I didn't think it was for me. This was a convincing argument, one which I had myself used to convince my family doctor of the rationality of such a decision on the part of one of my friends. The postulate and novitiate were periods of training and theoretically one could leave at any time; it was quite a lure to take a step in this direction as it did not seem irrevocable.

I really believed that if I did not like it, I could and would leave. What I did not understand at that time was that none of us would ever be given this freedom of decision. The decision would rest squarely with the superior who represented the Divine Will. It was she, with the advice of the sisters who worked closely with her, who would decide if a candidate had or did not have a "vocation". To decide on one's own, against the advice of the superior or without her advice, would never be possible. So while I may have thought that I was "buying time" before making an ultimate choice, I was in fact irrevocably committing myself.

It wasn't surprising that Sister encouraged me to enter the convent. She went on to tell me that the Provincial Superior (the Sister in charge of all the sisters in the United States) would be coming to Maine to visit the Sisters in a week's time. It would be a fine opportunity for me to have an interview with her. The interview, she said, was part of the screening process wherein the Congregation decided whether they would accept me as a candidate.

I was relieved. I no longer had the burden of making a decision. It was made for me. I would enter the convent. I continued to have misgivings, but the conflict that followed this February talk was mostly over resolving my sense of loss when I thought of giving up my freedom, my friends, and my family.

Mother Marie, the Provincial Superior, came to Maine as scheduled and I went in to speak with her. I barely remember what we talked about. She did not ask me any probing questions, nor did she impart much information. I had the feeling the whole thing was merely to get a look at me. As I left, she handed me a packet of forms to be filled out, personal questionnaires, doctor's forms, dental check-up and certification of legitimate birth. I thanked her for her time and left the room.

As soon as I got away, I opened the questionnaire out of curiosity."Why do you wish to become a religious?" The question starred at me.

"I don't know," I thought to myself. "What is it they want me to write?"
I ran up to Sister Mary Clare's classroom to tell her about my interview and show her the questionnaire, indicating that I did not know exactly how to answer.

"Well, why don't you put down, 'to serve the world for Christ'?"
"That's a wonderful answer." We giggled as I wrote it in.
June came suddenly that year. It was time to inform friends and relatives of my decision. I dreaded it. Despite the fact that priests and nuns were well respected, friends shared the stereotypic view of the nun as the quiet contemplative type. I anticipated that people would generally be shocked at my decision. Most felt that I was too lively to become a nun, that the structured life would be unsuited to my temperament. As I later discovered, they knew me better than I knew myself.

No one reacted to the news enthusiastically - no congratulations, only grudging good wishes. Friends and relatives alike viewed the religious vocation with certain aura of mystery. It was no ordinary decision to be tampered with. This aura of mystery eliminated the turmoil and consideration that should have gone into making a decision of this magnitude. It was mysterious to me that I had to enter the convent, yet I accepted it on the premise that God could so determine my life.

Though one cannot say that going to boarding school was the cause of my entry into religious life, it no doubt helped to nurture my decision. Yet, looking back on these early years, there were many influences on my decision to enter religious life. I was raised to believe that education was the supreme achievement in life, a goal attained with the college degree. My father was bright, energetic and cheerful, but suffered from a sense of inferiority at never having finished school and it became inordinately important to him. How natural it was for me in view of this respect for schooling that I model myself on those few college educated people in my small town of five thousand, namely the nuns and priests who held most of the teaching jobs in the local public schools.

I had the feeling of being apart. I was a bright child and came from a supportive and enthusiastic home. We traveled outside the area so that my horizons were broader than most of my classmates. We spoke English at home whereas the large majority came from homes where French was spoken almost exclusively. Most started school with a language barrier, and a large number of those in my generation would never lose their heavy accents. I was always effortlessly at the head of my class, even after being skipped a grade. In my senior year, I was class valedictorian; had placed 3rd in the Maine Science fair and first in the state in a United Nations Sponsored essay contest. Then there was my family situation. Life in rural America in the 1940's and 1950's was very traditional. Strong class-consciousness existed in the town and social distinctions, though rarely discussed, were quite evident. Prior to my father's death, I belonged to a better than average family, as most merchant families do in traditional societies.

To set us apart even more, we were outsiders, without kinship ties in a community where virtually everybody was interrelated. My mother's remarriage did not establish these ties, because my stepfather was not himself a native. Moreover, his financial position, however modest by national standards, was considerable for the place and time and served to isolate us even more. We had one of the nicest homes in the town and between us, we ran three businesses. My stepfather sat on the Board of Directors of the Savings and Loan Association which financed many businesses for the townspeople.

I did not think at the time I would ever find a man with whom I could share my life, because I had not, up to then, met anyone my age who was more intelligent than I was. To me, this was an important criterion in selecting a marriage partner. So I formed an image of my future that excluded marriage. I saw myself in the future as a professional single woman, most likely pursuing a career in foreign service. I never really thought it through. I don't believe that I spoke to anyone about it, except to mention the fact to a friend as an explanation for why I was entering the convent. My mother had strong religious and ethical values. She thanked God each day for her health and for the health of her children. She never placed any importance on money, except what was necessary to live, nor on social position. She never grieved the loss of anything material. Her only comment on learning about such losses would invariably be: "It's only money, it can be replaced." This utter detachment had molded me. We were raised with a tremendous sympathy for those who had less than we did, and my mother faithfully gave a goodly portion of her income to charity. Both my parents were honest, industrious and charitable. I remember my father rewarding a boy from a poor family for a kind act that he had witnessed by giving him a half-dollar, a great deal of money to a child in the 1940's.

How could I forget my mother's shocked expression when I gleefully told her that the clerk at J. J. Newbury's had made a mistake and given me too much change. She promptly sent me back with the money, and was mortified that I had not alerted the clerk. Such incidents helped to form my conscious and to instill in me a strong sense of integrity, of duty towards others, of commonality with the race, of fairness and sympathy for the plight of others.

I saw a life of religious service as a way of devoting my energies to God and to mankind. Instead of being a professional woman alone, I could be a professional woman along with others. When I was making my decision, the Peace Corps had not yet been founded. If it had, I might have considered this as an alternative choice for a life of service to others. The only sacrifice I felt was my freedom to travel, and the ability to make my own decisions. I did not understand the full implications of my decision to enter religious life, and how limiting religious life would be. I still had only a vague notion of what life behind convent walls would be like.

A strange incident had occurred when I was a senior that would have given me a clue to what was happening had I been more insightful. I had completely wiped it from my memory when it popped into my head during a therapy session years later. My favorite teacher remarked to me one day that though I gave the appearance of being a warm loving bubbly carefree person, easy to get close to, I was in fact quite distant and it was difficult to get close to me, that I didn't easily confide in others. I remember feeling uncomfortable as she spoke, recognizing the truth of her remarks.

"Everybody I love dies," I blurted out and burst into tears.
The remark was spontaneous. I had not reflected on it, in fact, it took me quite by surprise (My stepfather had died that spring.)

"But I'm not going to die," she said.

"You don't know that," I said defensively and left the room.

The experience was inexplicable to me. I don't know why it happened; I was not play acting, at least I don't think I was. It was not new to me that people felt close to me but that I did not reciprocate by opening up. I was aware of this aspect of my personality. I was not sure what it meant, nor what or how it related to my experience of death in those close to me.

Today, I believe that there was a clear relationship, making me self-protective and defensive. Could it be that it was a deep-seated fear of being hurt again that drove me to make a decision to attach myself to no one particular person by entering the convent?

At a party I attended shortly before I left home, I danced with a divorcee, a family friend, 40 years old, sophisticated, suave.

"Why would a young attractive, bright girl shut herself up in a convent?"

"Because I want to."

"I can't believe that."

"Well, it's not that I want to but that I have to. It's what I feel that I have to do with my life."

He laughed. "Nobody *has* to do anything with his or her life. You can do whatever you want to do."

"Well, *I know* it's something that I have to do."

He may have sensed my uneasiness because he stopped his prodding at that point. I felt tense and upset and was happy that he had stopped his questions. I buried my face in his shoulder and tried to fight back the tears. Why had this conversation upset me? I thought about it for a long time afterwards without being able to sort out the forces in me that he had touched. I thought that perhaps it was his insinuations that I was being irrational that had upset me, I who prided myself on my rationality and common sense.

But instead of more self-examination, I put all these disturbing thoughts out of my mind and attempted to ready myself for departure.

THE POSTULATE

I fled Him down the nights and down the days
I fled Him down the arches of the years,
I fled Him down the labyrinthine ways
Of my own mind and in the midst of tears
I hid from Him, and under running laughter
Up vistaed hopes I sped
and shot precipitated
Adown titanic glooms of chasmed fears
From those strong feet that followed after
But with unhurrying chase,
And unperturbed pace
Deliberate speed, majestic instancy
They beat and a Voice beat
More instant than the feet
All things betray Thee who betrayest me.

Francis Thompson,

The Hound of Heaven

My mother ultimately resigned herself to my decision. Though unhappy about it, she made few attempts to dissuade me. She too was of the opinion that God's designs on me must not be tampered with. My sister volunteered no comment that I can remember save to ask why I did not go to college first. I took all of her questions as unnecessary prying into my personal life, so I closed her off with some snide comment.

It was fortuitous that just as I was graduating from high school an opportunity to sell the family business presented itself. This freed us up to spend the summer traveling, visiting some of our relatives in Detroit,

Montreal, plus traveling on to Washington and New York. All was done in the spirit of this being the last time we would travel together. The summer passed quickly and it was soon time for my entrance day. I was happy and excited by the novelty of it, even if a bit scared. How one became a nun was as mysterious to me on the beautiful August day as it must be to most people. I knew that I would spend a year and a half studying to be a nun, but I would have been hard pressed to answer the question: "Studying what?" We were naive, not asking questions, taking with serenity what life doled out to us.

When I was dropped off in Connecticut to begin my postulate, it was not a wrenching tearful experience for me. After all, it was autumn, and I always went away in autumn.

The Sisters owned a choice piece of property three miles outside a historic Connecticut town. One hundred and twenty five acres of rolling hills, apple orchards, pine groves, babbling brook, woods, pasture, a corn field and exquisite formal gardens. The main building was a large red brick three story structure trimmed with white federal columns and shutters in an attempt to simulate a colonial appearance. These did little to temper its stern modern look.

Next to it stood the original rambling white farm house. Its graceful main entrance was wrapped in hardy violet wisteria woven into the lattice work with love seats to each side of the great door. A barn, stables, garage, greenhouse and laundry dotted the property. I was shown my bed, and assigned a place to deposit my possessions. There I changed from my worldly clothes to the long black postulant dress with its waist length cape. My mother and sister sat in the parlor waiting to get a last glimpse. When I had finished dressing, I neatly folded my pink chiffon dress and rushed to say farewell. The sister who showed me the way back to the parlor urged me to make it short to ease the pain. My mother continued to weep as she had done continuously for the last three days. I comforted her cheerfully, assuring her I was doing what I wanted to do and what God demanded of me. With this farewell, my new life began.

We had been instructed to arrive before 4:00 p.m. and, shortly after the last parents left, we were assembled in a large room to receive our postulant's headdress. It consisted of a white cotton cap (called a serre-tete) that clasped our head closely and had drawstrings to hold it firm. We stuffed our hair into this. Over the cap we wore a white fluted bonnet. Someone introduced us to Mother Marie Alexandre, the first Mistress of Postulants (as the sister in charge was called). She was a small blond French-Canadian woman in her late forties of ruddy complexion, sharp features and twinkling blue eyes. She gave us a brief talk to welcome us to the Congregation and to explain what we would be doing the next few days: "Many of you come to us believing that you already understand religious life, because you have been close to nuns all your lives, but you will find that you have many things to learn. In these first months, we will merely introduce you to the externals of the disciplined life. The real training will be the novitiate."

With these brief words, our first instruction ended, and we were marched to chapel to join the sisters in the recitation of the rosary. I found my first weeks in the convent easy. I was used to a regulated life. I was used to getting up with a bell, and going off to chapel in a group. I was used to being told when to take my bath and to being assigned housework. At least I was used to it all from September to June each year. I think it took me longer than the other girls to realize the weight of my decision because the routine was so much like boarding school. In the back of my mind, I think I thought of it all as temporary and that soon I would be on vacation and back to regular life.

The major difference between boarding school and the postulate was the significance attached to the rules and to one's actions. Though I had learned to be silent in boarding school, it was not through any religious motivation. I either obeyed through fear of punishment or because I had learned over the years to appreciate silence's disciplinary effect on the mind.

Silence in the convent was completely different. It was one of the keys in renouncing the world, one of the bases of religious life, the necessary means to the development of a deep communication with God. And to assure this development, we were taught to replace speech with signs. We learned a repertory of hand signals to be used in the dining room to express our needs, the cup for water, the handle of our knife for bread, and so forth. Speech was never permissible during Grand Silence, the name given the sacred time between night prayers and breakfast, unless of course one had a dire illness or an accident. We learned the meaning of the simple monastic phrase "a regular place" meaning somewhere one was never permitted to talk, even during the two hours of daily recreation, such as all convent corridors, stairs and refectory.

The bell was another instrument to help us renounce the world. Each time it rang, one was to hear in its special signal the voice of Christ, and with its first sound, each consecrated soul was to stop immediately whatever task was in progress. This went against worldly ways, to cut a word in half, to drop a pen without finishing the formation of the letter. The bell thus called us to renunciation of our willful selves.

Everything we did, even the clothes we wore, had religious significance. The headdress was boxlike and effectively cut off all side views, as though blinders had been saddled to our eyes. This was to help us remember that we must always be looking straight ahead toward God, never backwards, nor sideways to be distracted by worldly pleasures. It was so difficult to maneuver in this garb. How did the sisters do it so easily, I thought to myself? It was the same with the slippers which the sisters wore in place of shoes. One had always to press forward so as not to slip out of them- again a symbol of the inner thrust of the nun's soul. Explanations such as these helped all of us to justify to ourselves the irrational custom of maintaining a two hundred fifty year old habit as intact as the foundress had worn it even to the exact count and placement of each pin.

How easy and simple my commitment seemed on that glorious summer day when I arrived at the Postulate. I had no idea then how totally involved my life would become. Despite my six years of close proximity to the sisters in boarding school, many details about religious life had escaped my attention. At times, the regulations which were unfolded in the first months seemed silly and overdone. At other times, they seemed the result of the most eminent common sense.

Nothing in our lives was left to chance. Everything was regulated. For example, the way a nun was to hold her prayer book, never resting her thumb on the opened pages but rather covering it with a protective piece of clear plastic. This, to preserve it for the many years it would be in use. There was the sister's practice of eating out of a tin porringer with a wooden fork and spoon, as had the poor of the countryside where they had had their origins. This had been a startling discovery to all of us that first month, but as the First Mistress had predicted, it soon became second nature.

There was the practice of using one's napkin as a mini tablecloth. The table napkin was cut into a long rectangular shape. Each of us was taught how to roll it out onto the table to the approximate size of a placemat and pin it to our postulant dress at the other end. All crumbs would thus fall into it while we ate, and we could spoon them up at the end of the meal. Further, we washed our utensils at table and wiped them with our napkin. These two customs revolted me, seeming so unsanitary. The table napkins would become rumpled and stained as the week progressed. I longed for the week to end to have a fresh one. When I caught myself feeling this way, I felt ashamed that such worldly desires could find a place in me. I dismissed my feelings as worldly and unimportant.

It was usual for me to set aside my disappointments and difficulties and overcome them by acting as if things were fine. It was a psychological habit that I had acquired when I read the Pollyanna books shortly after the death of my father. I wasn't aware then and not until much later how large a part of my defenses Pollyanna's glad game had become. The game was simply to get into the habit of believing that if one looked for a glad aspect of any sorrow, one could find it. It became my chief mechanism for conflict resolution. It led me to deny that things were not right or that I had certain feelings of hostility. It became a key to my personality.

Very early in the Postulate I learned a rule which demanded an enormous sacrifice. It would prove to be a continual reminder of the "pinpricks" that made up religious life and that we were taught to look upon as help on the way to sainthood.

It was the rule not to smell flowers. I entered the congregation during the week, and the first Sunday that followed happened to fall on the first Sunday of the month. Customarily, this was a retreat Sunday, which meant that the sisters did not talk all day long and that whatever time was ordinarily spent on relaxation was spent in prayer and reflection. I had been "on retreat" many times before in boarding school, and though I found the silence difficult, it was a beautiful day and I remember feeling a sense of freedom not to have to rush about to keep a busy schedule.

I availed myself of the free time to walk around the grounds, admiring the elegant formal gardens. I plopped myself down in the midst of a large clump of roses, buried my face in them.

Suddenly I felt a tap on my shoulder. Instinctively, I smiled at Mother Michael, the superior and First Mistress of Novices. She returned a gentle and warm smile. "Sister Ethier, one of the things that we as Daughters of the Spirit have to learn to do is to mortify our senses. In order to do this, we give up smelling flowers."

I was stunned. Managing a weak smile, I mumbled, "Thank you, Mother."

Not smell flowers! Forever! My God! I wanted to burst into tears. I couldn't believe it. This was so unexpected. I walked to the apple orchard and sat under a tree. Oh God! Not smell flowers? I began to sob.

For goodness's sake, Rachel, I told myself. It's just flowers. What a little thing. Why should it bother you? You want to become a nun, so you have to give up smelling flowers. So what? For heaven's sake, you have already given up your family, your friends, whatever money you might have made. What's smelling flowers in relation to that?

Okay, I'll give up smelling flowers! I resolved with myself. That was that. There was a sense of finality about my decision. From that time on, if I did on occasion sneak near a clump of flowers to smell them, I felt guilty.

The resolution did not, however, take away my immediate strong sense of loss and resulting sadness. I decided to pray the psalms: "Out of the depths I cry to you Oh Lord, Lord, hear my prayer, and let my cry come unto Thee". . .

I found peace in the beauty of the psalms and in the landscape all around.

Some eight or nine months later, when we were given instruction on how to pray, Sister Mary Kathleen commented that often one goes out into the countryside on a beautiful day and communes with nature, deriving much emotional satisfaction from this contact. One is tempted to accompany these feelings with the recitation of the psalms.

"This is not prayer. This is a form of self-indulgence. Prayer is something stern. Prayer is something strong. Prayer is a matter of the will, not of the emotions."

I reddened as she spoke and hoped that no one had seen me sitting under the apple tree that first retreat Sunday or that if they had, they had forgotten.

You are now my dear daughters, clothed with the holy habit of the Congregation. Enter the novitiate and take your place in this house which you have chosen and in which you desire to remain all the days of your life.

Our days were regulated by schedule. We were awakened in time to dress and go to Chapel for Mass. After breakfast, we went about completing our assigned house chores. After which we went to classes in Gregorian chant, Theology, French language (this was the official language of the worldwide congregation), history of the congregation, and an instruction concerning the rules and customs of the order. During this hour, the first mistress, as the Directress of the Postulate was called, gradually introduced us to various customs and practices which we were then expected to put into practice. We were eased into the rule of silence, first requiring only evening silence from night prayer to breakfast, then breakfast was included and so forth until we eventually maintained silence all day save for the two recreation hours, one hour following each of the two main meals.

One of the principles of the American Novitiate was the belief that the way of life of the Sisters could not be imposed all at once on the new candidates. In Europe or in Canada, candidates were treated more seriously on the assumption that they were more mature and had the tolerance to lead an ascetic life. As a result, having entered the congregation one day, they were expected to do everything according to the rule the next.

In the American Novitiate, it was felt that candidates were too young for such expectations. Moreover, most had lived self-indulged lives and would find a disciplined life difficult to adjust to. The postulate was thus meant to prepare them for the more difficult novitiate year. Postulants were allowed to live less severely than the sisters in a multitude of ways. They were allowed to eat with restaurant china though the sisters ate with wooden forks and spoons and out of their tin bowls. They earned the "privilege" of eating in the manner of the professed or vowed sisters by mastering such practices as keeping silent for certain hours during the day. Once the group as a whole had satisfactorily learned the practice, the group would be rewarded with the tin bowl. And so it was with other practices. I resented the approach, and felt put down and humiliated by it. To me, it seemed unnecessary to offer us "privileges" to motivate us to silence. Most of us shared the common ideal of monasticism as a good and holy life, to give up the ways of the world was honorable. Moreover, I had learned a fair amount of discipline in boarding school.

I remember well the day we were rewarded by receiving our wooden ware. It was the feast of Mary, Mother of God, October 11, one of the days we especially celebrated. A scavenger hunt was arranged for us at the end of which we would be given our utensils, that is, they would be "found". I thought the whole thing stupid and silly and I told the sister in charge of us that I was 17 years old and insulted to be asked to play this childish game. She merely laughed and answered that it was indeed a bit childish, but that it would do me good to swallow my pride and play the game. I had half hoped that I would get out of it by protesting but to no avail. I hated every minute.

Postulants were particularly sensitive to the almost imperceptible ways we were being manipulated to foster a childlike and sometimes childish dependence on our superiors. We did a lot of canning of whatever fruit was in season, and as August was the peach season, we were soon set to the task of peeling, cutting and scalding the peaches in order to can them. On these days, all other activities were suspended in order to get the canning done quickly. It was reminiscent of old fashioned quilting or sewing bees. The day began at nine a.m. We mostly worked in silence while one sister read aloud or prayed. After lunch, we took a brief walk around the grounds for exercise, and then we were to return to our jobs until 5:00 P.M.

After we had been peeling for a time, Mother Michael, the head of the Novitiate, dropped by to check on our progress. She spoke a few casual words to the group to which the novices responded in chorus:"Oooh, Ma Chere Soeur!" in tones of adulation. (The French title for superior had been retained; Mother was never used. It was a strict differentiation of our order from other orders that in French the title Mother had not been given to the superior, but rather that she was dignified by being referred to as "My dear sister".)

The oohing and aahing embarrassed me. These young women acted like grammar school children. Mother Michael played into this. She turned to leave and announced in what I then viewed as a patronizing tone: "You may all have one peach." (We were not otherwise permitted to eat between meals.)"Oooh, thank you, Ma Chère Soeur," the novices chorused. The entire group of postulants burst into spontaneous laughter at this display of childishness. The novices and professed sisters looked at us with displeasure and confusion. Their looks told us that our laughter was inappropriate, and that they did not at all comprehend what we found funny. The behavioral patterns just displayed had become so commonplace that they no longer found them out of the ordinary. The sequel to the story is that one year later, we were behaving the same way.

Besides the customary practices described above, the superior's role as the representative of Christ was instilled in us not only then but throughout our religious lives. It was through our superior that Christ spoke to each of us. It was through her that God's will was made manifest. Sisters were asked to obey the superior following the example of Christ himself: "obedient unto death, even unto the death on a cross."

Contrary to popular opinion, obedience rather than chastity is the most fundamental obligation of the religious life. And that is why, as I was to understand much later, those persons who represented Authority, to whom obedience was due, were enveloped in so much ritual. One did not merely ask a superior permission to do a certain thing; one knelt to ask this permission.

Permission had to be granted for the most insignificant acts of everyday life: to open a window if one felt the need for air, to leave the room to go to the bathroom, to leave the room to get an item forgotten in the last room, to discard worn underwear, to read any book whatsoever. And this in spite of the fact that each day the community of sisters as a whole knelt to the superior and asked in unison: "Permission, Ma Chere Soeur, for all my actions." One was not to be content with a mere compliance with these practices, one's obedience had to be pure in motive and in action, as the rule stated: "Obedience the sisters owe their superiors and their constitution should be entire, admitting of no reserve, prompt, brooking no delay, cheerful, without trace of sadness, holy, excluding all human motives, blind, that is without reasoning and persevering without interruption."

These were the "grand lessons" of the postulate- silence, the bell, obedience, some of the fundamental rules, and we tried to assimilate into our daily routine. These attitudes and behavior changes were buttressed by the things we learned in theology, and Church History.

Yes, we had begun to learn the ways of God's chosen and to leave behind those of the world.

****

It was in the Postulate also that we deepened our knowledge of the Congregation we had joined. We read biographies of the founders, and histories of the congregation. All of this was meant to instill in us a deeper sense of loyalty and commitment to our congregation as well as an understanding of its spirit. The religious order that I had entered was a papal congregation founded in the early 18th century by a colorful and eccentric French Priest. Young, idealistic, and fully committed to the task of alleviating the suffering of the poor and to providing them with an opportunity for schooling, he gathered around him a small band of devout men and women who shared his idealism and energy. He placed his female followers in the alms houses of Poitier doing primitive nursing. Later, he founded free schools for the poor. The sufferings of the poor truly pained him and his whole life was dominated by an earnestness and urgency to found as many schools and hospitals and to preach as many missions as he possibly could. It was, above all, his preaching missions that drove him, because, to his way of thinking, sin was the ultimate and worst enemy, worse than poverty and class distinctions. He was one of the high minded men, spirited, animated the likes of which one may chance to meet once in a life time. He was a whirlwind for God's work.

The women he had grouped around him suffered derision and insults because of their association with the poor. Their works of service forced them to partake in the life of the community to an extent that was considered shocking in its day.

His critics spoke up against his foolish schemes: "Nuns belong in convents to be silent and pray for the sins of mankind."

But the founder responded: "The streets are their cloisters" and admonished his sisters to lead a balanced life of prayer and service. He was a man with an idea that had met its time.

The order flourished and eventually spread to about half of Western Europe, to North and South America, to Africa and to Borneo. It kept its central government and maintained French as its official language. And the founder's personality continued to dominate his congregation.

When I entered it some 250 years after its founding, it was a well-established European Congregation, much respected as a serious and highly disciplined body. It was headed by two superior officers, a priest and a nun. These were assisted by a council of six elected members, all of whom resided in Rome. Their jurisdictional powers extended over all members. The Congregation was then divided into administrative units, called provinces, which were governed by three full time officers, a provincial superior, her assistant and a bursar. These offices were filled by appointment by the higher superior for three years. Territorial boundaries of Provinces were usually co-terminus with the political boundaries of the nation-state. Thus, there was an "American Province," a "Canadian Province," "a Colombian Province," and the like.

Within each province, there were a number of establishments referred to as the local communities. These consisted of the schools, hospitals, orphanages, etc. of the Congregation. The American Province oversaw approximately 25 local communities, 3 Hospitals in Brooklyn, two on Long Island, and a Nursing School in Virginia; numerous schools in Maine, Connecticut, New York and Virginia.

American sisters were also responsible for staffing certain missions in Africa and South America. The head of the local community, the local superior, was appointed by higher superiors, and was held responsible for the financial administration of the house as well as the spiritual care of the sisters in her community. Thus it was her duty to see to the strict enforcement of the religious rules.

It was a historic time to enter the congregation in August of 1957, because it was a historic time for the Church. The church was in ferment, the eruption of which the world would witness when the Bishops of the world would gather in Rome for the Second Vatican Council. Many members of the Church were already experiencing a certain malaise with the way things were and had been for centuries. There had been a lot of experimentation by the French Clergy during the War. Priests had gone out as workers in factories and construction jobs in order to maintain contact with their parishioners. When the war ended, seeing the value of this kind of involvement in the daily lives of those who were in their spiritual care, many had continued this work begun under the necessity of war.

Applications of this experimentation to the religious life had been suggested, emphasizing the point that it was time for nuns to restructure their cloistered lives and to "enter the world". War had touched people in Europe in the most fundamental ways. When one is struggling to survive, living in cellars and wondering where the next meal is coming from, or whether one will be alive to eat the next meal, getting up on schedule, saying prayers in a routine manner, and other monastic practices seem of little importance. If anything, their "sacred character" seems ridiculous.

It was this perspective that European theologians were bringing to the Church and that European nuns in my congregations were bringing to its governing body. In the fall of 1957, the Congregation was preparing itself for its General Chapter. Held every six years, the Chapter was the law making body in the Congregation. Delegates were empowered to make necessary changes in the constitutions and/or customary laws. The Chapter always brought some kind of change, and in 1957, everyone expected these changes to be major.

There were several issues to be discussed. One of the central issues was the habit.

The habit worn by the Postulant consisted of a simple ankle length black dress with a waist length black cape worn over the dress. Our hair was covered by a quilted cotton cap covered by a fluted bonnet (achieved by heavy starching then curled with a curling iron. NOTE: In 1957 when I entered the convent there was a well known cleanser with an image of "the Dutch Cleanser girl".) We often remarked how much we resembled that image. I have inserted a photo of myself on visiting day, sitting with a friend from high school who preceded me into the convent nt. As we were not permitted to pose for photos, most of the ones taken were not clear and they are so dark, it is hard to differentiate details –

As postulant, Visiting Day October, 1957

Up to 1951, no changes had been made in the religious habit. It was worn exactly the way the foundress had worn it in the early 1700's, with the same number of pins, the same number of pleats, and the same kind of fabric. Furthermore, the same kind of whale bone corset and coarse muslin tunic were worn underneath the coarse woolen outer garment. The changes of the 1951 chapter had consisted of allowing the sisters to use the sewing machine to make the habit (up to that time considered too sacred to be sewn by machine), and snaps were permitted to replace pins in some places. But as to the habit as a whole, there were no major revisions.

The religious habit worn by the novices and professed sisters consisted of three main pieces: a skirt, a bodice and an apron. These were made of heavy coarse wool, over which was worn a white heavily starched cotton kerchief and on the head a complicated peasant coiffe, also of three pieces. The headpiece required long hours of mending, starching and ironing after each washing.

Unlike the religious garb of most orders, ours was not a free flowing dress with endless folds but consisted of a tightly fitted bodice with long large sleeves. The skirt had twenty pleats, ten in the front, and ten in the back. Each pleat completely overlapped so that there was a triple thickness. The white starched kerchief went down the back, coming to a point, and was held by a long two and a half inch steel pin. At the neck a small half inch pin held it together. It crossed over slightly the rest of the way down and tucked into the skirt. Over this, each sister wore a gray bibbed apron pleated in the same fashion as the skirt. The skirt and bodice were of heavy coarse wool, much like an army blanket, the apron of lightweight wool. For nurses and missionaries the habit was made of white lightweight cotton. For us, a white apron was exchanged for the gray whenever we worked, for example, when we taught, laundered, etc., in fact at all times except prayers and community exercises, such as meals.

In order to achieve a proper fit, each sister wore a whalebone corset about one inch thick laced in the back. The front had a long stick that protruded down over one's stomach so that if you did not sit upright it jabbed you in the abdomen. On the inside of the front were two small gussets, sewn on each side, and laced together in the center. This formed a pocket and allowed one's breast to be protected from the corset. The stick was padded and covered with muslin, as was the rest of the corset.

This is an example taken from Wikipedia circa 1730-1740 France

Ours had the addition of a long stick in the front (this gave shape for our crucifix and ours did NOT have straps.

We dressed in this order (eight layers of clothing): a man's T-shirt, our whale bone corset, a long white muslin tunic (think of it as a slip) two long pockets sewn to a tape which we tied around our waist, the woolen skirt, with its 20 pleats, the woolen bodice, the white heavily starched kerchief, the grey lighter weight woolen apron.

When we received the habit on February 2 1958, it was constructed in almost the exact same way as the habit of the foundress in 1703, including the use of long steel pins to hold all together. On our right side from the waist we hung a long white rosary. This completed the novice's habit.

Later upon taking vows, the white rosary would be exchanged for a black one and the crucifix would be added to slip in between the kerchief and the grey bib.

Rachel Novice, Marlene Professed Nun

The corset could be laced as tight as one wanted and functioned to give shape to the whole, so that each Daughter of the Spirit had the same hard round barrel-like appearance. Since we were not allowed to wear girdles, the effect of the tight upper corset over the loose flesh of the abdomen and buttocks and the overlapping pleats gave us a strange tied at the center balloon-like appearance.

In keeping with the vow of poverty which was faithfully adhered to, each sister had only 1 habit. Once a year the community seamstress took the dress apart, laundered the wool and put the dress back together making the hem the waist area and the waist area the hem, thus the dress would wear out more evenly and last longer. Now it was understood that during the upcoming General Chapter, the Europeans would press for more radical change.

Then there was the question of "apostolic work." Should the sisters continue to engage in works which no longer met the needs of the times? Free schools for the poor were now supported by the state. Should sisters continue to staff schools? Is that what the founder would advise were he alive to guide his flock?

The American and Canadian sisters prepared themselves to defend the status quo and sought in tradition the answer to questions raised by the European nuns. One week prior to the start of the General Chapter, the Dutch-born Father General was killed in a motorcycle accident. This superior, a priest, would have presided over the meetings and his position would have allowed him to set the tone. He was a vociferous advocate of change.

His death was interpreted by the American superiors as a sure sign that God was on their side and, though sorrowful over his death, they prepared with renewed vigor their defense of tradition at the coming chapter. The air of excitement over the chapter set the tone of my six months of postulate, and I felt privileged to have entered the community during such an exciting time. I looked forward with relief, however, to the end of this probationary six month period, and eagerly awaited my entry into the Novitiate.

THE NOVITIATE

"My dear Daughters, what do you ask?
We ask to be admitted to the Novitiate…
What motives induce you to make this request?
The desire to be trained in the religious life and to acquire Divine Wisdom."
****

What Am I asking of thee? Children: Priests free with thy
Freedom, detached from all things, without father or mother
or brothers or sisters, without relations according to the
flesh, without friends according to the world, without means,
without worry, without cares and even without any will of their own.

Founder's prayer for followers.

I entered the Novitiate with all the fervor and eagerness of my seventeen years. Now at last, the serious work was about to begin, There would be no more childish games. We would be instructed in the rules and the vows and at the end of the year, we would "graduate" as Daughters of The Spirit.

And what would I be in the end? How did I picture myself in those future years? Perhaps, I thought to myself, I might be a great missionary, and I imagined myself conquering the hearts of all I met in the jungles of Africa. Or maybe I would remain here in the states and become a master teacher, astonishing all, not only by my command over the hearts and minds of my students but also by my revolutionary ideas in education.

But these were only dreams. I saw them as such and dismissed them brusquely. I must first set about the task of becoming a nun.

There was very little change between the postulate and the novitiate, or so it might have seemed from the outside. We got up early, went to prayers, and ran through a similar daily schedule. Nevertheless, there was a fantastic change, not so much because of what we did, but because of the image we developed of ourselves. This image had been carefully nurtured in a variety of ways during the previous six months. The novice wore the grey habit of the professed sister, similar in every way save two: the rosary was white, not black, and the large ebony crucifix that decorated the chest was missing. The rooms set apart for the novices were considered sacred rooms. To enter them was to step into the cloister. As postulants, we had been allowed to enter them maybe twenty times, each on a special occasion. Thus becoming a novice, having access to the rooms, wearing the religious habit, symbolized our new status.

We approached the novitiate with a sense of: "This is it!" "This is the big year!" "This is the hard year!" To prepare ourselves fittingly, we made an eight day retreat prior to our admission.

There were rules that we would be asked to obey in the novitiate that we would never again have the "opportunity" to obey. For example, the rule requiring complete silence was one that couldn't possibly be maintained if one became a teacher or a nurse. Yes, life during our novitiate was going to be very different. Moreover, we were made to feel that if we made the most of it, it would serve us well for the rest of our lives.

There were twenty-three girls in my group, fresh out of high school except for two nurses, Barbara, 25, and Dorothy, 26. We were very young, very idealistic and ready to do anything. The only clear vision all of us shared was that we wanted to be nuns. We were isolated, healthy and willing. We were training for our vocation under the most ideal conditions.

Life in the Novitiate, as in the postulate, was highly regulated. Its description is perhaps best embodied in a chronology of daily events. Rising was at 5:30 a.m. unless on some special occasion we were given the privilege of rising at 5:00, like the professed sisters. Privileges such as these were dispensed only to the fervent, to those whose zeal prompted them to obey all the rules and regulations in their most minute detail.

Being fervent and being "disponible" spelled the height of success as a novice. "Disponible", a French word meaning malleable, had the connotation that one did not resist the molding process at hand. None of us, that I can recall, ever questioned the virtue of this characteristic. Rather, accepting it as a desirable trait, we strove to be thought of in this way.

From the very first sound of the morning bell, we were trained to jump out of bed and direct our thought to God: "*Our Lord Jesus Christ be Praised!*" the novice mistress said aloud as she flicked on the lights. "Through Mary.",we chorused in response, jumping out of the bed, and rolling back the covers all in one motion. Each novice knelt by her bed and renewed her consecration: "I am all Thine, and all that I have is Thine."

The next half hour was given over to dressing, making beds and straightening up our cells before getting down to the chapel. Dressing was ritualized, though not much was made of it, except that we had to stand to put on our stockings. That was to develop virility, an important virtue in the convent. Virility was the stuff saints were made of, virility meant one did not cry when one felt like it, and that one did the opposite of whatever one felt like doing. If you liked sleeping with a pillow, then you slept without it, and if you liked sugar in your coffee, then you had it without, and so on. In short, virility meant that one was strong enough to control one's impulses.

Despite the modern conveniences in the convent, each sister was furnished with a small white porcelain basin which hung on the back of her three-drawer night stand. We were instructed to fill the basin, wash from it, and then brush our teeth from the water in our glass and spit out into the basin. Early on, I dispensed myself from this practice which I considered to be archaic. Besides, I was repulsed at the sight of my saliva and tooth paste floating in the water. Instead I went to the nearest communal bathroom and brushed my teeth in the sink as I would have done at home. Thankfully, no one ever stopped me or remarked on it.

The bell marked the end of the half hour allotted to dressing and called us to chapel. We quietly made our way downstairs to take our place in line outside the chapel doors, along the long shiny convent corridors, oldest first, youngest last. The mistress with an almost imperceptible nod of her head signaled us to enter. We filed down the center aisle, genuflected as one, and took our assigned seats. If we had arisen at 5:00 a.m., the prayer hour began with morning meditation; if at 5:30, then meditation was reserved for 8:30. Morning meditation during these first years of religious life seemed to be a perpetual struggle with sleep. Perhaps it was the strain of leading a regulated life, or perhaps it was the early rising, but many of the novices and sisters slept, or spent the half hour fighting off sleep. Unwittingly, the chapel, warm, dark and quiet served as our accomplice. One of my superiors later confessed that she engaged in a game of imaginary chess with the sisters who sat before her in an attempt to keep herself awake. Meditation, Morning Prayer (a series of vocal prayers said in unison, or read aloud by one prayer leader) Mass and Thanksgiving (more meditative silent prayer) formed the first of the chapel exercises.

Despite the early hour and the constant interruption of my thoughts by the vocal recitation, I treasured this early morning meditation. I used the time to reflect on some passage I had read the previous evening or to take stock of my plans for the day as yet to be unfolded. I especially loved the earlier rising, because on these occasions, Mother Michael often took us for a brisk walk outdoors to recite the first of our vocal prayers. Contact with the fresh air was meant to wake us up. It suited my romantic nature to imagine myself with all the multitude of saints praising God at sunrise. I imagined that I knew what Christ's glorious return to earth would be like - hosts of the faithful, singing God's praises at sunrise. In the winter, we prayed in the presence of the stars, and I saw in it a unique form of adoration that we broke the stillness of the night to chant our hymns of praise.

After Chapel, we filed down to the refectory for breakfast. We said brief graces and heard the daily maxim: *"If I intend to be a true Daughter of the Spirit, I must guard all my thoughts against the encroachments of the devil..."* the reader began. We sat heads bowed, hands in our sleeves, and listened to the advice of the founder read to us each day. When it was over, usually in a minute, we began breakfast. The reader would then read from some current theological work. Breakfast was followed by housework, or ménage as we called it, a duty that we carried out whether the house was dirty or not.

Ménage gave way to mediation if we had arisen at 5:30 or to a brief half hour study period if we had gotten up early. Theology class was at 9:00. This was conducted much like our High School religion classes. It centered on understanding and memorizing the points made in the Baltimore catechism, i.e., the official United States Catholic version of basic tenants of Catholicism. When it ended at 9:45 we were allowed to rush down to the refectory for a drink and for some ten minutes of recreation, the first time during the day that we were allowed to talk. It was then that we exchanged the silly remarks that made up our still largely adolescent conversations: ... "Did you hear Sister Gagnier snoring last night?" "I thought I'd die when..."

Study period began at 10:00 a. m. and lasted until 11:00. This was our most lengthy and profitable study period during which we busied ourselves memorizing the constitutions and the "catechism of the vows" in preparation for the central event of the day, the eleven o'clock instruction. Everything was focused on this sacred hour, during which the head mistress instructed us in the constitutions and the catechism of the vows. It was at the heart of our novitiate training. The catechism of the vows was a "canon-law-made-easy" book written by priests who were canon lawyers. It dealt with those points of law which the Church had laid down to govern convents and monasteries. Each congregation had to guide itself by these broad guidelines within which some small variation was possible. Each order described and defined these variations in its particular constitutions.

Typically the head mistress would discuss a topic, starting with the general regulations of the catechism, and then go on to explain the specifics affecting the sisters of the order as outlined in the constitutions. For example, though canon law only required a sister to renounce the free disposition of her property (if she had any) when taking simple vows of poverty; the congregation placed more stringent demands on its members.

We were forbidden to have any pocket money whatsoever, even for necessities. Thus each time a sister needed a dime or a quarter for a bus ride, she had to kneel before the superior and ask for it. This practice, specific to this congregation, was explained at this time.

Besides imparting information, the eleven o'clock instruction was intended to give the novices a feel for the spirit of the congregation. A congregation's spirit was expressed by the way it formulated its rules, and how it practiced them. More difficult than the mere presentation of facts, the duty to impart this spirit to the young candidates rested squarely on the shoulders of the novice Mistress.

I greatly admired and respected Mother Michael, our head mistress. She was a Victorian lady, quite "old school" who sometimes did not understand young people. But I liked her nevertheless. She was a highly intelligent woman who had been one of the progressive superiors of an earlier day. Trained as a High School teacher, she received her PhD in English in the 30's at a time when for women in general it was an extraordinary feat. For the congregation, it was so extraordinary that in 1957 when I entered it, she was still the only sister in the American Province to possess this degree.

Mother Michael came from a large Canadian family of Irish descent. She was bright, confident and alert. Of medium height, graying hair and rosy complexion, she had a sharp incisive mind, and one felt she could have mastered anything she might have undertaken. She was a controlled woman, with a fine sense of humor, betrayed on occasion by the gleam in her eye. She spoke with a slight brogue and an Irish lilt to her voice and her French, though impeccable, was amusing with its Irish r's.

She was a veritable storehouse of poetry, and on special occasions, would entertain us by her recitals of Tennyson, Shakespeare, Browning, etc. She had such a command of English and American literature that she constantly made use of literary phrases to illustrate a point. I found it exciting to listen to her. Typical was her use of Tennyson's <u>Charge of the Light Brigade</u>: "*Ours is not to question, nor to reason why......ours is but to do and die.*" She would literally shout out with much vigor when she explained what our attitude would be vis-à-vis a superior's command. I laughed much later when I realized that the next line was: "*And into the valley of death rode the five hundred.*" Chastity, a subject hardly discussed at all, demanded an attitude which she found reminiscent of Rebecca's in <u>Rebecca of Sunnybrook Farm</u> "*It's the dearest thing in life to me, but it's an awful care.*"

Despite her Victorian reticence, she had a profound sense of life and a capacity for enjoyment that was greater than that of any other superior I ever had. As young superior of the boarding school which I later attended, she had made St. Patrick's Day a holiday that rivaled all others. When I became a boarder, twelve years after she had left the school, it was still a day of general festivity, with plays, skits, choral singing and general fun for all. The important thing to note is that the school was in the midst of a French-Canadian community for whom St. Patrick meant nothing culturally and very little religiously. Her personality and ability to draw people to herself was so strong that it had lasted all those years.

I never felt ill at ease with Mother Michael. I trusted her judgment. I felt that if she made a decision, she would make it according to principle, that I could know why she was making a decision, and that I could argue with her on the principles. Her decisions did not seem arbitrary. She was eminently rational and even if I did not always agree with her premises, I had to acknowledge her consistency in thought and action. Moreover, she did not do things to get even, or exercise that kind of power play; she was above that. Finally, she never got lost in detail; she could set it aside when something important was at stake.

When I entered the congregation, postulants were allowed to see their parents monthly. Though my mother came to see me the first visiting day, the trip from my home town to the novitiate was a long and strenuous one of 15 hours. It seemed unlikely that I would see her every visiting day. Mother Michael understood this without explanation. She came to me unsolicited, and told me to allow my mother to return the next day if she wanted. That just seemed like good common sense to me, and exactly what I expected from rational older people. I thanked her and informed my mother of the decision. What I had not yet discovered was that it took an extraordinary person to be able to set aside the "sacred rule' when circumstances called for it. She was one of the few superiors that I came to know who could do it with ease and assurance.

Mother Michael was named Provincial Superior after I had been in the Novitiate six months. Her nomination meant that she would leave for New York. While I felt that she would be an ally for me in the future, I regretted her departure because it left me without a friend in the present. I had found her especially sympathetic to those of us from Northern Maine. She had spent the greater part of her religious life in that far away place. Because of this she had seen firsthand the difficult financial straits most rural families had coped with in the second quarter of the century, she knew the sense of inferiority that can plague those of a minority group whose language is different. She understood the prejudices that place real obstacles in their paths. I felt that without explanation she understood what it meant to be French-Canadian. In time, I came to believe that my training would have been different if it had continued under her supervision for, despite her old-fashioned ways, she was a mature, well-rounded, stable person. A rare breed indeed, even though we were a generation apart.

Eleven o'clock instruction ended at 11:50. The bell summoned again, this time to chapel for our particular examen. This was a device for personal growth, a check book to help one keep track of how well or how badly one kept a particular rule. Rules like promptness in answering the bell, fidelity to the rule of silence, etc. were among the first to be picked as material for the examen. A page of this little book would be divided into days and hours and at 11:50 a.m., one would run through the day in one's mind and check for infidelities. Because these dealt with external control, they were judged easier to conquer. If, for example, one had spoken twice between ten and eleven in the morning, it was recorded in the appropriate slot: A reduced sample is below

	S	M	T	W	T	F	S
9:-							
10							
11:							

The hope was that if one "broke silence" 15 times a day in the beginning, as time went on, this could be cut to ten to five and eventually down to zero by sheer dint of will. Once you achieved the zero goal, another point of the rule was picked to work on. This method bore a lot of similarity to Ben Franklin's well described system for strengthening his character by an hourly check on his behavior

The angelus ended the brief examen time and signaled the lunch hour. The dining room was located in the basement as it was in all the convents (with the exception of Christ the King where the entire convent was on the fourth floor over the school). The cinder block walls were unpainted and bare save for the life size crucifix that hung in the front of the room, behind the raised estrade where the superior and her assistants sat.

The Sisters sat in order of seniority at these long tables placed perpendicular to the raised estrade:

Raised podium for Reader	ESTRADE, or raised table for Superior and two assistants

Sister s	Novic es	Postul ants

Prie Dieu (kneeler)   Prie Dieu (kneeler) Prie Dieu
At the back were three kneelers (called Prie Dieu or "Pray to God" in French)for the Superior and her two assistants. They intoned grace

before meals and blessed the reader who took a bow from the waist and then went to the Reading Podium. Following this the Superior walked down one of the two aisles to the raised dining table (estrade) to take her seat. The sisters bowed from the waist as she walked up the aisle.

It was not permissible to be late for meals. If by chance you had to slip into the bathroom on the way from chapel to the refectory, and did not make it on time to say graces, then you had to report to the superior eyes downcast, hands in sleeves (or under the cape if a postulant) to explain the reason for your tardiness. Usually the superior dismissed you with a nod of her head. Thereupon, you went to your place, knelt down and kissed the floor in reparation for being late and thus breaking the holy rule.

All meals were eaten in silence. One sister was assigned to read aloud, this time from a lighter book usually some biography of a saint or renown Catholic person. Refectory reading was as ritualized as were the sacred Chapel exercises. One did not simply read. First the assigned reader had to step out into the center aisle, bow from the waist to the crucifix, turn and bow to the superior and ask for the traditional blessing. This was asked in Latin in chant tones similar to those used in the Divine office: *"Jube Domne Benedicite"* to which the superior would respond.

The sister would then bow again to the Superior, to the crucifix, and walk to the reader's stand. The Superior then walked to her seat at the estrade in the company of her assistants. As she made her way down the aisle the sisters faced the aisle and bowed from the waist, eyes downcast, and hands in sleeves. When the Superior reached the front the community stood erect, facing the estrade, waiting for her to be seated. This accomplished, all the sisters followed suit. Each meal's reading began with a short solemn passage to which the sisters listened motionless in their seats, eyes downcast.

At breakfast, it was the maxims; at lunch it was the gospel of the day and in the evening, it was usually a biography of a saint or some light theological reading. Occasionally letters from the Mother General would be read aloud. The reading was done in a high pitched monotone which struck the listener as odd at first but which eventually seemed normal. Try reading the following in a high pitched monotone and you will understand the fit of giggles we got into as postulants when we encountered this passage in Father Flanagan's Boy's Town: *When he knocked the hat off his head, the whiskey flask went flying. Ha! Ha! Roared Father Flanagan.* These outbursts among new postulants were tolerated but never condoned; usually we would be ignored, and the giggles would quietly pass. As novices, we had already become very serious and giggles were a part of our past.

Food took on an exaggerated importance for us during those early years. This was caused by a strange belief that a hearty appetite was a sign of happiness in one's chosen way of life - the sign of a true vocation.

Overeating as compensatory behavior had not yet penetrated the psychology of the religious superiors. Thus, we were required to eat two slices of bread at each meal, to have a hearty breakfast of cereal, fruit, occasionally eggs, a farmer's lunch of soup, two vegetables, meat and a big dessert, and a supper lightened only by the absence of the soup. Added to this was the obligatory snack at four o'clock which consisted often of two slices of bread with jam or peanut butter. We were encouraged to finish dishes and often the serving sister would bring the dish to be finished back to the head of the table, so that each sister could partake again.

These rules had been put in place in the early days because the sisters would often deprive themselves in order to give food to the peasants they were serving. Despite the fact that over 250 years had passed since the founding of the order and the peasants were not in danger of starvation as they had been, the rules continued to be enforced.

Each time my mother visited me during that year she expressed her anxiety over the weight I was gaining, but I assured her that I was happy, and my hearty appetite was a sure sign. (I gained 45 pounds by the end of my first year and a half. We were weighed before vows.)

But even for a good sturdy girl like me, the habit of overeating became a problem. One lunch, a novice returned from the kitchen with a full serving bowl of leftover vanilla pudding with instructions that it was to be finished. I had been the serving sister at the meal and had already finished the previous main dishes. Moreover, as I had served during the meal, I was the only sister left in the dining room to eat the dessert. My stomach felt stretched with the food that I had already consumed. I knew I literally could not eat another thing. I told the sister as much, but in response to my remark, she merely set the dish before me and walked out.

I sat before the dish, tears flowing, wondering what to do. If I returned the dish to the main kitchen myself, I would probably be given an argument. If I went to the Mistress... well, one did not trouble the Mistress with such matters.... There was only one way out. I stood defiantly, picked up the dish, went to the garbage pail, lifted the cover and dumped it out. My act was to bother me for a few days, as I thought of the unnecessary waste, but I chose to live with my guilt.

Lunch was followed by our first hour of recreation. In the Novitiate, as in the postulate, this hour was usually accompanied with some task to be done. For example, we did most of the gardening during this time or we refinished furniture, or canned fruit. Occasionally, we went for a walk. We hardly cared what we did, as long as we could talk. Talking, like so many other facets of our lives, had to be controlled and molded. We were no longer worldly people who could talk about anything and anyone, and in whatsoever fashion. Our recreation had to be sanctified. In order to do this, several suggestions were made. There follows a list of these as they were presented to me when I became a novice.

These lists are detailed prescriptions to which we were bound if we wanted to become nuns. A reading through them will illustrate how controlled all our actions were expected to be. Many of these are mere common courtesy suggestions. Others specific to the vow of poverty and practices meant to enforce ways to remind the sister that she had to care for the physical items in her care, such as her one habit. A sample page follows. (A scanned copy of the entire 8 pages of customs can be found in the appendix).

Mary Immaculate Novitiate
_____, Connecticut

SPIRIT'S 'little' CUSTOMS

FIDELITY is the outgrowth of LOVE. "La fine fleur de
1'Amour" (Marmion)

Virgin, Most Faithful, pray for us.
Tres pur Coeur de Marie, je me confie en Vous!

THE CHAPEL

1.Do I always answer the-bell promptly and take my line for chapel
noiselessly?
2 Do I always go into the chapel in grey, with my sleeves down?
3. Do I always hold my Rosary when entering (asking Mary to enter
with me)?
4.Do I always take Holy water when entering?
5.Do I make an inclination when passing in front of the Superior's
place? AVE CHRISTIE
6.Do I genuflect together with the others?
7.Do I keep any books I may be bringing into chapel in my sleeves?
8.Do I lift my skirt a little when about to kneel?
9.If I arrive late do I remain in the back until the Veni Sancte, etc.,
is said?
10.When late, do I report to the Mistress or Sister in charge?
11.Do I always kneel and make an act of adoration when I arrive at
my place in chapel?
12. Do I always cover my hands with my sleeves whenever
possible?
13.Do I pick up my cloak (if wearing it) when sitting down and pull
it down when standing?
14.If I am obliged to leave, do I ask permission?(except for regular
charges)
15.Do I always bow to the Tabernacle when I pass in front of it?
16.Do I always go into Chapel prepared?
17.Do I sit at the right time if I feel the need, during the rosary?
18.Do I stand at the right time *if I have been sitting during the Rosary?*
19.Do I sit and stand in a manner befitting the Divine Presence ?
20. Do I kneel correctly, not leaning on my arms nor slouching?
21.Do I avoid turning around to look when someone leaves or
enters?
22.Do I ask permission to open and close windows

23.Do I pass the paten correctly?

24.Are all my books covered?...with the right type of paper?

25.Do I avoid loud yawning and any other impoliteness or indelicacy?

26.Do I avoid making useless noise ?...turning unnecessary pages?

OFFICE AMD PRAYERS

1. Do I answer all vocal prayers?

2. Do I say my prayers aloud but not shouting? "Pray your prayers, don't say them."

3. Do I say my prayers piously and distinctly?

4. Do I do my best to keep the tone neither raising nor lowering it myself?

5. Do I always hold my book when praying or reading?

6. Do I always put something under my finger when using a book?

7. Do I follow my prayers in the prescribed book? (for 5 years)

8. Am I careful not to change the wording of the prayers?

9. Do I pause for two counts at the median of the psalms?

10. Do I endeavor to maintain a proper speed?

11. Do I bow and incline at all the places indicated?

12. Do I make all the necessary signs of the Cross, finger to lips, hand on heart, etc.?

13. Am I faithful to bowing reverently during the Gloria Patri...to Spiritu Santo?

14. When it is my turn to say prayers, do I prepare carefully checking on special intentions, list of the dead, special feasts, examens, meditations, etc.?

15. Do I always read an examem on Mary on Saturdays

16. Do I make use of the card giving the directions for saying the prayers?

17. Do I ask for a penance if I have said the prayers badly and given cause for distraction?

18. Am I persuaded that Community Prayers depends largely on the care and preparation I take in saying the prayers?

One cannot stress enough the force of these practices on the formation of the candidate. We did not become "robots" but our behavior nevertheless became highly routine and ritualistic, so that the slightest deviation seemed grotesque and unpardonable. We were jarred by non-conformity. While only an external control, these practices did nevertheless effect some changes on us in the long run. Their immediate effect was to make us different. We perceived that they made us different, and we did not resent this, because after all, we considered ourselves different, and this only served to mark us. We were, as we were often reminded, the specially chosen ones, the first who were called.

Recently, when I viewed Jean-Luc Goddard's film "Alphaville", I was jolted by the sense of familiarity I had with the surroundings. The members of the new city began each conversation in this way: "Hello. Good-bye. I am fine. Thank You. Please."

And after concluding their conversation they repeated their initial greeting: "Hello. Good-bye. I am fine. Thank You. Please."

It was several days before I could make the association. It had the ring of the mechanical greeting we used each time we spoke to each other in the convent: "I greet your good angel." "And I yours." Now the conversation could begin.

Singing practice followed the recreation hour, an exercise that I found totally relaxing, and one that I looked forward to each day. During this time, we sang Gregorian Chant and some of the early polyphonic music of the first centuries of the Church. We learned and practiced the chants for the Sunday High Mass, and whatever big Church feast that was coming. Three days a week, at 3:00, we went to a workroom in the novitiate for sewing. Mostly, this consisted of learning to mend the religious habit and the coiffe in particular. The coiffe, made of cheesecloth like fabric, had to be mended after each washing, a tedious process of replacing each broken thread. We were also introduced to the basics of machine sewing and the remarkably skilled method of darning our heavy woolen stockings.

The remaining two hours were devoted to French language lessons as this was the official language of the Congregation. Because I was already fluent and a good student, Mother Michael had assigned me to tutor the three sisters in my group who had not had any French language lessons in high school, Sister Dorothy, Sister Fiorella, and Sister Amarillo. I had never taught and like many native speakers had not analyzed the language structure sufficiently to understand how to present the material. The best I could do was to repeat to them what I had myself learned in grammar school, not realizing that the teaching methods used to teach a language were different for native speakers.

A welcome break arrived at 4:00 P.M. This was the only free time of the day. One could go to the bathroom without kneeling and asking permission, or open a window without asking, or run out for a breath of fresh air. Besides, we could talk again for a brief period.

Unfortunately, the belief had arisen that if one were truly fervent, one would use this free time to go to chapel on one's own, or at least use this time wisely. Thus it was that we usually ran down to the recreation room in the basement, had our collation (i.e. bread with jam or an apple with juice or coffee) and left to do some useful thing for fifteen minutes of the half-hour's time.

At 4:30 p.m., the second most important instruction of the day was given. This was the customs instruction. The task of the Eleven O'Clock instruction was to impart the essential information about what it meant to be a nun and specifically what it meant to be a Daughter of The Spirit. At the Four O'Clock instruction one learned the fine points as these were embodied in the customs. Customs were of two types: long-standing practices in the Congregation which accordingly had the force of customary law, and modern customs. All had to do with the externals of daily life. The first were universal in the Congregation and small in number. The latter usually varied greatly from country to country and consisted of numerous practices and exhortations.

On her first day, each novice was handed a prepared booklet of these latter customs. Many were common sense dictums which should have been left up to the individual's judgment; in fact only a few could be considered helpful for people learning a new social role. Somewhere along the line, a false piety had crept in allowing exhortations to be added to the list in order to help one become holy. Most had nothing to do either with piety or common sense. Given the length of these lists, it was easy to lose sight of the ultimate goals that these individual points were meant to help one reach. On pages 44-45, samples of "customs pages" are presented. At the end of the book, a photocopy of the eight pages given to me during my novitiate have been scanned and reproduced.

The customs had become elaborate- completely out of all proportion. I later came to believe that Mother Mary Kathleen was responsible for this over emphasis on little things. She was the second mistress of the Novitiate. A short, plump, freckled faced woman with large eyes, prominent teeth and light brown hair, Mother Mary Kathleen hailed from New York. Her father, at one time a wealthy business man, had lost a fortune during the stock market collapse of the thirties. The pampered little girl had grown up to resent her loss of wealth and status and this was evident by stories she told of her family and friends. Her best friend, whose family had retained their wealth, had always gone to school in a chauffeured car and ended up becoming a nun in another order dedicated to the education of the wealthy. She was, at the time of our novitiate, the superior of an exclusive girl's school in Connecticut from which Henry Ford's daughter, Charlotte Ford had recently graduated.

No longer buttressed by family connections, wealth and prestige, Mother Mary Kathleen had found a new security provided by the confines and rigidity of convent life. Her ardor and devotion had been rewarded by her elevation to the rank of second mistress of the Novitiate and she did her best to devise a scheme for holiness which she could pass on to her young charges. She was the type of person who felt a sense of accomplishment by checking off a list of duties when completed. Moreover, she seemed to believe that others should do things in exactly the same manner as she did in order to have an ordered existence. It was she who had compiled the list and it was she who gave the instruction.

Four o'clock instruction was also used to give pointers on "how to grow in virtue", i.e. how to become humble, how to become charitable, etc. I was completely absorbed by these instructions. I gave myself over to an intensive attempt to understand and fully practice what was taught. As I saw it, virtue was to be the staple of my life as a nun. It was essential that I understand it and learn it. I think I approached its acquisition with the monotonous concentration of the drill sergeant. I really tried.

Practices of humility were often artificial and too self-conscious. For example, there was the custom of never beginning a sentence with the proposition I more than three times in a letter. All our mail was screened and if we had forgotten to omit I, the letter would be returned to be rewritten. It was believed that we would get into the habit of being less self-centered if we did not speak or write of ourselves so frequently.

Another instance was that out of humility one submitted one's judgment to the superior and asked her to make the judgment. In this way, the sister's maturity was halted because she was deprived of the ability to make mistakes and to learn by them.

I have inserted here a re-typed copy of the practices of humility which we were advised to practice.

D.S.

<u>HUMILITY</u>

Self-Knowledge, self confidence and self control

1st Degree – refrain from Mortal Sin

2nd Degree - Refrain from venial sin

3rd Degree -To do our utmost not to offend god even in small imperfections.

1. Avoid Dispute and any vain success they bring
2. Too quick and ready words often leave behind a sting
3. Do not excuse yourself even when not to blame
4. Add nothing to the truth, be simple in your aim
5. Born poor conceal it not; let none your riches see
6. The good you do forget but grateful always be'
7. An independent spirit shun as a dangerous snare
8. Let every regulation be kept with zealous care
9. To those God places over you blindly obedient be
10. Hide nothing in your heart your mother may not see
11. Your many imperfections be glad that all should know
12. Abhor the world's opinion and false shame never show
13. Be glad to find a critic both truthful and severe
14. Whatever be the verdict accept it as sincere
15. Rejoice to be reproved even when you do your best
16. See that your slightest faults in public are confessed
17. Far from the eyes of all, act always quite the same
18. Speak little of yourself either to praise or blame
19. Successful in your labors, to God the glory give
20. Never distrust the Master for Whom alone you live
21. Extraordinary graces like St. John Berchman's fear
22. Devout in your actions, do nothing to appear
23. Always regard yourself as least and last of all
24. Think little of your talents; your misdeeds oft recall
25. Seek not to gain attention, but serve with humble grace
26. All honors to your sisters
27. Be truly kind and gentle to each and everyone.
28. But wisely guard your heart and be attached to none.
29. Never allow suspicion to rest within your mind
30. For those who contradict you have feelings ever kind.
31. Be glad that others' merits should gain their praise due
32. Accept when (go) called by duty, the hidden life for you.
33. For others' faults and failings, find always an excuse

34. Ne'er speak of them in public unless it be of use
35. To every low employment, with willing footsteps go.
36. Wear garments poor and humble, thankful to have them so.
37. If pleasure be in question, let labor be your share.
38. Assist the sick and gladly another's burden bear
39. Your service in the kitchen, render with joyful heart
40. Always believe another could better be your part
41. Accept those trying duties which others seem to dread
42. Unworthy you the Holy State, to which you have been led.
43. Never a word of murmur- be ready at each call
44. to place yourself the lowest and at the feet of all
45. In fervor and exactness a novice try to be
46. It is your lot to be despised; the justice of it see.
47. Believe yourself unworthy to bear the light of day
48. If all looked down upon you a "Deo Gratias" say
49. If words of praise should reach you smile at the strange mistake
50. Pious not worldly, converse is what you should hold
51. "I'm prouder than a peacock", for your motto take
52. Thirst for humiliation as misers do for gold.
53. We're told by St. Ignatius to ask them of Our lord
54. Let come what may His Holy Will in all things be adored.

D.S.

HUMILITY

Helpful Hints on Humility.....Boylan,
"The Tremendous Lover*

1. Abandonment to Divine Providence, the outward expression of Humility,

2. Pray for the Grace.   Co-operate with it by accepting humiliations, our own limitations, defects, lowliness, etc.

3. Place the utmost confidence in God; no trust in self,

4. "Humility is not so much self-depreciation as self-forgetfulness."

5. "It is our emptiness and thirst that God needs, not our plentitude."

6. Put no value on personal achievement .Fr. Clerissac

7. Do not think well of self nor wish others to recognize your value.

8. Humility is acquired by keeping good company: that of Jesus and Mary.

9. Frequent meditation on the Passion will bring us more quickly to humility than anything else.

10. Self-knowledge, so conducive to humility is better acquired through study of God than study of self.

11. Humility of heart is acquired by living the Mass, whereby we offer sacrifice to God ' He is all...we are nothing,

12. Avoid all manifestations of pride; therefore:

    1. speak as little of self as possible
    2. attend to one's own affairs
    3. avoid curiosity.
    4. do not seek to manage other people's affairs.
    5. accept contradiction and correction.
    6. do not insist on one's own opinion.
    7. pass over, cover up the mistakes of others.
    8. yield to the will of another when possible.
    9. hide one's ability; do not seek to shine.

13. There are higher acts than the above:

    1.Accept blame, insults, injuries, being slighted, forgotten, not especially loved or admired,
    2. Be kind and gentle under provocation.
    3. Do not be put out by one's clumsiness or mistakes.
    4. Yield in discussion, be not opinionated, nor self-assertive.

14. One may go still further:

    1. Be glad at being despised, thank God for humiliations,

lowliness, etc.

2. Be patient with one's own failings, glory in infirmity.

Now love is becoming ardent, union more intimate.

3. Practice humility and its sister-virtues in one's thoughts.

4. Do not brood over humiliations, failures, etc.

Above is s a sampling of pointers that were given us and elaborated during the instruction hour. Most of the statements are true, but for the most part, they were the summation of a whole life experience and could not be passed on to others by some glib phrase that one could simply memorize.

Doing things to forget oneself was illusory. We were encouraged to pursue tasks that were unwelcome such as helping the sister in the laundry during the 10 AM or 4 PM coffee break, instead of using this limited free time to relax and chat with friends. In fact, such behavior led to feelings of hostility toward the other sisters who interpreted life differently, resenting them for enjoying themselves or unconsciously resenting the system that required such inhumane practices.

If the resentment became conscious, then it too had to be transformed into sanctity by suppressing it as base - unworthy of a person devoted to God.

When I matured, I came to believe that one doesn't become humble by practicing humility. Humility is a comparative estimate of oneself that is rounded out by life and can't be taught by practices of humility. Humility comes from experiencing one's own weakness. One makes judgments which turn out to be bad, or one volunteers for a task which it turns out cannot be accomplished and others are let down. These are the experiences of life which truly teach one to be humble. I came to view it as tragic that these middle-aged women who were my teachers had not grasped these simple truths.

The customs instruction had still another function. This was to explain the special practices of penance in the Congregation as well as the Chapter of faults. There is already some public knowledge of the latter. It is a ritualized ceremony where individuals publicly confess their personal failings. In the Congregation of the Daughters of the Spirit, it took a simple form. The sisters knelt in a semicircle, facing a crucifix lit by two candles. The room was darkened and sisters wore their black chapel capes, giving an aura of mystery to the room.

The oldest sister began: "In the name of the Father, of the Son and of the Holy Ghost. Mother and Sisters, I accuse myself of. . . For these and for all the faults I have committed against the Holy Rule and you my sisters, I beg forgiveness. A penance, if you please."

The Superior would then assign a penance, such as saying a number of specified prayers begging for one's supper on one's knees, or other practices. She might at this time also take the opportunity to lecture the sister on her failing.

Sisters did not accuse one another as was the practice in some other congregations, but only themselves. The ceremony took place monthly. It had to do with the external aspects of the rule. In other words, you never confessed an interior fault such as jealousy, but only an external one like breaking the rule of silence, or not moving at the first sound of the bell. It had as its fundamental principle to restore the damage done to community morale and commitment by such open flouting of the rule. One had to acknowledge the break in solidarity by one's behavior and express one's regret for such failure.

It was common among the sisters to choose as subjects of exposure the least innocuous of their failings so that after a time, one became familiar with the repertory of common failings which no one seemed inordinately ashamed of admitting. Occasionally we would be jarred by an uncommon accusation such as gossiping or criticizing the superior. On these occasions our respect for the particular sister rose that she should be so honest as to admit so heinous a fault.

Similar to this was the custom of public accusation of faults that took place each evening during supper. At an appropriate time, usually after the main meal and before the dessert, the superior would ring the bell next to her to give the reader a break. Any sister who so desired could at that time stand up, kneel, kiss the floor and accuse herself in the same manner as at the chapter of faults. Before beginning, the sister glanced around the room to see if there were others, because in this, as in all things, we proceeded in doyenne(seniority) order. According to custom, it was incumbent on each sister to accuse herself in this manner at least once every two weeks, be it at the chapter of faults or at the evening meal.

I hated this custom. Whenever my turn approached, I had to struggle with myself to do it. I could put it off a day or two, during which time my meals were disrupted by nervous regurgitation. After the sisters had finished, they usually knelt there for a few minutes, arms outstretched in the form of a cross, saying their assigned prayers of penance. My stomach always tightened when the time for such public accusations began.

The special practices of penance were three in number. They were performed in times of Lent and Advent or on the occasion of some special public failing for which a sister or superior insisted on making extraordinary reparation. The first of these was begging for one's supper. When assigned this penance, the sister, instead of taking her usual place at table, knelt by her seat and accepted whatever the sister sitting next to her chose to dish out. Over time the practice lost its severity; all it really meant was that you ate kneeling instead of sitting. Nevertheless, it was humiliating.

A second practice involved kneeling at the refectory door,

shrouded in the black chapel cape and asking for the prayers of the sisters as they filed into the room. If one was of perpetual vows, the cincture given at the ceremony would be removed from one's waist and slipped over one's head to hang from the neck like a noose, signifying one's guilt.

The third practice was the one I found the most difficult. It involved kissing the feet of a sister. One had to kneel, kiss the floor, then rise, tap the shoulder of a nearby sister, who then rose and joined the sister in the refectory aisle. The penitent lifted the shoe of the sister to her lips to kiss the shoe, kiss one and then the other. These customs bore little resemblance to the flagellant practices of medieval monasticism from which they were derived. Nevertheless, they were humiliating.

Finally, it was at the four o'clock instruction that we learned the practice of asceticism. Like most virtues, asceticism had become systematized and translated into a behavioral index. It had as its governing principle: Whatever you like to do, do the opposite. If you liked salt on your food, you ate it without, and so forth.

What I said about humility does not apply to the practices of asceticism. It is in fact true that one learns to be disciplined by acts of discipline. I did however have an argument against these practices. Most were too out of the ordinary to be truly disciplining, and too much emphasis was placed on external practices. What could one possibly learn that would make one a more disciplined controlled person by the few extras below?

MORTIFICATION

1. Eat dry bread occasionally
2. Serve yourself with a slight amount of jelly or peanut butter
3. Wait for a while before drinking
4. Use slightly less milk (or more)
5. Eat less of food you prefer and more of food you dislike
6. Eat food as served – no salting
7. Never show likes or dislikes
8. When the reading is funny, do not communicate impressions
9. Do not examine food on the table
10. Decide on how much food you need and eat it constantly
11. Eat dry bread after a very tasty morsel of something
12. Help to finish dishes
13. Eat dry bread at collation
14. Refrain from adding water to hot drink at 10:00
15. Eat brown bread if you prefer white or vice versa
16. Wipe plates clean
17. Eat crumbs
18. Hang towels neatly
19. Help clean the tables

RECREATION

1. Keep busy- a bit of sewing, a book—knitting on walk if possible
2. Accept companions Providence sends you
3. Do not seek certain Sisters
4. Do not talk much of self
5. Mortify moodiness
6. Turn tongue before saying an unpleasant word. Then avoid the word.
7. Don't become impatient if the place is crowded. Or if you are pushed about.
8. If a conversation is begun do not question as to what went before.
9. Mortify curiosity
10. When cold, avoid shivering
11. Do not rush to radiators

12. Do not show that you are inconvenienced
13. Accept suggestions from others At 10:00 or 4:00 sacrifice recreation for a visit to chapel
14. Refrain at times from a witty word or a joke
15. Wait until recreation to give news

DORMITORY

1. Rise on signal – promptly
2. Kneel for offering
3. Stand while putting on stockings
4. Wash with cold water.
5. Do not turn on useless lights
6. Do not open or close windows without permission
7. To avoid noise, put Rosary in pocket when making bed
8. Sleep without a pillow or use one if you do not like it.
9. Retain one position in bed
10. Do not keep turning about in bed
11. Perform no unnecessary secular works during Grand Silence.

CHAPEL AND PRAYERS

1. Occasionally, do not rest hands on pews
2. Or the back on pews
3. Or the feet on pews
4. Occasionally, raise feet from floor, when sitting
5. Or step on toes while standing.

When the 4:30 instruction was over, we reported to our study room for a half hour of private spiritual reading. We were not permitted freedom of choice in any of our reading matter, though one could submit a request to read a certain book one had heard about in community discussions. Each of us read the book picked for us by Mother Mistress, a choice designed to give us the most enlightenment on our particular defects or ambitions.

Meditation followed. Various methods of meditations were introduced to us by the second mistress during the customs instructions. Whether the Ignatian method, the Sulpician or others, each had a structured approach, consisting of placing oneself in God's presence, chasing away all thoughts of the day's activities, troubles, etc. and focusing either on one attribute or gospel story, or virtue to be attained. From prayerful reflection on the topic chosen, one was to derive lessons for personal life. In those early days of our religious life, the assigned sister actually read aloud a passage to be meditated on and in the end read aloud a suggested resolution that one could draw from reflection on the passage. "Nosegays" or catch phrases were selected as reminders of the resolutions taken.

Up to this time, the form of prayer most of us had engaged in was classified as "prayers of supplications":

Oh God, give me an A in the exam...

Oh God, don't let my parents hear me come in so late…

Now we were led into a more ascetic approach to God. Prayer as a means of modeling oneself on the Divine, prayer as a means of self-control.

Frankly, I always found this structured meditation artificial. There were just so many resolutions one could make. And along with the particular examen, just keeping up with the new strains placed on us seemed ample.

Evening meditation was followed by the recitation of the last five decades of the rosary and then dinner. Like lunch, dinner was taken in silence except for the reading of some light biographical work.

The evening hour of recreation was meant to be more relaxing. We often just sat and talked, mending our personal things as we talked, without being pressed to work. The Novice Mistress and her assistants rotated supervision. We sat in a circle and the sister in charge often attempted to engage us in a general discussion. The result was that, to be polite, many listened when they would have preferred to spend the time talking in small groups. At 7:45, it was customary for a novice to make a spiritual remark. This was done by simply standing, waiting for silence and delivering one's comment: "Sisters, I remarked that God provides for those who place their trust in Him."

These remarks were taken either from spiritual reading one had done, from the public reading during the meals, or from the Gospel of the day. They were meant to elevate the minds and hearts of all the sisters to the spiritual realities, even for a brief moment. During advent and lent, sisters were encouraged to recite by heart the founder's daily maxim. All these things served to place one more constraint on the sisters instead of helping them relax.

At 8:00, we went to the chapel to recite the last vocal prayers of the day, after which, we proceeded to our cells to prepare for bed. Lights out was at 9:30, a welcome relief after a full day.

It was during the novitiate year that we got to know one another as much as we could, given our guarded structured lives. Ours was a happy, fun loving and lively group with several strong personalities. By the time we had finished the postulate, we had been dubbed the group with all chiefs and no Indians. We worked well together, despite the arguments that only half concealed a struggle for leadership. Because we were go-getters, we were singled out as particularly suited for intensive training in obedience. The attitude of the Congregation toward those with initiative was ambivalent. On the one hand, they repeated many times over that taking a vow of obedience did not mean foregoing one's reason, nor one's initiative and common sense. On the other hand, they seemed unable to deal with anyone who actually did exercise initiative and common sense, even punishing for it. Independent thinking was far too threatening. An example of this ambivalence was demonstrated early.

Each six months, as one group made ready for vows, the next group would arrange a farewell party. The party consisted of having a special meal, usually hamburgers, French fries and coleslaw; because these were foods we rarely got to eat. Afterwards, the junior novices would entertain the outgoing group and the postulants with skits, songs and games written for the occasion. Usually the songs celebrated the virtues and/or idiosyncrasies of each of the senior novices. It was lots of fun and we looked forward to our turn to do it.

The first step was to decide on a theme for the occasion and get it approved, and then the writing of the songs and skits could begin. We decided on such a theme and got down to writing. When the big day arrived with just a few minutes to go before curtain time, a novice came running into the kitchen where some of us were preparing the meal and in a nervous and excited tone exclaimed that Mother Mistress wanted us in the next room.

Tension filled the room as one of the sisters asked if we were in trouble.

"I don't know, but I think so!" She answered and hurried out.

As soon as we stepped into the room, the answer was obvious. Mother Mary Kathleen and a grim faced Novitiate staff stood at attention in front of the room.

"If it wasn't for the senior novices, I'd call the whole thing off. Imagine! Who do you people think you are? Going ahead with everything without permission?"

I was stunned. Without permission? But, we had asked permission.

As was customary, we knelt to accept the reprimand. Sister Fiorella, the spokesman for our group, protested that we had received permission long ago and that there must be some misunderstanding.

"There's no misunderstanding! I never saw the songs, nor did I read the skit." Mother Mary Kathleen continued angrily. She went on about how typical this was of our group, always wanting to take over and do everything our own way.

How could she hold us responsible when we didn't know that we had to get the finished product approved? I thought to myself.

We had no choice but to apologize and so we did. Then and now the whole incident seemed so trumped up. If they did really want to teach us obedience, then the thing to do was to make clear what was expected of us. It was disconcerting to be informed after the fact that a rule existed, to be pounced upon with an "Ah ha! we caught you!" attitude.

We no sooner got out of one mess then we were into another. It was that same week, during the Senior Novices' retreat, that we received a donation of furniture. Mother Mary Kathleen who was with us during the evening recreation, suggested that we look it over and decide what needed to be done, whether pieces needed to be refinished and the like.

"Wouldn't that make a good desk?" Mother suggested as she pointed to a buffet in the corner. "We could saw down the legs and remove the middle section and it would be just perfect."

We agreed and she got the saw to begin the job.

"Don't you think that we should do the sawing?" several of us asked our oldest member.

"No," replied Sister Fiorella, "she probably enjoys the work. It must be a welcome change for her. Besides, if she were tired, I'm sure that she would tell us, or quit." That sounded reasonable enough so we let her continue.

The next day at the eleven o'clock instruction, we got the reaction. Not only had we not submitted copies of the songs and the skit we had written for approval, but we had the nerve to stand around and watch the first mistress saw down a cabinet without offering to assist her. Who did we think we were?

We stood up as a body and knelt down to listen to the accusation. The only way to cure us, she continued, was for us to go on a special campaign of obedience. All the sisters would be advised to be very careful not to let us "take over" tasks and would report on us whenever we showed signs of inordinate independence.

I was confused by the whole thing, though I was not really aware of my confusion at the time. I felt uneasy, and uncomfortable. I couldn't reconcile the fact that the Congregation was happy that some of their best students entered the convent, girls who had shown a lot of initiative in High School and who were by most standards brighter than average. Why then did they proceed to strip us of any opportunity to exercise our talents?

In addition to the group effort to achieve some virtue, each sister, with the advice of the head mistress, decided on what it was in her character that needed polishing. She would then be encouraged to read the proper books, meditate on certain subjects and focus on the eradication of her fault through her particular examen.

My first encounter with Mother Mary Kathleen after Mother Michael left Connecticut was typical of our future meetings. She informed me that my problem was arrogance and pride. She spoke to me of humility and ended the talk with the recommendation that I read Tanqueray's Chapter on Humility and Pride. Tanqueray's volumes were an authoritative theological discussion of the Christian virtues with a commentary on the practice of these, not the kind of book that inspires one to change one's life. I did as suggested, and read it. Even with my limited experience and lack of maturity, I knew that one would not make any progress in humility by reading a book; wisely, I kept this opinion to myself.

The ambivalence toward talent and initiative manifested itself in a variety of ways and intruded in the most innocent endeavors. When I was assigned to clean a basement bathroom where the towels were well worn, I decided to cut some down, patch some and hem others up anew. Finally, I matched the colors to give the sisters the feeling of entering a pleasant clean room. Satisfied with the job I had done, I was shocked to be reprimanded for showing a worldly interest in color. I remember kneeling before Sister Montfort, one of the novitiate staff, and struggling within myself to feel sorry for what I had done. She took the occasion to state that not only had I matched the colors of the towels in the bathroom, but I had color matched my own towels in the dormitory. I listened to her comments without understanding how this was contrary to religious spirit. Nevertheless I forced myself to produce tears for the occasion. Deep inside me, I was uneasy and resentful, though not aware of it at the time.

Of all the incidents in the Novitiate, one in particular stands out in my mind. It had to do with "setting up" a picnic supper for the sisters. Sunday night picnics were fairly usual in the summer. By eating out of doors, we got around the rule of not talking in "regular" places such as the refectory. The menu, special to the occasion, was usually summer fare: hamburgers, hot dogs, corn on the cob, and watermelon.

One Sunday, during the recitation of the evening prayers, Mother

Michael came over to me and whispered:"Sister Ethier, would you go to the refectory and organize a picnic for tonight's supper?"

"Yes Mother," I answered.

It was to be a surprise for the sisters and I was honored to be picked for the task. As it was already late, I hurried to carry out the heavy wooden tables and chairs before the bell rang for supper. I congratulated myself on having everything ready when the bell rang and I waited for the sisters to file downstairs to discover that we were to eat outdoors.

I was so busy with my own thoughts that I failed to notice Mother Mary Kathleen's approach."Sister Ethier, did you take the tables out?"

"Yes, Ma Chere Soeur:"

"Whose permission did you ask to take out the tables and chairs to set up for the picnic?"

"No one, Mother Michael asked me to prepare for a picnic supper."

"Yes, I know, but you are supposed to ask permission to take out tables, chairs and dishes."

Ask permission? Why? I had been told to do it by the superior of the house whose authority superseded all others. I refrained from answering the charge, knowing full well that to answer back was considered insubordination, and asking questions was answering back. At that moment, Mother Michael came into view and I breathed a sigh of relief.

"What is the matter?" she questioned addressing herself to Mother Mary Kathleen.

"Well, Sister Ethier took out all the chairs and tables and dishes for the picnic without asking permission." Mother Michael looked a bit confused and I suspect she was wondering why this was so important to Sister Mary Kathleen.

"We'll see about this tomorrow." she said, half dismissing the problem.

The scene was reminiscent of the inferior officer catching the superior officer cutting corners or not enforcing the rule.

The next day I was told that at the eleven o'clock instruction, I would have to confess my error before the novices and ask for a penance.

The novitiate room was rectangular with a raised platform at one end of the room. It was here that the Mistress sat to give her instruction. Behind her on the wall hung a large life-size crucifix with mottos from the founder printed on the wood in large characters. Before her were rows of chairs where the novices and sometimes the postulants would sit and listen to instructions.

The front row chairs were pushed back for the occasion and I knelt before the sisters and the mistresses who sat on the platform before me. "Sisters, I accuse myself of being disobedient by taking over and taking things out of rooms without consulting the sister in charge of these rooms. For this and for all the faults I have committed against the Holy Rule and you, I ask forgiveness. A penance if you please."

I forget the penance, but I remember kneeling there wondering what it was that I had done wrong. I felt confused, hurt, and angry. I could not muster any feelings of guilt. I certainly had not been disobedient. How could I be disobedient when I was following orders? How frustrating religious life was. I felt that I would have to pray harder, listen more, and make more sacrifices, if I were to understand this mysterious life.

One of the keys to molding us in this period of training was our psychological isolation. There were several mechanisms to effect this. We were forbidden to read letters to one another, forbidden to keep family pictures, forbidden to exchange small gifts, forbidden to talk to each other when only two were present. It was a safeguard to prevent gossip and close friendships that three were necessary to recreate.

Furthermore, we were admonished not to seek out companions during the recreation hour but rather to recreate with whomever it was that we came out the dining room door with. Cells were rotated every two months and "roommates" were carefully scattered. All of these things served to isolate each of us from one another and though we got to know each other's behavioral characteristics quite well, we were guarded and hardly knew each other. It took us a long time to learn to trust one another. In fact I believe that this trust never did have a chance to mature in the novitiate year. Though for those of us who stayed together long enough, real friendships did develop.

There was a deeper reason, which I did not then understand, used to isolate us one from the other - the underlying fear of homosexuality. We were often warned about particular friendships, how these were destructive to community life. At the time, I interpreted it as a warning against cliques, a phenomenon I had recognized in high school. How cliques might encourage the development of homosexuality never entered my mind because on this matter I was completely innocent. Later on, this realization helped me to interpret the following incident which I had found very confusing at the time.

The sisters had maintained the European practice of having their day off on Thursdays instead of Saturdays. Once we were professed, we would be allowed to speak all day Thursday and Sunday. In practice, this meant that if a sister had an assignment such as sewing, laundering, or cooking, she could then recreate with the sisters around her during these days. For the teachers and nurses, Thursdays were such busy days it hardly was different from other days. But during our novitiate days, Thursdays were wonderful. We could talk from 12:30 to 4:30. How we looked forward to this time! Activities would usually be arranged. In the summer we gardened and in the fall, we canned the particular fruit in season. It was also on Thursdays that the starching and ironing of coiffes would take place - a two day project. And if there was nothing special to do, we went for long walks in the Connecticut hills.

During these free hours, I had become friendly with our doyenne, Sister Fiorella. She stood about five feet seven, of square build with a strong angular face and a masculine walk. She was a handsome woman with her jet black hair, fair skin, hazel eyes and wide smile. Her manner was engaging and her laugh infectious. When serious, she assumed control of the group with a natural ease.

She was very affectionate with me, laughing at my jokes, helping me adjust my coiffe (something each new sister struggled to learn), noticing if one of my pins was out of place, or if the point of the pin was not turned in. (We had thirteen pins in the coiffe, and much was made of the custom of always placing them in the proper location with the points turned in). Her eyes reflected a state of perpetual amusement when she looked at me. Occasionally, I felt uncomfortable because Sister Fiorella would single me out of the group. All my life, I had tried to minimize my uuniqueness in order not to be alienated from my school mates. I continued to do my best to avoid standing out.

In December, Mother Mary Kathleen called me into her office for a serious talk. Sister Fiorella and I were becoming too close. We were often together despite the custom of having recreation with whomever you happened to walk out of the dining room with. Whenever we gardened or had some other project going, we managed to work together. This behavior was suspect and if I wanted to make profession of vows in February, I would have to show that this friendship was not a particular friendship, such as we were often warned about. I would have to discontinue talking to Sister Fiorella, to seek her out, to work with her unless it was completely out of my control. It was a warning as well as an injunction, and without my compliance I would be denied profession.

I was stunned. The warning came down on me with the suddenness of a thunderbolt. I went to the chapel and cried. Why was this happening? Was this one of God's inscrutable designs? Did I want to be a nun? My tears subsided and I resolved to do my best to avoid my friend despite my lack of understanding why. I knew that I had no choice if I wanted to reach my goal of becoming a nun.

Perhaps they had an inkling that Sister Fiorella had lesbian tendencies. As it turned out, several years later, she did leave the convent with another sister and they set up house together. But at barely eighteen years old, I did not know about such matters. I never felt physically attracted to women and would not have recognized it in another.

That evening, I arrived late for recreation because I had dishes to do. I noticed two possible places for me to sit. One was near Sister Fiorella. Faithful to my warning, I chose the other seat. Sister Fiorella motioned me over, but as the superior had told me not discuss the warning with her, I kept my eyes down and acted as if I did not see her. It became obvious as time went on that the superior had not discussed the matter with Sister Fiorella and that all the effort had to be on my side. What conclusions were drawn by my friend I would never know, because I never felt free to discuss the matter with her. After some weeks, she stopped initiating contact with me and it became easier. I bitterly resented the interference of Mother Mary Kathleen into my personal life. Still I felt that I had no choice but to obey.

This incident is a good illustration of the inability of the superiors to confront problems. Often superiors allowed things to be left unsaid when it might have been better to explain what they thought and/or why they took a certain course of action. This aspect of convent life added tension and uncertainly to a life that was already strenuous and demanding. The psychological isolation that kept us from forming close friendships and sharing our thoughts guarded us carefully from a discussion of sexual drives, needs and feelings. It was as if sex had disappeared from our lives. We never saw men except the priest who said daily Mass, the weekly confessor whom we saw through the grill, and the elderly caretaker. We dressed alike without vanity and decoration. We possessed no mirror wherein we might for a moment reflect on our appearance. We were forbidden to speak of our past. Our mail was censored to avoid contact with ex-boyfriends or even casual male friends. (Letters written by a first cousin were confiscated and I only discovered years later that he had written to me during this time.)

All of us considered a life of sexual denial a good life, a better life than the married state because it freed up the individual to devote all energies to God totally or to God's work. This belief was clearly expressed in the letters of St. Paul, and the writings of Augustine. We were able because of our beliefs to channel all energies in one direction, to sublimate, suppress and repress all conflicting needs and desires. Personally, I reasoned that I had made a decision to live a life of consecration to God while actively working in the church. Because my decision demanded that I put all other conflicting needs aside, I did it. I did not understand then, nor did I fully comprehend later on, the full extent of my decision. I was used to male attention and took it in stride as a normal part of my life. I did not believe that becoming a nun would cut me off from this. I had some clues to contradict my belief but I did not grasp the implications.

The first incident that I remember which indicated that relationships with men might be different for the sister than the unmarried came early. The parents of the sisters had founded an auxiliary organization for fundraising purposes. This organization was set up so that the members shared in the spiritual benefits of the congregation. In return, they held bazaars, Bingos, cake sales, rummage sales, and trips, all for the financial benefit of the congregation. Because of their efforts, the sisters had been able to pay off most of the construction mortgage of the novitiate house and the expenses incurred in renovating a summer house to serve as a rest home for the aged members of the congregation. These parents deserved a just reward, and this was granted them in the form of a bus ride to Connecticut. On a certain day, three or four buses would carry the members of the auxiliary to the novitiate. Ostensibly the trip was to view the fruits of their efforts, the new buildings, repairs and the like but what it really did was to provide an opportunity for parents and daughters to see each other. It was a gay time for all, and the novices were given a free afternoon to take the parents around the grounds. What usually happened was that the fathers soon tired of these endless tours of the grounds. They would leave their wives and daughters and gather together in some corner to exchange stories and to plan future activities. Three of four of these men had gathered on the back stoop of the postulate making ready for an activity later on in the day.

They motioned to me to get them a bell. At their invitation, I gladly sat down to chat with them. They were such fun. They entertained me with tales and jokes. I had such a great time that I did not hear the bell. Suddenly I noticed that the novices were nowhere in sight so I jumped up, excused myself and ran up to the novitiate room.

The novices were already quietly at work when I walked in. I went directly to the desk to report to Sister Montfort but before I had a chance to say anything, she demanded to know why I had not come in when I heard the bell.

"I'm sorry, Sister, but I didn't hear it!" I answered, a bit breathless. "When I noticed that the novices were not there, I ran up."

"You must have heard it. I saw you in the yard."

"No, I didn't hear it." I said in self-defense.

Isn't it funny, if she saw me sitting in the yard talking, why did she assume that I had heard the bell and chose to ignore it? Her attitude was strange. If I had been a high school girl with an attitude of trying to get away as much as possible, then I would have made sense of her assumption, but I was seventeen, a perfectly serious young woman. I felt hurt that she was so suspicious.

"You realize you were alone with a group of men?"

I was amazed by the question. I never thought of them as a group of men. I thought of them as people, just people.

"They are the fathers of the Sisters," I answered in an amazed and hurt tone of voice.

I knelt down and kissed the floor in penance for being late and breaking the rule. I remember trying to make myself feel bad about the incident, and in a way, I did feel bad about it, without really knowing why.

Almost all matters that were related to guarding us from sexual temptations were left unexplained, and seemed enigmatic. For example, there was the rule that read:

"A Daughter of the Spirit must keep her hands over the covers when in bed."

The only thing that I could think of when I read this rule was that my arms would get cold and that I would find it difficult to sleep. I questioned the mistress to understand the rationale of the rule. " Because, that's the way sisters sleep" was the explanation. I only understood much later that it was meant to safeguard us against masturbation.

Then there was the line in the rule that read: "When they are obliged through charity or necessity to converse with a man, it must be if possible in an open place, you must be able to open the door at any moment."

A Charlie Chaplin-like scenario popped into my head whenever I reviewed these lines. Blaring music in the background, the superior in a sweeping gesture breaking into the room with a smirk on her face and declaring: "Ah! Ha! caught you!!"

It seemed so ridiculous to me. I simply could not imagine what people could be doing in a religious parlor that would demand that kind of rule.

We were not only isolated from each other and kept in the dark about problems a sister might encounter because of her sexual drives; we were thoroughly isolated from the outside world. We never listened to the radio, saw no TV and read no newspapers. We were so carefully guarded from the outside world that it was in May 1958 before I heard for the first time that a Russian satellite, Sputnik, had gone into orbit. I remember well struggling with an analogy a priest was making in a lecture.

"Sputnik?" I kept repeating to myself. Sputnik? I wonder what he means?

"What is sputnik?" I asked one of the mistresses after the lecture was over.

"Sputnik?" She repeated incredulously, "Why it's the name of the first Russian satellite that went into orbit last October." She said it in a tone that seemed to say, "Why, everybody knows that!" I remember feeling bitter that such startling scientific news had been kept from us.

"A satellite in orbit! My God!" It frightened me to be so unaware of what was going on.

A year is a short time and we soon found ourselves in January, one month away from the taking of vows. It was really not an exciting time, these days of preparation. Life was much too serious for that. One had to be busy about the spiritual readiness of one's soul.

Just as being admitted to the novitiate had been surrounded by ceremony and rite, so too was the taking of vows. The first of these and the most impressive was the hair cutting ceremony. The ceremony had been kept a secret up to this time. Nine days before January 21, the feast of St. Agnes, Mother Mary Kathleen informed us that we were to have our heads shaved. To prepare for this holy ceremony we would engage in nine days of special public prayers. The eleven o'clock instruction would be given exclusively to those preparing for vows, to impart to us the significance and solemnity of the occasion. Hair cutting was a symbolic gesture, a sign of our giving our womanhood to God, since hair is one of a woman's most feminine and personal possessions.

On the feast of St. Agnes, directly after lunch, we were summoned to the dormitory where we were directed to sit in a circle. Because we had not been allowed to cut our hair even an inch during the previous 18 months of our stay, most of us had lengthy and full heads of hair. We sat there and stared at each other with heads uncovered for the first time in these many months. The three mistresses took their places at the head of the circle and someone intoned the prayers. We had our hair cut as we did everything else, in doyenne order - the order established by our entry the first day of the postulate. The one who arrived first was number one and the spokesman of the group, and so on down the line. I was number 12.

Mother Mary Kathleen took out a pair of scissors and proceeded to cut the tonsure. The cutting of the tonsure dated to the medieval initiation rites of monks and the clergy. It is in the center of the back of the head and its cutting symbolized dedication to God's Service. In pictures of saints and monks during the Middle Ages, one often sees an even amount of hair on the sides of the head and none in the center. That was the result of having been tonsured.

After Mother Mary Kathleen clipped the center, the novice moved to the next seat and the second mistress finished the cutting with electric clippers, leaving a slight ridge of hair on the back of the neck (which could be seen once we had our coiffe on so that the public would not suspect that we were bald). Once the hair was completely cut off, we went into the bathroom where Sister Charlotte, an old and venerable sister would brush your head and help you place your coiffe back on. She stuffed it with newspaper to replace the space your hair had previously occupied and also, according to her, to keep you from catching a cold. No sooner had Sister Fiorella had her hair clipped when Sister O'Shea began to cry hysterically, wailing so that it drowned out the sound of the hair clippers and the prayers. Her wailing made clear to all of us how difficult turning back would be for any of us. Who would go home bald?

The novitiate had a very subtle effect on me. If someone had asked me at that time if I were happy, I surely would have answered yes. Nevertheless, I experienced a faint discomfort about myself that I had never experienced before. I felt inadequate to the task of becoming a nun. That in itself was a shattering reality. I had never felt inadequate before. Everything I had attempted to do up to this time, I had done and I had done well. My parents took pride in our achievements, and I experienced a sense of well being as I faced the world at seventeen, sure that I could do anything I put my heart to do.

Now, one year after my entry into religious life, I often engaged in self-doubt. While Mother Michael had ruled, I had felt more secure. I felt toward her as I had toward my parents. Displeasure was always passing and, moreover, it was understandable and predictable, not an arbitrary whim. I felt trusted and respected. When she left the Novitiate I lost my security and found myself full of fears and insecurities.

But more basic than this was my own discomfort with a system that demanded so much in submission and restraint. Despite my constant rationalizing that: "it was a little thing to give up" each time I had to kneel to ask permission to go to the bathroom, I resented it. Each time I had to kneel to ask to open a window, I resented it. I resented having to hold my hands in my sleeves when I wanted to swing them at my side. I resented walking up or down the stairs when I would have preferred to run. I resented not being able to express an opinion of my own. I wasn't submissive by nature, and I never became so by practice. But I wasn't insightful enough to recognize what my feelings were.

Mother Mary Kathleen, who had replaced Mother Michael, must have sensed my feelings and interpreted it as an underlying hostility. I remember her saying to me on several occasions, "Sister, I know you disagree with me on such and such a matter..." then she would go on to justify her reasons for believing to the contrary. I had so successfully suppressed my feelings that I was no longer aware of what they were and her approach only made me feel more insecure and fearful. Little did I realize that there was a harsh inspector in the midst. I realized it least of all because I was the inspector, unconsciously taking the measure of all the sisters I dealt with, of the sisters, of the rule, of the way of life. I was learning a lot and sowing the seeds of a conclusion that was to germinate and bear fruit much later on.

Mother Mary Kathleen may have been only responding to my straightforward and forthright manner. Prior to my arrival in the convent, my reputation as an active youngster in High School had preceded me. I had participated in everything that was available and often took leadership roles in these various activities. I had graduated as the class valedictorian, I had placed third in the Maine Science fair, I had placed first in Maine in a

United Nations-sponsored essay contest on the United Nations. As a result the sisters anticipated a highly critical and difficult candidate in me. On the contrary, it was as if the critical part of my nature had ceased to operate. On a conscious level, I only felt uneasy and uncomprehending.

There was another reason for my uneasiness, and that was the lack of praise for anything done well. Always an energetic worker, the type who annoys others because I never tire, I felt crushed when Sister Mary Kathleen looked at a picture of the novices cleaning the barn pointed me out and said: "Typical of Sister Ethier, leaning on her rake." Perhaps she was joking, but I felt unknown and unappreciated.

At the solemn chapter of faults that took place just before we left the novitiate this image of myself as inadequate received its final seal. We knelt in a circle in the darkened room lit only by one candle, and each novice in turn, draped in her black cape made her final accusation of faults. We had been advised to pick faults that typified our behavior so that the First Mistress would then give each one a penance as usual, but add her last spiritual advice.

When my turn came, Mother Mary Kathleen addressed me as follows: "Sister Ethier, remember that unless the grain of wheat fall into the ground and is crushed, it will not bear fruit. So too you must be crushed and humbled. Though you have many talents, you will not bear fruit for the congregation unless you conquer your pride."

No word of encouragement that I had done well, or at least that I had tried.

The next in line was Sister Matthews. She was a moody girl, strangely restless. Her behavior had been shocking during part of our novitiate. She had starved herself on the pretext that food was an unholy thing and eating was to be avoided. She had to be rushed to the hospital for blood transfusions. She was often irritable and ill tempered.

"You, have many talents and can be a great blessing for the Congregation. You must have the strength to continue..."

I listened to it without understanding. What was the criterion of judgment on which holiness was based? If that was holiness, behavior which I had always considered childish, uncontrolled and whimsical, yes, even unbalanced, then I had not understood anything about holiness, and I did not know where to begin to go about learning it. Still, it never occurred to me to find my superiors wrong, or to see them as the unwitting victims of an interpretation of Christianity that was dehumanizing. I felt that it was my fault that I did not understand. It was not that it did not make sense, but rather that there was some block in me, some imperfection in my understanding that made the whole thing seem beyond comprehension, even mysterious.

I began our eight day retreat with relief. The days of preparation had entailed cleaning, sewing, etc. to make the convent ready for the grand occasion. The retreat would provide us with a much needed rest. As it progressed, I wondered what name I would be given. We had been asked to submit three names in order of preference, explaining the reason for our choices. Fearful that I would be given my deceased father's name, I wrote a lengthy explanation of my first choice, Sister Rachel Mary, my baptismal name. My mother was a widow, and would want me to keep it as a reminder that it was both her and my father's choice for me. I hoped that my argument had been strong enough to overcome the customary practice of giving sisters the names of their deceased parents. I did not want to live out my life as Sister Henry.

It was during these last days of our novitiate also that we were given a group name. As each group made profession, the group would be given a name which had some symbolic religious significance and which served to cement the group identity. We were to be called "The Candles". This was Mother Mary Kathleen's favorite symbol, and since we were the first group to take vows since she had been named Mistress of Novices, she chose it for the group.

The retreat gave way to profession day, and I looked forward to the ceremony with half a hope that I would somehow experience that fullness of joy that would permeate my being, that I might even feel a certain giddiness. A French magazine in an issue dedicated to the Gospel parables had so impressed me that I had copied out two passages and used them as book markers. They were:

"The Kingdom of God is a passion stronger than that of alcohol."

"The Kingdom of God is to waste one's money, talents and strength for others."

Here I was giving up my life for this kingdom and I had wanted to feel a bit of this passion. But I went through the ceremony feeling more like a spectator, not at all carried by the emotion of the day. With relief however, I received my religious name: Sister Rachel Mary of Jesus. Rachel, I had kept my name. Still, I was disappointed that the ceremony did not move me.

THE JUNIORATE

Within a few days after the ceremony we packed our few belongings and moved into the graceful farm house that had served as our postulate. It was now being used to house the sisters during the Juniorate, a one-year extension of their training established in implementation of the changes wrought at the 1957 General Chapter. Prior to this time, the sisters had been sent out to work the day after the taking of vows. Thus, a seventeen or eighteen year old high school graduate would be assigned to teach in a grammar school after receiving only the training provided in the novitiate - training in prayer and communal life. She had to cope with her new role of sister and teacher at the same time. Adding to these pressures, she often attended college in the evenings or on Saturdays. While the sisters had established a house of studies in Brooklyn in 1951, only a small number of sisters could be spared for full time study. It was hoped that the Juniorate year would give new sisters a longer period of adjustment to their roles as nuns, and give them time to begin their college education.

Because the Juniorate was new, our expectations of it were less clear than if it had been a long established part of the formation of the young nuns. All was in a state of experimentation. We believed that because of this we would help decide the form of this new phase of training. This belief lent some measure of excitement to the year.

Mother Mary Ambrose, our new superior, was a bright, handsome woman in her late forties. The white coiffe framing her square face heightened the olive tone of her skin and her sharp, dark eyes. She was of medium height, about five feet five inches, but always seemed taller because of her erect posture. She had joined the Novitiate staff as the third Mistress of Novices just at the time that we entered the postulate. Prior to her novitiate assignment she had spent three years in theological studies at Regina Mundi in Rome. Regina Mundi was an institute founded by Pope Pius XII in 1953 to train sisters in theology and the social doctrine of the Church. At the time of its founding it was considered an avant-garde institute. However, in light of Vatican II, and what transpired in the Church shortly after Pope Pius's death, it came to be viewed as a bastion of conservatism. Nothing seemed to have been done to update courses, so these newly trained sisters, shining lights of convents, returned ready as never before to elucidate the theology of Aquinas as it had been maintained by the hierarchy of the Church over the centuries.

Mother Mary Ambrose was no stranger; she had taught us theology while we were novices. Though a basically warm and loving person, years of control and suppression added to her own natural reserve had made her a cold, and repressive person. She was one of the convent's most successful products.

Our new superior did not try to hide her resentment of our arrival into her community. The previous six months had been joyous ones for her surrounded by a small group of admiring and loving young sisters. They had been the founders. Now she was being asked to absorb fifteen new people. She made known her burden by referring to us as the young sisters, laughing gleefully with the sisters of the "first" group at "in" jokes which left us out, and joining them more often than not to relax during the two daily recreation hours.

Her usually cool manner could in part be explained by her physical state. Three months prior to our arrival she had undergone a complete hysterectomy, which left her weak and distraught. It was neither unusual nor unexpected for her to feel attached to the sisters who had been with her at that time and had in a sense "seen her through." Despite my attempt to understand the situation, I found her behavior painful.

One of the goals of the Juniorate was to bring together the sisters who now stood divided in the local communities, i.e. the "house" sisters who took care of the kitchen, laundry, and sewing, and the "professional" sisters, i.e., the teachers, nurses, and social workers. This was difficult on at last three counts: the educational differences of the two groups, the prevailing low esteem of manual labor, and the traditional enclosure of the house sisters that kept them isolated and ill-informed about the simplest affairs of the community, the state and the world.

Precaution had been taken by the founder to prevent the development of a class system within the order. To do this, many rules centered on points of precedence and ranking.

Precedence in the Congregation apart from that deriving from authority or office is determined according to the date of profession and in the case of parity of profession by the date of arrival in the postulancy. (#70 Constitution of the Daughters of the

Spirit)

Thus members would not achieve leadership roles through any personal gifts nor because of their family's social status. Moreover, the members were enjoined to accept without question the work assigned to them, hoping to prevent thereby the development of ranking according to occupational status.

Obedience, which is the supreme law of all religious actions, must in a particular way regulate the work of a religious. Consequently, a Daughter of the Spirit should be quite indifferent as to the type of work assigned her in the Congregation. She should do it in the manner indicated following the directives of her superior. All the members were advised for the sake of humility.   . . . to willingly chose the most menial and despised occupations. (#240)They were further enjoined to accept no personal payment for their labors: They may engage in manual work, but of their own, they do not seek work outside the house. They do not determine the price nor receive personally the payment thereof. They derive no benefit from the work except in common with the rest of the community. (Primitive rule pp. 259-260)

Finally, the constitutions pulled all of these elements together and specified the following:

The Congregation of the Daughters of the Spirit comprises but one class, the sisters, at the discretion of the superior, are assigned to the different works of the institute according to their individual aptitudes and the needs of the various houses.

To bolster these rules, a heavy stress in the training was put on the monastic ideal epitomized in the phrase of Thomas a Kempis: *"Flee, hide and be silent."* This life of hiding primarily referred to those who engaged in housework, such as cooking, sewing, laundering for the sisters. If one could not remain hidden de facto because of one's occupation, then one should cultivate the mental habit of removing oneself from the bustle of life and withdraw to heavenly thoughts within.

Mary, the Mother of God, was held up as exemplar par excellence, she whose entire life consisted merely of house chores, and who, according to Catholic theology, achieved the highest rank after Christ in the supernatural order.

In the words of the Founder: *God wishes to reveal and make known Mary the masterpiece of his hands...#1 because she hid herself in this world and put herself lower than the dust by her profound humility, having obtained from God and for his apostles and the Evangelists that she should not be made manifest.* (True Devotion P. 320)

Thus, in keeping with the spirit of the order, we were told that the junior sisters would be assigned various house chores, i.e. doing a stint of time in the laundry, the sewing room, the kitchen. It was hoped that this would acquaint the sisters with the life of the "house sisters" and make us more sympathetic to their problems. Each junior sister would enroll in college classes, regardless of whether she would continue on to get a college degree. In this way, each sister, regardless of future occupation would, for this brief time, be allowed entry into the life of the other.

The Juniorate was the first year that I was *consciously* unhappy. I probably had been unhappy in the novitiate but I had not been aware of it then. I can't say that I understood why I was unhappy at that time, but I was at least vaguely aware that I was.

Mother Mary Ambrose had intrigued me from the time I met her, as I would have been by anyone who had studied in Rome. I was in awe of people with international experience. Perhaps it was the result of growing up during the war, or of growing up on the border of Canada. Whatever the reason, I had an intense curiosity about other peoples and absolute fascination with the intelligentsia.

I don't think that Mother Mary Ambrose understood the interest that I displayed in her. This interest, coupled with my spontaneous, easy manner made my approach too strong for her. I can't determine even now what it was she really felt for me. Nothing in my relations with her later on clarified that. What is important is that I felt that she did not like me and I felt bad about that; being liked was important to me.

Though I remember many incidents about the Juniorate, what colors and dominates my memory of that year is the feeling of being misjudged. I had not experienced it with Mother Michael. Though it had begun with Mother Mary Kathleen, it had been restricted to comments about my person that did not agree with the picture that I had of myself, the picture in fact that others' seemed to confirm.

With Mother Mary Ambrose, it was more than that, and different. She actually accused me of doing things that I had not done, or of wanting to do things that I would never have thought of doing. It was totally confusing to me. A great part of my feeling of discomfort with her can be ascribed to my dealings with her over my particular examen. Whatever my examen had been in the novitiate, none were traumatic or intrusive. They all centered on externals things like keeping silence at specified times, or keeping the holy habit neat.

When I arrived in the Juniorate however, Mother Mary Ambrose indicated in our monthly meetings over my spiritual progress that she had studied me while she had taught me theology and in the informal occasions when she had been with me, and she had come to the conclusion that my greatest problem was my pride and arrogance.

She told me, "A person cannot conquer her arrogance and her pride unless he or she is aware of how much their whole life is dominated by it, thus our first task is to make you aware of it." She then went on to describe what she thought would be a method of eradicating my self-centeredness. I was to examine myself hourly, writing down the specifics of each time I became aware of thoughts of self-praise. At the conclusion of the examen, I was to kiss the floor for as many times as I had had such thoughts. This was to make reparation.

I was tense and expectant throughout the talk. I knew, more or less, that I thought highly of myself, though I'm not sure that I was convinced that this was a bad thing. I greatly respected Mother Mary Ambrose. She was an intelligent and educated woman. I trusted adults. I believed that she, like many older persons, had something to teach me: lessons that they had learned from life. Without question therefore, I submitted to her plan.

Because my examen was different from the usual, instead of using a graph system, I kept a log in a small loose-leaf notebook in which I made daily entries that might have look like any of these:

8:30: I congratulated myself on doing a good job scrubbing the floor.

9: 15 felt proud about making an interesting comment in class today. Realized that Father got my point while others missed it because it was too subtle.

10:45 Went out of my way to help a sister find some books in the library and thought to myself that I was good for doing so.

This was the kind of miniscule self praise that I indulged in. I look back now and see it as a healthy self-confidence. However, at that time, I reasoned that since it was being pointed out to me that I was exceptionally proud, surely these thoughts must also be out of the ordinary and exceptionally vain. So I struggled to overcome my way of thinking.

I had no way to determine whether this perspective was a healthy one. We were not allowed to discuss our examen with one another; and even if we had been allowed to do so, all of us were under the influence of the same belief system. We had no contact with other adults who might have served as a sounding board for our ideas and feelings and who might have presented us an alternative way of thinking.

There is one positive thing I can say for the exercise. It enabled me to get to know myself so well that I learned to anticipate my thoughts. Surprised at first by the degree of the self involvement, I considered this to be bad and felt ashamed of it. I did not realize then that such self-centered thoughts were common to all persons.

Aside from the feelings of disgust and shame that I experienced each time I became aware of my inner self, I had to deal with the humiliating experience of sharing this newly acquired self-knowledge with my superior. Each month, I would sit at the side of Mother Mary Ambrose's desk while she pored over the book I had written. Occasionally she would comment: "Well, so you think this..." or she would shake her head and smile. I reddened and grew more miserable.

I don't believe that Mother Mary Ambrose acted this way out of inordinate curiosity. She was not the voyeur type; at least it did not appear so to me. But she was energized by power, the power that she held over the lives of the individuals under her care.

My reaction was mixed. On the one hand, I resented the intrusion into my very private inner life, but on the other hand I was grateful for the opportunity to grow spiritually. Each month as I stood outside the superior's door waiting to go in to discuss my spiritual state I would run through my mind all the possible reactions she might have to what I had written that month. I felt humiliated, while at the same time, I felt I had to expose myself as fully as possible in order to grow spiritually.

Writing was not all I had to do. For every proud thought that I recorded, I had to kiss the floor in reparation. This practice was repulsive to me in the beginning. It was not so much because of the dirt on the floor as because of the kneeling position that one had to take in order to do this. I felt tightness inside of me each time I had to do it. Later, it became so routine that I looked back in amazement that I had found it so difficult in my early years.

Mother Mary Ambrose detected this reluctance in me and made it a point to check each month to make sure I had not omitted my acts of reparation. When I reported that I had skipped the act of penance a few times, she would do one of three things. She might kneel down immediately and kiss the floor herself, explaining as she did that it was in reparation for my weakness and in the hopes that her example might give me the courage to do it in the future. Or she might command me to kneel down and kiss the floor in her presence for as many times as I had omitted to do so in the month. Her worst tactic however was to wait for a public occasion, such as during the evening meal, when she would publicly announce that she was about to kiss the floor for one of the sisters who did not have the courage to do so when it was her duty. At the sound of this announcement, it was expected that the guilty sister would rise and join the superior in kissing the floor in asking forgiveness for causing her such a humiliation.

The examen became for me a sort of "damned if I do, and damned if I don't" dilemma. It dominated a large part of my thinking, i.e. feelings of shame over my thoughts, feelings of guilt at omitting my acts of reparations, feelings of uncertainty about my progress. The harder I tried the more imperfect I became.

Sometimes, I wondered about my superior's motivation. She seemed to delight in finding fault with her subjects. On one occasion, I remember her ending our monthly meeting (referred to as Direction) with the comment that she thought that I had had a good month and I showed some progress.

I was so happy to get even some small hint that I was doing well, like a trickle of water on a parched throat. I thanked her for her words of encouragement and knelt to receive the traditional blessing. She traced the cross on my forehead in the usual manner and I got up to leave.

As I placed my hand on the knob her voice broke the silence: "Did you have proud thought just then?"

"Yes, I guess I did."

"Then you had better kneel and kiss the floor in reparation," she answered with a faint smile on her face.

Why couldn't she have let me go out happy just once?

It was during these months that I began to cry a lot. I would either begin crying just before my monthly talk with my superior, or once I had opened the door. I did not sob. Rather, tears would quietly flow down my cheeks. I felt pressured, anxious and inadequate. I felt that I was being asked to be someone very different than who I was and who I was capable of being.

I was ashamed of my tears, a sign of weakness. I wanted to be strong. I tried to think of funny incidents to spare me the humiliation of my tears. But my body refused to obey because crying was my only outlet for the anger and frustration which I had buried deep inside.

The examen, representing as it did continuous and unending pressure, was the most difficult aspect of my Juniorate year. However, many other incidents added to my tension and increased my self-doubt. As was the custom, both our assigned house charges and sleeping quarters were rotated after three months. During one such rotation, my new assignment was to ring the bell for the sisters announcing the beginning and end of all common exercises such as meals, prayers, Mass and the beginning of Sacred Silence. I was given an alarm clock to enable me to ring the rising bell at 4:55 AM.

That afternoon, Mother Mary Ambrose motioned me into her office. My stomach tightened as it always did when I had to enter her office and I could feel my body tense up. I tried to steal myself for the tears I felt surging within me.

"You will be sharing a bedroom with Sister Constance Mary (formerly Sister Fiorella) as of this evening," she told me, "and I wanted you to know that I am aware the two of you are friends. You will be tempted to talk and perhaps joke during Sacred Silence, but you must remember your obligations, those which you took when you made vows."

She mentioned the warning that I had received in the novitiate concerning our friendship, and decided to take this occasion to point out that while playing touch tackle during recreation, I had twice touched Sister Constance Mary's backside.

I was stunned. It's not a thing that I would have ever thought of doing, even before I had entered the convent. It was a crude gesture as far as I was concerned. I did not even remember being near Sister Constance Mary while we were playing. I had been concentrating on the game and admitted that I may have touched several sisters, but that this was involuntary.

I told Mother Mary Ambrose as much in a halting, choking voice. But she continued to look at me in a stern way, insisting that she had seen me, implying that I was lying. "I wish to warn you of your tendencies, Sister, so that you can be on your guard."

I knelt next to her desk listening intently, not comprehending. What had I done to warrant such as accusation? I had barely spoken to Sister Constance Mary since that December day when Mother Mary Kathleen had warned me.

"There's another thing also; if anything funny happens during Sacred Silence, Sister, you must control your impulse to tell the sisters in the community because making light of such things publicly diminishes the sacred character of the evening hours"..

I left her room in a daze.

As things are often wont to happen, something funny happened the very night of the warning. When the alarm went off at 4:55 a.m. to waken me, I was so completely disoriented by its harsh ringing that I frantically jumped out the wrong side of the bed into the white curtains that separated me from Sister Constance Mary; upon realizing where I was, I attempted to locate the clock, climbing onto the walls in the process and eventually tumbled onto Sister Constance Mary's bed.

She was already in a fit of giggles and I soon found myself laughing uncontrollably. We finally located the clock and silenced the alarm.

That evening, when we walked into the recreation room Sister Constance Mary called to me from across the room. "Sister Rachel Mary, tell the sisters about your first day ringing the morning bell," chuckling to herself as was her habit.

I ignored the remark.

"What's the matter? Come on. Tell us. It was so funny."

That was all the other sisters need to hear, so they joined in.

"Tell us, come on."

"I don't want to talk about it. It wasn't that funny." An unconvincing response on my part, so atypical of me.

Mother Mary Ambrose sat there in silence taking it all in. I remember glancing at her to see her mending her stocking as if unaware of the drama that was taking place. She made no motion to change the subject of the conversation, as if unmindful of the difficulty I had in maintaining my silence. At that point, the phone rang, and one of the sisters left the room to answer it.

She returned in a few seconds to fetch Mother Mary Ambrose. "Come on. It was so funny that you just have to tell the Sisters," Sister Constance Mary began again.

"You tell the story; I'm not going to tell it."

"You know you're a much better story teller than I am. Come on."

"Listen, it was nothing, and I want to forget it."

"It was so funny," Sister Constance Mary persisted, beginning to recount the tale.

Forgetting myself, I laughed and joined in, adding details of what had happened.

"Sister Rachel Mary!" Mother Mary Ambrose's voice was sharp.

I jumped and turned to face her, kneeling to receive the inevitable reproach. "Yes, Mother."

"What did I tell you about Grand Silence, Sister?"

"You told me not to tell funny stories, Mother."

"Well, because you've been so disobedient all the Sisters will go to bed early tonight. Ring the night prayer bell."

I felt miserable. Not only had I been weak enough to give in to my impulse to tell a funny story, but because of my weakness the entire community of sisters would be deprived of a half hour of recreation.

Incidents like this one made it increasingly difficult for me to be my own judge. Because it contradicted so much of my previous experience and education, my religious training decreased rather than increased my self-confidence. Moreover, I felt myself to be under increased suspicion.

A few weeks later, I woke up in the middle of the night with a terrible headache. Soon it was accompanied by a throbbing in the base of my head, nausea and dizziness. I got up and walked around the house trying at intervals to vomit, as I felt I would do at any minute. No success. We had no access to medication, not even to aspirin. I hated to humiliate and single myself out by rousing the superior. I continued to pace hoping thereby to lessen the pain, but the throbbing worsened.

"Mother, I have a headache," I meekly mumbled at the door.

"A headache! How selfish can you be? Do you know what you did? You woke me in the night because you are so weak and soft that you can't bear a simple headache! Well, Sister, you go right back to bed and sleep your headache off! And with that she slammed the door.

I was shocked. I replayed the scene in my head, deciding the fault lay with my presentation. I had not been assertive enough; I had not made known how bad this was. I did not dare knock a second time. I didn't feel guilty this time. I knew myself to be a basically considerate person, not one to indulge my weaknesses at the expense of others. I felt as if my head would burst with pain. With no recourse, I took a long bath and cried myself to sleep.

I had other kinds of personal struggles during my Juniorate year. My sister had graduated from college that June and as a graduation present my mother sent her to Europe. When I got the letter bearing the news, Mother handed it to me with this admonition: "Sister, you will read in this letter that your sister is going to Europe for the summer. Most of the sisters come from families who cannot afford this luxury, so you must not tell them about this trip. This would only accentuate differences between you."

I was crushed! Not to talk about it! My sister and I had always discussed our world tours together. It was bad enough that I was not going with her. The command to be silent made me more resentful that I was not with her, and it served to accentuate my losses. I found myself constantly warding off fantasies about my travels with her.

Despite my general inability to exercise critical judgment over what was happening in my life, my common sense occasionally surfaced. When we had entered the convent, we were asked to bring a foot locker with us, as the sisters were not allowed to use suitcases. The General Chapter changed this, allowing the sisters the use of several suitcases which would be kept by the superior.

In keeping with the new rule, my mother gave me a beautiful Samsonite suitcase for the profession. It was a good size, black with a scarlet lining, probably her way of giving me some little touch of the world I had left behind.

As with all gifts, I brought it to the superior. When she opened it, she gasped."That will never do sister. The suitcase is far too nice for us and the red lining is inappropriate. I will exchange it for something more suitable. This is not what sisters who have vowed themselves to poverty should be using."

I thought she was wrong, but I refrained from saying so. Some time later, she returned from a trip into the nearby town with two large cheap zippered suitcases. I took one look at them and confirmed my original judgment that she was foolish to exchange a sturdy suitcase which would give years of service for those two flimsy ones. She was going to Notre Dame University to study for the summer, and she declared that the suitcases would suit her fine. I thought the whole thing had been a ruse on her part to get two matching suitcases for herself. When she returned at the end of the summer, one suitcase was ripped on the side and the other had a broken zipper. A strange way to practice poverty, I thought to myself.

While Mother was away I noticed Sister Constance Mary became friendly with Sister Caitlen. They would walk together, garden together, sew together; in short everything we had done together the year before. I was jealous of this friendship and angry that I was left out. Hiding under the cloak of charity I took advantage of Mother Michael's visit to our house to tell her what I had noticed. I told myself it was my duty to do so as we were enjoined to report to our superior cases of particular friendships. I tried to hide my true motivation from myself, but I was unable to do so. The result of my act was to make me feel worse about myself than any false accusation from my superior could have done. I tried to console myself with the thought that Mother Michael had seemed completely unmoved by my words, and I did not think that she took it seriously. Still, the memory of this vindictiveness haunted me for years, making me feel guilty each time I saw Sister Caitlen and Sister Constance Mary.

In the fall, we were initiated to college, though allowed to study only subjects that would not distract us from our religious training, such as philosophy, theology and Church history. I loved philosophy and gave myself to its study wholeheartedly. Our teacher, a brilliant priest, kept us in absolute fright of himself. He taught quickly and succinctly and expected us to keep pace with him. He assigned us our first research paper, which became our major preoccupation. With it came a different kind of personal struggle.

I chose Hegel as my topic and began the collection of bibliographic materials. I was about three weeks into the preparation for the paper when one of the sisters in my class asked me what topic I had chosen.

"Hegel."

"Oh, I'm interested in Hegel too."

I questioned her to find out if she had begun work. "No, I've just decided on it."

The teacher had specified that each class member should pick a different topic so I told her that as I had already begun the paper, she had better look for another topic. She made no protest.

A few days after this conversation, my superior called me into her office and told me that she heard that both Sister Louis Mary and I were working on Hegel."Sister, you must change your topic."

I protested meekly, stating that I had started the paper more than three weeks before and that I had done a lot of work on it. On the other hand, Sister Louis Mary had only begun and it would be easier for her to change her topic.

Her response to me was that since I was a good student, it would be easier for me. It was clear that the period of discussion, if there had ever been one, was over. It was not a question of asking me to do this, she merely told me to give over my notes and bibliography to Sister Louis Mary and to find another topic.

I was angry. I reflected on the injustice. What could I do? If I fought to keep the notes and the paper, I would be accused of being selfish. I did as I was told.

During this year, I became close to two of the sisters with whom I had entered the convent, Sister Elena, and Sister Florence Jane. Though older than me by fifteen months, Sister Elena's small petite stature gave her the appearance of a twelve year old. A hazel-eyed blond with round rosy cheeks, she had an air of innocence about her. Naturally shy and retiring, she was a loving and supportive person. We had embarked on a project of typing and mimeographing philosophy notes and discovered through working together that we complimented each other. We became pals. She was my sounding board, the person to whom I would read all my term papers, discuss all my surface anxieties and on whose shoulders I would cry.

For my part, I tried to encourage her to do things she wanted to do but had felt lacking in confidence. She had refused to teach me how to operate the old mimeograph machine; later confiding that her reluctance was due to the belief that by sharing her knowledge she would be deprived of her one area of superiority. It had never occurred to me to view anything in this way.

Sister Florence Jane was a high strung wiry person whom I considered a spoiled brat. Sporting a pencil thin figure and sallow complexion, her step bounced and jerked her from place to place. Treated by the superiors as a misguided person who associated sainthood with fasting, she resisted all attempts to have her gain weight. I suspected that she was simply afraid of becoming fat and I refused to be taken in. She later admitted the truth of my suspicions. Despite my difficulty in forgiving her vanity, couched in holy terms, I enjoyed her quick wit and pun studded humor.

In addition to our studies we undertook the renovation of the Farm House to better suit our needs. This involved removing old wallpaper, scraping off the glue, washing the walls with TSP, rinsing the walls with fresh water, scraping the paint off the doors and windows, sanding all and finally repainting walls, windows and doors. We were inspired by Mother Mary Ambrose's 6-week summer course at Notre Dame to surprise her by getting most of the work done in her absence.

We were all kids together, growing up in the convent. The struggles of identity which our contemporaries faced, we also faced. Our friends sought to resolve their identity by marrying the right guy or by getting the right job. We struggled to become holy by carrying out our rituals of rule and custom and thus find ourselves. But this did not separate us from the everyday human experiences. We laughed, we joked, we sang, we worked until we plopped down with exhaustion.

Despite our inability to share our deep personal feelings, our good will and good faith enabled us to feel a warmth and concern for our sisters. Our practice of fraternal charity enabled us to tolerate surface idiosyncrasies of others that we might not have done otherwise. We laughed heartily at silly things, the sight of someone's backside before you as you bent over to kiss the floor, our medieval appearance as we readied for bed in our night clothes and night bonnets. We found joy in simple things, the satisfaction of a job well-done, the taste of a hot cup of cinnamon chocolate on cold fall Thursdays when we came in from harvesting the apples, or from a long walk in the Connecticut hills. We were sincere, and we tried to be selfless, loving, and just representatives of Christ. And we waited with patience to be delivered from these years of probation. We were anxious to go forth and spread the message of Christ's love and hope that filled our hearts.

During this time, we were introduced to yet another aspect of monastic life: The "*grand practices of penance.*" References had been made to these practices in the novitiate, but these were often vague. When questioned on the subject, Mother Michael had dismissed our queries with the reply that a Daughter of the Spirit was to obey the little points of the rule exceedingly well. If and when this task was accomplished she could ask about the more difficult external acts of penance. These were never given except to Sisters who were exceptionally fervent, and only after final vows.

It was quite a surprise when we were told that we would make disciplines as Christmas gifts for Mother Michael. She would distribute these to willing sisters. The discipline was a whip of five strands in honor of Christ's 5 wounds on the Cross. It was made with a clothesline, cut into five pieces of uneven length. These ranged from fourteen to twenty inches in length. At the end of the cord, a slip knot was made and the pieces were attached together to a loop in this fashion.

The discipline illustrated by Abbie Wanamaker

The loop was large enough to place three (in honor of the Trinity) fingers through it to enable one to get a firm grasp on it. After explaining its construction Mother got us started on our tasks.

We questioned our superior about its use and she agreed to demonstrate it. She stood in the center of our circle, fully clothed and with a back swing hit her buttocks. I cringed. I knew I would never be fervent enough to ask to use one. The discipline was to be used only under instruction from one's spiritual confessor. Usually a sister was not allowed to use it more than three times a week (three in honor of the Trinity) and sometimes five (in honor of the five wounds). Besides this, the sisters were usually restricted to three strokes on these three nights (always the Trinity).

Encouraged by our interest, Mother volunteered to show us yet another instrument of penance.

"It's spooky," I whispered to Sister Caitlen when Mother left the room.

"I know, who would have thought it?"

Mother soon returned with an iron bracelet in hand. "Here is the clasp. You fasten it on your upper arm with just enough pressure to feel it. When you get used to it, you can tighten it with this chain."

She held it up for our inspection. It was fairly lightweight, about three inches wide, with tiny blunt points protruding on the inside so that, if fastened tightly enough, you would get the effect of nails in your arm. I was horrified. I never saw one again, nor did I ever hear it discussed. Mother Mary Ambrose may have been the only sister who ever felt fervent enough to ask to wear one.

It was October already and I felt a relief that the year was soon to be over. Uncomfortable with my superior and with myself, I had felt despondent for some time. With this cloud of gloom constantly over me, forcing myself to meditate, laboring over my examen, Mother called me into her office to discuss renewal of vows. She talked and I listened. My year had been a bad one. Though I would be allowed to renew my vows, I would be put on probation. If I didn't show any improvement in the next year, I would be asked to leave the congregation.

I was frightened and confused by what I saw as a threat. First of all, what had I done wrong? Why was my year a bad one? How could I improve if I did not know what I had done wrong to begin with? How was I different from the other sisters? I was given no explanation other than a vague reference to my attitude. I sobbed, promised to try harder, and left her office.

The meeting left me with an overwhelming sense of failure. I didn't seem any different from the other sisters. How was it that they seemed so serene while I was being threatened with dismissal. I was too ashamed to discuss the threat with anyone.

"Why are you so unhappy?" My mother questioned me when she visited me.

"I'm not unhappy," I protested. I felt that it would be disloyal of me to tell my mother. Besides, I couldn't explain if she asked me why I had been an unsatisfactory sister. So I said nothing.

My mother was not that easily satisfied. She took advantage of the Provincial Superior's visit to the Novitiate to go over to discuss the matter. She had known Mother Michael as my Mistress of Novices, so she felt quite at ease with her.

The next day, Mother Michael called me over to the Novitiate. "What's the matter?"

"Nothing."

"Well, Sister, your mother got the impression that you are unhappy here and you know that your mother is a widow. She probably worries more about her children than she would if she were not alone. If you are not unhappy why don't you write her a long cheery letter to ease her mind."

I felt her warmth and interest in me. I wanted to open up to her to tell her that I did not understand why I had been told that I had been an unsatisfactory candidate. She had long before told my mother that I would be an important superior in the Congregation some day. But what could I say? I didn't know what to say or where to begin.

"Okay, mother, I'll write to her." I left without saying another word.

One of the last events that I remember about the Juniorate was the reading of The Nun's Story. It was Advent when Mother surprised us one evening by suggesting that we spend fifteen minutes of each night's recreation reading the book. It had appeared on the book stands just as I entered the convent and I had not had a chance to read it. I was curious about it. Many of my friends had written to me, wondering what I thought of it.

And so it was that those winter nights while we sat knitting, sewing or making disciplines, we listened to the Kathryn Hulme novel. Mother felt hostile to the sister whose revelations had enabled the authoress to write so vividly and so convincingly of the rigors of convent life.

When the character Sister Luke placed a black cape behind her window to have it serve as a mirror in an otherwise mirror less convent, Mother shuddered. "You see how this sister was being unfaithful to God and to the demands he was making on her from the very first days of her religious life!"

She read on and we listened. Every time the character Sister Luke expressed difficulty with the rule, Mother would comment on the negative attitude shown by her complaints. When Sister Luke described her feelings of fright at her own needs when she recognized a man glancing at her with a certain flirtation, I caught Sister Caitlen's eyes across the room and we smiled knowingly at each other. "What were you thinking when you looked up last night?" she asked

"That we would have that same kind of problem." "And you?"

."The same." "Her eyes twinkled as she laughed in her gruff way

It was only a hint of insight into our natures, our needs, not sufficient to dissuade us from the chosen way.

Prior to the taking of vows in the novitiate and the renewal of vows in the Juniorate, the group made an eight day retreat. Mother Mary Ambrose had a unique sense of drama and in keeping with it she insisted that we stay up to finish the novel the night before we were to begin our eight day retreat. The novel ends on what I then considered a sad note. Sister Luke is led to the parlor where she finds street clothes laid for her. She is expected to clothe herself and leave without an opportunity to say good bye to anyone. We said night prayer and went to bed.

The next morning after breakfast, Mother gathered us into her tiny office. "Sisters, just as we read of an infidelity to God in the novel last night, so too in our very midst is a sister who has chosen to be unfaithful to God. Sister Ruth Mary has asked for a dispensation from vows this week and she is returning to her family today."

It was retreat and we were in silence, so no one spoke. She urged us to pray for her and we filed out of her room. Sister Ruth Mary was one of the youngest sisters in our community. She had taken vows six months before, which meant she had to obtain a special dispensation from Rome in order to leave. This type of departure was most unusual and a jolt to all of us.

I resented the harsh comparison on the superior's part. It was, however, a fitting note on which to end our Juniorate year, with this judgment rendered against a nineteen year old girl, a judgment which, in its severity and condemnation, embodied in it the atmosphere of the past year, that religious life was a lonely struggle against pride and self will, that religious life was a life of faithfulness to one's calling no matter what the cost.

THE COLLEGE YEARS

Old friends cannot be created out of hand,
Nothing can match the treasure of common
memories of trials endured together, of
quarrels and reconciliations and generous
emotions. We forget that there can be no
hope of joy except in human relations.

Antoine de St. Exupery

I had grown more eager each day to leave Connecticut and to try my wings in the wide world outside the convent. What a great disappointment to learn that our order was to establish a college of its own and locate it in Connecticut. This move, along with the establishment of the Juniorate, resulted from decisions taken by the General Chapter in the fall of 1957. Prior to this time, the sisters had been assigned directly to teaching and went to school part-time, usually on Saturdays and in the evenings, plus the summer months. Very few were given the opportunity for full time study. Nurses went to the nursing school run by the sisters in Virginia. I was quick to realize that my college education would suffer from partaking in such an experiment, and I resented it. Separate quarters would be designated (a new wing was already under construction) and a new superior named. Until then, we were to stay put. Twelve of us were assigned to full time study and formed the nucleus of the new College Community. It was hard to say what upset me most, the new college, or the decision to stay on with Mother Mary Ambrose.

Eight months passed before a new superior was chosen. During this time, I got to know Mother Mary Ambrose somewhat better. She informed me that her annual report to the Superior General regarding my performance was much better than the previous year. In fact, I had shown a dramatic turn for the better. I felt relieved and thanked her. Still, I was puzzled. Had I been different? I was less nervous and tense. I thought I had even been a little lax in carrying out the rule. Her judgments continued to seem so arbitrary.

What happened in the next two years of my life can only be understood in the light of our new superior's inimitable personality. She was one of the most unique and engaging persons I have ever met. Living with her could be delightful, and at the same time infuriating, confusing and traumatic.

Mother Marie Mathilde was a short rotund woman whose French Canadian parentage was betrayed by her heavy French accent. A highly emotional and volatile woman, she had never learned to control her temper. To this day, at gatherings of former Daughters of the Spirit, the very mention of her name evokes the memory of the most outrageous emotional outbursts. It is hard to know where to begin in describing her. She was one of those strong peasant women fashioned in the old school where virtue was a composite of hard physical work, prayer and utter faith in God. A fantastic creature, she was full of surprises. Her character seems best revealed by anecdotes.

It was decreed in those early years of our religious life that thirty minutes would be set aside for public spiritual reading. Mother would often lose track of time and continue reading for an extra ten or fifteen minutes. As she always insisted on doing the reading herself, it was difficult if not impossible to call her attention to the time. If one succeeded in doing so, she would remark, with a holy disregard for the details of our scheduled life, how interesting the reading was. "Just another few minutes", she would say in pleading tones, and continue. We read her favorite authors, Father Faber and Father Vincent Dion, over and over again. We got so we could recite by heart passages of Dion's book - such as his advice: "When someone hands you a lemon, open a lemonade stand." We privately commented that we had had our fill of lemonade.

Mother read passionately, pausing every now and then, grunting and groaning to express her delight with a particular passage. Her pronunciation of bosom as "boosum" in the recurring phrase, "the bosom of the Father" would send us into fits of quiet giggles. Her eccentricities were not limited to spiritual reading. To conquer her tendency to sleep during the evening half hour of silent prayer (a phenomenon, by the way, which was quite common due to the time of meditation, between 5:30 p.m. and 6:30 p.m., after a long day's work), she had taken the habit of meditating in a standing position, often holding a book. Occasionally, she read aloud as if she were alone. Her reading sharply broke the silence of the Chapel. At times, she fell asleep and as she struggled to balance her massive frame, would waken and grunt loudly. She may have secretly believed that since most of the sisters were asleep anyway, it would do them more good than harm to thus startle them.

Mother held the firm conviction that the mind conquers all and coupled this belief with an incredible zest for life. A few days after having cancerous ovaries removed at the age of sixty seven, she organized a cleaning party to rake leaves, carry off dead wood, and lead the way in chopping down a diseased tree. She had spent most of the 48 years of her religious life teaching French in High School. Later, as the superior of the study house in Brooklyn, she had returned to University to get an advanced degree. She was thus qualified for college teaching and as my superior she taught me a course in nineteenth century French Romanticism - a course so unique that I shall never forget it. She would read a line from one of Lamartine's poems and moan over its poetic beauty. Then, she would violently slam a hand on the table and declare, "To think! He wrote this for his mistress, not even for his wife! How disgusting!"

This led Mother to a lengthy discourse on the perversity of human nature. Then suddenly, in a flash, she would brighten up and recount an anecdote such as the following: "A young priest came to his pastor one day to ask for advice about sexual temptation. All these beautiful young girls would come to confession to him and confess their desire for him and he just didn't know how long he could resist these advances. The wise old pastor smiled at the young priest and said: 'Well, son, it's a long hard road, but take courage in the knowledge that youth doesn't last forever. When you're 80 these matters are of no concern to you.' The next day the pastor called the young priest into his office, and with a big grin on his face, said: 'You'd better make that 81.'" Hardly finishing the story, she shook with laughter, pounding on the table as she laughed.

These engaging contradictions showed her common humanity. Mother Mathilde was not the only unique and eccentric person who formed our small college community. She headed the tableau of elders, each of whom represented a neurotic type that one would later encounter in religious life. Even though these older sisters were our college professors, we were all subject to the superior's authority and to the Holy Rule.

There was Sister Herman, a peasant girl, Canadian by birth, who because of her lack of education was destined to serve the Church by doing the "hidden tasks," i.e. kitchen and other household chores. Though a bright and ambitious woman, by the time I knew her she was in her forties and the life of "servant" had taken its toll. Her humiliating position in the convent, her insecurity and lack of self-esteem, led to a neurotic show of power over the areas of life that she controlled. Sister Herman had had a painful back operation some years previous and she used this as a ploy for attention whenever she met with frustration in daily life. She would begin to cry and sit in the large overstuffed chair provided especially for her. We were not permitted to sit in anything but straight back chairs, and never supposed to lean against them. She would then complain that "no one cared for her." Mother Mathilde, who normally had no pity for whiners, was moved by these demonstrations and sided with her.

Sister Mary Francis, also in her forties, was a mousy, sickly, scared human being. Though intelligent and educated, she found it difficult to make decisions. Teaching served to further undermine her self-confidence. She had been unable to handle unruly adolescents, and even now, with disciplined sisters, she seemed unable to exercise enough control to command the class. She took refuge in mystical experiences and took delight in recounting the details to Sister Florence Jane. The latter, always groping for some entry of the Divine into her life, once made me the unwilling recipient of these privileged communications. I remember flatly stating in comment: *"Maybe Sister Mary Francis sleeps with Jesus, but when I go to bed, I sleep alone."*

Visionary experiences left me skeptical and though only 20 years old, I regarded this "older sister" as a neurotic, sick individual. It worried me that Sister Florence Jane was being unduly influenced by her. Nevertheless, she was a kind person, and more often than not she agreed with us that Mother Mathilde and Sister Herman's behaviors were erratic and irrational. Thus, we sought and received comfort by airing our views to her.

Sister Catherine, the third elder, suffered the ignominy of having recently been removed from the office of superior. Usually superiors were renewed in office or sent to rule in another house. Removal was unusual except when illness or old age prevailed. A vain and arrogant woman, she saw herself as the upholder of rationality vis-a-vis the neurotic entanglements of Sister Herman, Sister Mary Francis and Mother Mathilde. She would chide Mother for keeping us too long at some task to the detriment of our studies, or shake her head visibly and disapprovingly when Sister Herman displayed her whining self-pity. Though she was often right, her obnoxious manner made it difficult for us to be sympathetic with her.

It was with these three hardly healthy, older sisters that we twelve young sisters and the superior formed a community.

There must be a thousand stories that I can recall about Mother Mathilde and our days in the college community. Space and purpose restrict me to a few. Externally, our life was pretty much the same as it had been, but the whole tone of it changed, due to the personality of our colorful superior. The first incident I remember should have been a forewarning of the kind of behavior that we soon learned to expect without ever being able to accurately predict it.

About one week after Mother Mathilde arrived, the Juniorate sisters celebrated Mother Mary Ambrose's feast day. (Instead of birthdays we celebrated the day of the saint whose name we bore in religion). As we were temporarily housed in the Juniorate building, we participated in the festivities. Though Mother Mary Ambrose was a cold, fairly repressive individual, we had grown accustomed to her, if not attached, and enjoyed common memories and jokes. Unable to share in these, Mother Mathilde seemed to bristle over our repartee. Later that evening, when we separated ourselves from the Juniorate sisters and went to our separate recreation room, the tension between the two superiors was much in evidence.

We often played board games on Sundays and Feast days, so two sisters and I joined our superior in a game of Chinese checkers. In her gruff way, Mother made it clear that we were to take the game seriously. There was to be no talking at the table. As I recall, I did not feel like saying much that evening, so I did not find her demand for silence too oppressive.

Soon Mother Mathilde was tapping her fingers on the table, muttering to herself: "I'm going to kill her; I'm going to kill her."

I wondered what she meant and turned quickly to see if anything out of the ordinary was going on. No one seemed to be doing anything out of the ordinary, so I shrugged my shoulders and turned my attention to the game once more, humming as I had been doing.

Mother Mathilde was breathing faster and louder. "I'm going to kill her - I'm going to kill her," she repeated.

 Suddenly, she grabbed the tin checker board with all the marbles and flung it into the air giving the marbles movement in all directions. With this show of disgust she announced that we were going to bed early.

It was then that Sister Mary Francis who had been playing with me turned and whispered: "That was your fault."

"My fault?! My God! What did I do?"

"Mother can't stand any kind of noise when she plays a game. You were humming and that annoyed her."

If it had not been so tragic, it would have been funny. In fact, I wryly smiled to myself over the incident, but made a mental note not to play games with her anymore.

Mother had other idiosyncrasies. For some inexplicable reason, she became completely unnerved if a Sister broke something. It was customary in the congregation to report each broken item to the superior. In so doing, the sister knelt- broken dish or whatever in hand- and asked the superior for a penance. The vow of poverty was practiced very strictly and faithfully in the order and breaking something, even accidently, was seen as a breach of this vow. Most superiors realized that the humiliation of bringing the damaged item to the superior, of kneeling to ask for a penance, was, for most sisters, quite enough reparation. They usually noted the broken item and prescribed some simple prayer as penance in a matter of fact way. Not Mother Mathilde! She would yell, groan and moan, showing her displeasure. One day, while I was sitting in the study room opposite her office, she let out such a cry that several sisters and I jumped up and ran in to see what had happened. A sister had brought in a crucifix which she had just accidentally broken. It was a clean break of the Christ figure's upper left arm, easily repaired with glue. Undeterred by her audience, perhaps even spurred on, she pleaded with the sister to recognize the gravity of her act. So as not to further embarrass the sister we left the room, casting knowing glances at each other that said, "Well, it was just another of Mother's tantrums."

This behavior made us feel tense despite our ability to see its relative unimportance. When a sister broke something, especially if it happened in a public gathering, everyone froze.

One such incident is indelibly imprinted on my memory. It occurred the last few months of my college days. It was my week to wait on tables, i.e. bring the hot food from the kitchen to the tables, pick up the serving dishes after the meal and return untouched food to the main cooking kitchen. It must have been a feast day, because we were talking at lunch. Suddenly, a loud crash interrupted our conversations. I went dashing into the small galley kitchen to see what had happened. A younger sister hurriedly leaving for college classes had brushed against a stack of platters near the edge of the table and knocked them down, shattering the lot. I knew Mother Mathilde's wrath and realized that the sister would miss her ride to school, so I said: "Go! I'll explain what happened to Mother!"

Everything had happened so fast that I had not paid much attention to what was going on in the dining room. I stooped to pick up the broken pieces when another sister came to the door and in breathless voice warned, "Get out, Mother is coming!"

Without thinking, I jumped up and made for the door. Too late! She grabbed me by my two shoulders and gave me such a forceful shove that I involuntarily went backwards, knocking myself against the sink and falling to my knees on impact.

Without a word, she then picked up some of the broken pieces which I had gathered on the counter top and- venting her anger -proceeded to crack them further against the edge of the counter top, inches from my head.

I was petrified. I was angry with myself for being petrified. I was angry at her for being so childish. I felt powerless to do anything about it. After her outburst, she walked out into the refectory and intoned the Latin after dinner prayers with the most peaceful countenance and sweetness of voice. I stood in the kitchen and cried, disgusted that I had to be treated in this manner without chance to explain what happened. So irrational!

It was in this atmosphere that we attempted to set our minds on our studies. Our schedule was simple:

5:00	Rising
5:30-	Mass, prayers
7:30-	Breakfast
8:00-	House chores
8:30-	Classes
12:00	Lunch
12:30-	Recreation
1:30-	The Rosary
1:45-	Study
5:15-	Spiritual Reading
5:45-	Meditation
6:15-	The Rosary
6:30-	Supper
7:00-	Recreation
8:00-	Night Prayers
8:15-9:30	Lights out

Our professors were either our own sisters who had been named to the college community, e.g. Sister Catherine, Sister Mary Francis, and Mother Mathilde, priests from the nearby seminary for certain courses in theology and philosophy, or lay teachers hired for specific courses from nearby colleges, or universities. We never left the convent grounds, thus we met no new people except our teachers. We accumulated a certain body of knowledge and we did so in the same structured way that we had gone through the Novitiate and Juniorate. We were not introduced to literature, historical interpretation, and/or philosophies that might in any way contradict Catholic traditional theology. If some dangerous teachings were encountered in class because of their importance, they were always presented with a strong defense of traditional Catholic views. Unlike our contemporaries, our college years were not a time for challenging tried and true ideas.

It was in this matter that Mother Mary Ambrose found her saving grace - her intellectual curiosity. Because of it she understood it in me. She was not threatened, as others were, by exposure to new ideas, and even considered the possibility that they might reflect a portion of the truth. At her suggestion, I wrote a paper on Freud for a psychology class. Sister Catherine, observing me read Freud's case studies, gave me a tongue lashing for allowing myself to be exposed to such abhorrent ideas. She even reprimanded Mother Mary Ambrose publicly. Feeling that Sister Catherine was not the guardian of my soul, I ignored her. But this basically anti-intellectual attitude was typical of the sisters of her generation and it hampered our growth during those years. I could nevertheless justify my need to read by my duty to learn and just as I was to do much later, I read to escape and to release tension.

While I had been a novice, Mother Michael and I had discussed the possibility of majoring in French. She wanted me to do so, pointing out the singular advantage of being completely bilingual and fluent. The problem was that I did not want to. I disliked the study of grammar and could not see myself teaching French, a boring repetition of simple phrases all day long. It was near the bottom of my list of preferences.

Shortly after we were named to the college community, we were asked to select our major. I selected History, my first love. A few days later, Mother Michael, who was visiting us, called me in to see her. When I got to her office, I found myself with another sister. Mother looked at us and announced that we were to major in French. She offered no explanation nor did she give us a lecture, she just announced it simply and dismissed us. As this was God's will, made manifest to us through the Superior, there was no ground for us to argue. I was crushed. But like the other disappointments that I had had along the way, I talked myself into accepting it as being for my spiritual good. I reasoned that this was a small sacrifice, that I would still be a teacher, that I could have been forced into nursing, as so many would-be nurses had been forced into teaching in bygone days, that I was lucky to be studying full time instead of having to go to school part time, and that finally this was the risk I had taken when I entered the congregation, and now I had to suffer the consequences of my decision.

We struggled through our first college year, juggling our duties to God, to our studies, and to our superior's whims. Our good times were in laughing at the incongruities of life and at Mother Mathilde's foibles. Sister Elena, Sister Florence Jane and I deepened our friendship through what we later termed our combat experiences. These were usually disasters over which we met to sound off, to laugh off, or figure out how to avoid. We enlarged our circle to Sister Helen, one year our senior. Sister Helen was a sturdy girl with chestnut hair and vulnerable hazel eyes. Mild mannered, she seldom spoke and when she did her remarks were careful and spare. One could easily confide in her without fear of betrayal. When she relaxed however, she had a raucous laugh. She was the other French major, so the

90

two of us had much in common.

At the end of our first college year, Mother announced that summer school would be held in Connecticut. We had to be prepared to receive eighty sisters who would attend summer school. We began a frantic house cleaning. Over the previous months, Mother Mathilde and I had developed a unique relationship. I felt that she liked me better than most. Perhaps it was because we belonged to the same ethnic group, a minority in the American province. She often told me that I reminded her of herself as a young sister. To my tense and angry tears, she would say: "For the first seventeen years of my religious life, I too was always in tears; then I grew up. You'll see; you'll get over this." She thought I should be made of the same stern stuff that she was and she despised any show of weakness on my part.

In some ways, I was more mature that the others. I had a strong sense of responsibility, and I had excellent work habits due to my years in boarding school. Mother appealed to these virtues and burdened me with more responsibility than I should have had in those early years.

As it happened, I was enrolled in three courses that summer when Mother called me into her office to announce that I would have two house chores (ménages). I would help Sister Mary Francis in the laundry and Sister Herman with the kitchen. She gave as her reason for this decision the fact that I got along well with both of them. "It may be true," I protested, but to take the two of them at once was more than I would have liked and more than I thought I could manage. Furthermore, I continued, why was I assigned two major house chores when sister Florence Jane's assignment was merely to sweep the stairs daily, a hardly significant or time consuming task.

"Sister Rachel, you are a strong girl. Sister Florence Jane, as you know, is weak physically and she really can't do more."

"Weak! More like manipulative," I thought to myself. "Weak and lazy; she doesn't even sweep the stairs as she should. Why should I have to do more than my share?"

"But why two ménages?" I said aloud. "Sister Herman will surely place enough demands to keep me busy full time."

"You realize, Sister, that you are one of the only young sisters who is sympathetic to Sister Herman. She is difficult, I know, but her back bothers her a great deal and she is in pain a great deal of the time."

"Pain my foot!" I thought. "Sister Mary Francis needs a person like yourself who is well organized and who can truly work. Remember, 'To whom much is given, much is expected.'"

To be appealed to on those grounds was flattering. We were all schooled in the belief that God required more of some than of others. It was true that I was intellectually gifted, having always been at the head of my class. Moreover, I had a good temperament (a gift from my father). For these things, I had to "pay" according to the ideas of holiness being instilled in us.

But even more than this, I truly believed this philosophy, so I tried to understand God's mysterious ways in treating me thus, never stopping to question the underlying premise that it was God who was willing my life to be such.

A pattern soon developed. When I worked with one of the two sisters, the other would watch me to assess if I worked as hard for her. Had this been my only source of pressure it would have been bearable. However, to add to the confusion, I was taking a course in French literature taught by my superior. One day she would scold me for not doing my homework properly, and the next day, she would, upon inspection of the kitchen, get me out of study to scold me for not washing the kitchen floor, a task which did not necessarily have to be done, and for which I really did not have the time.

Strong feelings of jealously existed among the sisters of the American Province toward those of us who had been selected by the superiors for full time study. Why should some, especially the youngest members of the congregation, be chosen to study full-time, while the older sisters supported them by working and going to school evenings? All of us in the college community knew that we would have to contend with these feelings when the sisters arrived for summer school.

This made Mother Mary Ambrose's action on the first day of summer session inexplicable. She had called a meeting of all the sisters attending courses, and in the course of explaining several administrative details, she elaborated on the grading system. To illustrate, she chose my grades from the previous semester: "For example, taking Sister Rachel Mary's grades, three A+'s and three A's her grade point average would be ..."

I was embarrassed. How could she? Our grades were normally kept a closely guarded secret. None of my friends knew exactly what grades I ever got. Was it her distorted way of helping me rid myself of my pride? I wondered.

As the session broke up, I hurried to greet two of the sisters who were to teach me summer courses. Both had taught me in high school, and I had liked each of them. "Well, you won't get an A from me this summer, Sister," one said to me angrily as I approached.

I was too stunned to respond. She walked off, leaving me standing there wondering how I would overcome the hostility that was the inevitable result of my moment of singularity.

My summer schedule was unusually rugged. Up at 5:30 a.m. (we were permitted an extra half-hour sleep in the summer), we reported to chapel at 6:00 and participated in prayers until seven thirty. Breakfast followed immediately, so I had to leave chapel early to prepare breakfast for the sisters. Afterwards, I had to put away the extra food and set the table for lunch. Moreover, I had to prepare juice for the 10:00 a.m. break. That consisted of pouring cans of juice into a large five gallon canister, watering it down and sugaring it a bit. I put away the breakfast dishes and attempted to leave the kitchen in order. All this had to be accomplished in a half-hour since I had a class at 8:30.

After the first class, I would run down the stairs to carry up the urn of juice and the milk for coffee break. This was followed by two other classes. After the last one, I ran down to put out lunch. Repeating the breakfast routine after lunch, I put away the dishes, cleaned the kitchen and washed the floor - if I had not done so in the morning. I rarely got out in time to participate in our shortened recreation, often missing the recitation of the group rosary as well.

Class or study was the first order of business in the afternoons. But two days a week, my study time was cut into by my laundry duties. On Tuesday, I had to separate and distribute clothes which were returned by the laundry. On Thursdays, I went to the laundry building to iron the large squares of cotton which formed part of our habit. These were heavily starched and had to be ironed on the commercial mangler (ironing machine). During this time, Sister Herman would watch me and invent stories about how I was slacking off in my kitchen duties.

When I felt overwhelmed by it all, I characteristically talked myself out of my feelings. Still, as the summer wore on, I became tense and nervous, laying the grounds for the inevitable explosion. This came unexpectedly early one morning. I had washed the kitchen floor hurriedly and, realizing that I did not have the time to rinse out the mop, I decided to leave it outside temporarily.

I was late for class and hurrying to grab my books when Sister Herman beckoned me. I turned to ask what she wanted, hoping she would not attempt to delay me for long. She had taken the mop in and was waving it with her right hand as she began a tirade, attacking me for not doing my work properly. Then, to "teach me a lesson," she proceeded to wring out the dirty mop on the highly polished floor. I couldn't believe my eyes. Such irrational behavior! I was sick and tired of this kind of behavior, and felt aggravated by the "demonstration lesson" as I remembered the long hours spent washing, scrubbing and polishing the floor.

"Sister Herman,'" I screamed, "You're nothing but a big baby. You want your own way all the time. Why don't you grow up."

She stood defenseless for a second. I had never spoken to her or to anyone else for that matter, in that way before.

"These young sisters! I'm going to tell our superior how you speak to older sisters."

"Good! Go right ahead!" I screamed, "Tell her, Tell her everything. But I'm going to get to her first."

The two of us charged off, running up the stairs with me in the lead. I continued up beyond the superior's room to my class for which I was now very late. I caught the look of annoyance from Sister Mary Brandon, the professor, when I walked in. It was time for me to give my report.

Report! I had forgotten all about it. Luckily I had prepared it carefully a few days previous. The report was on a series of articles in Tests and Measurements. I had found them mediocre and had a lot of negative criticism to make. Had I been more mature, I would have recognized that I was in no state to deliver a report and would have asked to be excused for the day. (Not that my professor was mature enough to have understood.) Instead I walked to the front of the class with a fierce determination. I vigorously listed the points with which I disagreed adding, with wry humor, applications that reduced their arguments to the absurd.

I caught Sister Elena's worried look from her front row seat. I knew that I was sounding off and I didn't seem to be able to stop. I finished and sat down. Though I felt the audience to be tense, the class ended without incident.

It was unlikely that Sister Mary Brandon would allow the tone of my presentation to pass unnoticed. That afternoon, she sought me out. "What has happened to you, Rachel? In high school, you were such a cheerful and happy girl. You are not the girl you used to be. If you are looking for justice in this world, then don't, because there isn't any."

She did not want an explanation. All she wanted was to lecture me. Under so much pressure, I couldn't very well be the "jolly, bouncy, happy girl" that I had been in High School. Why couldn't she understand this? I did not know what to answer.

She proceeded to drag out some feelings she had harbored against me over the years, insisting that I had been the spoiled child of the family, the gifted one, insensitive to my sister, usurper of my parent's affection. I felt tense, nervous and exhausted. I did not understand why she chose to attack me in this way. I chose not to attempt to answer, but to let her say what she had to say.

As she talked, I caught a glimpse of Mother Mathilde passing by in the hallway and wondered if she would come in to scold us for talking during silence time. Though Sister Mary Brandon was my senior and my professor for the summer course, we were both equally bound to the rule of silence, and equally subject to the superior. After a few minutes, I realized that Mother Mathilde would not return and I breathed a sigh of relief. I ended the conversation with Sister Mary Brandon, excused myself on some pretext, and left the room.

That night, exhausted with the more than usual harassments of the day, I hurried down to the community room to gather some clothes from the shelves reserved for my use, intending to rush up to bed early. If only I could get some sleep, I reasoned, things would seem better. I had yet to talk to Mother about the incident with Sister Herman earlier that morning and the conversation with Sister Mary Brandon bothered me.

Suddenly Mother Mathilde's booming voice filled the silence of the downstairs floor: "Soeur Rachel!"

Oh My God! My stomach tightened as I hurried to the kitchen where she was waiting for me. I wished I had gone to her office to give her my side of the fight with Sister Herman. No doubt, she had heard a twisted version of the incident.

"Yes, Mother," I said meekly as I entered the kitchen.

Without a word she flung the refrigerator door open and pointed to the milk pitchers neatly stored for the morning's breakfast. My heart sank. I knew without looking into them what the problem was; they were empty.

This forgetfulness had become more frequent recently and my efforts to check and double check my actions did not seem sufficient. I was terrified not so much of Mother's scolding, but terrified that I was losing my mind. I swallowed hard, trying not to cry in front of her again. I hurried to the main kitchen to get an urn of milk. By the time I got to the end of the long corridor, tears were flowing freely.

I closed the door of the large refrigerated room and sat on one of the milk urns, grateful for a bit of privacy to sob. "What should I do? I can't stand to have her scold me tonight. Maybe if I sit here for a while, she'll go away before I get back. Why am I forgetting things? Is this what it means to be crazy?"

I suddenly became aware of movement on the other side of the refrigerator. The novices were coming down from the chapel to check lights, doors, locks, etc., and most likely someone would open the door. I quickly brushed aside the tears and picked up one of the large milk cans. My back ached as I carried the urn down the long corridor, not from the weight of the milk, but from the fatigue that had seized my whole body.

Mother Mathilde stood in the doorway of the galley kitchen and watched me carry the urn in. I filled the pitchers and rinsed out the urn. I tried to avoid looking at her and hurried to finish my task so I could get away for some much needed rest.

Just as I turned to leave, Mother let out a terrible grunt and raised the cover of the coffee urn with a dramatic flourish. I felt paralyzed. It just couldn't be that I had also forgotten the coffee. God! I didn't want to look. Mother's face was contorted as if she was trying to exercise tremendous control over an insurmountable force. I looked in. No coffee. I sighed and walked to the pantry to get a can of fresh coffee, opened it and filled the urn's basket.

If I could only get out of here and not have her breathing down my neck, I thought to myself. Mother Mathilde had the habit of breathing heavily to demonstrate her displeasure. It was probably a technique she had developed to let off steam all those years when verbal assaults were not permitted her.

"Soeur Rachel," she said again as I went to step out the door. Her tone was one of "What's going on?" and I knelt down in anticipation of a scolding. Sure enough, she began softly at first but her huge voice eventually dominated the quiet of sacred silence. I could hear the sisters scurrying out of sight, embarrassed to witness the scene. I began to cry.

As she talked I realized that her displeasure was not over my fight with Sister Herman but rather over seeing me speak with Sister Mary Brandon earlier that afternoon. She had misinterpreted the conversation as a complaining session on my part. "What right did I have to discuss community affairs with a sister who was not a part of our community?" she went on. It never occurred to her to ask me if in fact that was the content of our conversation. She assumed it to be so, because, in the past, sisters under her care often complained of the treatment they received at her hands. The sisters most likely to receive this information would be those they had known prior to entering the convent, former teachers. Just because I had known Sister Mary Brandon in high school, she went on, I was not to expect nor seek sympathy from her.

"So that was it," I thought to myself. "She thought that I was getting sympathy from Sister Mary Brandon. God, if she only knew."

I was too tired to explain and besides one did not "explain" anything. So I knelt there and cried softly, hurt, angry, frustrated, confused and helpless.

"You're soft, a weakling, Sister Rachel, not able to stand up to what God is demanding of you."

"Thank you, Mother," I said when she finally finished. I bent over to kiss the floor in gratitude that it was over and I could at last go to bed. I climbed the stairs slowly, almost as if in pain. "God, is this what one has to do to become holy. It doesn't make sense to me. Why can't I understand what I have to do - why must it be so hard?"

"Someone must have gone to bed early this evening," I thought to myself as I entered the darkened dormitory. It was customary to dress and undress in the dark if a sister was asleep before the usual bed time hour. My cell was next to Sister Mary Brandon's. What irony! I hated her then, as I was reminded by her proximity of our afternoon conversation. Why hadn't she minded her own business instead of unduly complicating my life? The smell of Johnson's Baby Powder, with which she customarily doused herself, had a suffocating effect on me as I undressed in the dark. It was the one semblance of luxury and vanity that we were permitted.

I lay out on my bed. It was an unusually warm night and I found the heat oppressive, especially as the curtains which divided our cells one from the other cut off any cooling breeze.

My legs twitched incessantly and my jaw was set. I suddenly realized that my teeth hurt from being held together so tightly. I had a pain in the back of my neck.

"I have to relax," I told myself, gripped with a momentary panic that I would not be able to sleep. "I have to relax. I have to sleep." I rubbed my chin and my jaw as I contemplated the possibility of spending a sleepless night. The twitching seemed to increase. I rubbed my legs, hoping to relax my muscles. I have to get up tomorrow and live through another day, and if I don't sleep I won't be able to live through the day.

I don't remember how long it took me to fall asleep but whenever it was it was early morning. When I got up, I felt battered; my face was drawn and my body ached. The fatigue seemed unimportant however in relation to the fear that maybe I was slowly losing control over my mind. I must talk to someone about it, I resolved, and watched for an opportunity to meet someone who might help me.

Meanwhile I knew I had to address myself to my fight with Sister Herman the previous day. At morning coffee break, I sought out Mother Mathilde to explain my side of the story. She was very mellow; perhaps she had decided after the scolding of the previous night that I was in no state to be scolded further. She admitted that Sister Herman had acted irrationally and perhaps even out of jealousy that the young sisters were being given an opportunity for schooling which she had been denied. Mother Mathilde asked me to apologize to her because she felt I should not have yelled at her the way I did, but primarily because it would make Sister Herman feel better.

"Sister Herman likes you a lot, Sister, and she was very hurt by the remark you made."

"I couldn't help it. She really is a baby."

"I know," Mother Mathilde admitted, "but we all have our failings."

I was relieved that no scene had taken place. I swallowed my pride, ran downstairs and apologized to Sister Herman in as lighthearted a fashion as I could muster. She was, after all, a creature to be pitied. I found her in her large overstuffed chair, most probably indulging in some moments of self-pity. She cried, wiping her tears with a flourish. Yes, all was forgiven. She knew I was tired and she probably had been too harsh herself. I should learn better control over my temper, she advised however. We parted friends.

As the end of the summer session approached, I was confronted with another problem. One of the visiting sisters attending school approached me, remarking that I was a good student, and that writing seemed to come easily to me. Would I help her with a term paper?

I felt I had no time, but I dared not refuse. Mother Mary Ambrose's publication of my grades placed a burden on me not to "*hide my light under a bushel*" but to share my talents with others. I felt this urgency not to be selfish, so I helped first one sister, then another.

After I had given assistance in this way to a few sisters, I found a handwritten term paper on my desk. The attached note stated that since the author noticed I was a fast typist, would I please type the paper for her.

I felt angry. Besides imposing on me in this way, the sister had not even had the courage to ask me face to face. I complained to my college community buddies, Sister Helen and Sister Elena. They were as angered as I was and suggested that I put it back on the sister's desk. In the end, rather than chance the anger of the little known sister or in any way give cause for saying that I was selfish, my false pride triumphed and I typed it.

Sooner than I had expected, I had the opportunity to discuss my state of mind. Mother Michael, the Provincial superior, and my former Mistress of Novices, came to Connecticut. I made an appointment to see her and tried to rationally explain to her that I thought we were being treated inhumanly and that I couldn't stand the pressure. I told her how forgetful I was becoming and confided that I was afraid that I was losing control over my mind.

Though she appeared to understand what I meant by the pressure, and the tension, instead of being upset by what was happening, she seemed proud that God was seeing fit to test me in this way.

"Just as gold is tried by fire, so too are the saints tried by suffering," she answered. I was growing strong, not weak, by this experience and I should stick it out. She re-assured me that I was sane and very normal. It was not unusual for me to feel tense and to become nervous. I would look back on this time of trial and be grateful for it because I would be a strong woman on account of it.

She amused me with tales of her own experiences as a young sister with another irrational superior, Mother Theophile. She asked me about my family and dismissed me. I can't say that I was fully convinced by her argument, but I did feel better, having had the opportunity to complain and to feel that someone understood. With this reassurance, I managed to get through the summer. The full extent of my confusion, tension and fatigue was yet to be felt. For the first three weeks following summer school, I walked around the grounds crying for no reason at all, feeling tired and depressed. There was no class to rush to, no floor to wash, no dishes to put away. My duties, now that summer school was over, seemed unbelievably light. I felt dazed, immensely fatigued and incapable of enthusiasm about anything.

Upon receiving my grades, Mother Mathilde called me into her office to demand an explanation. I had received three B's. She was sorely disappointed and lectured me on not wasting God's gifts. I was an A student, everyone recognized that, but this was a gift of God. Why then was I not returning to God the things of God?

I was aghast at her lack of insight, and incapable of even beginning to explain. And after all, what could I explain? How could I explain? I hardly understood myself what was going on in my life. I felt beaten down. The normal élan of my nature seemed irretrievably lost.

One afternoon during this three week period, I stood in the kitchen drying a pitcher with Sister Renee, a Canadian Sister who was studying with us. We were talking, taking advantage of the new regulation which permitted us to talk between 4:00 and 4:15, if one so wished. Our superior, who was uncomfortable with this evidence of laxity on the part of our higher superiors, had shortened the period to ten minutes, which she sincerely believed was time enough to talk if one insisted on it.

Mother Mathilde walked in, and addressing herself to Sister Renee, said, "There she is again, wasting her time as usual," shaking her head in my direction. Again she revealed that she expected more from me than from the majority of the sisters in the community. She was disappointed that I did not feel fervent enough to do without the period of talking. Despite the fact that the rule had been changed to permit it, deep down she still felt it was a breach of the rule of silence, understandable in view of the fact that she had lived 48 years of her life in this religious community, during which time very little had changed.

I knelt down automatically, put the pitcher on the counter, kissed the floor and walked out of the room. I was numb. "Wasting time! My God! I can't live here anymore. I can't take it. How could she say that to me after imposing two demanding ménages on me, while all the other sisters had only one?"

I felt so alienated from Mother Mathilde; the whole way of life suddenly seemed so hostile to my nature that I felt over whelmed by it. What could I do? I had been walking. Now I began to run down the hill, onto the major highway, running and sobbing. "I have to get away. I have to leave here." I was like a wounded animal running for cover where I couldn't be hurt anymore. So I ran blindly.

It was at least twenty minutes later before I suddenly remembered the phrase in the Constitution: *When a sister leaves the house with the intention of not returning, she is a fugitive from religion and an outcast from the Church. The apostate from religion incurs by the very fact itself the excommunication reserved to the Ordinary of her place (i.e. the Bishop) of residence.*

"*A fugitive from religion? Excommunicated? My God! What am I doing? Where am I going?*" I suddenly realized that I was dressed in a religious habit, running away from a convent, running on a major highway. To where? I had no money. What would I do? Where would I go? What if somebody saw me? What would they think? The strong sense of loyalty to the Congregation instilled in me during my years of training compelled me to hide my own misery from the "outside world" so that they would in no way misjudge the Congregation. I must go back.

I walked back, whimpering, afraid to sob too loudly, for fear that someone in a passing car would stop to ask me what the matter was. I entered the convent grounds with some trepidation.

"*Would Mother Mathilde have been searching for me?* By this time, I had missed evening meditation. I had no intention of joining the sisters for supper. I sat down under a tree to rest for a while and think about what I was going to do.

"Oh good! Thank God!" I heard Sister Florence Jane's voice. She came over and gave me a hug. "I was so worried," she said. "Sister Renee told me what had happened and I've been looking for you ever since."

"Does Mother Mathilde know you are out here?"

"I don't know. Anyway, that doesn't matter. Are you ok?"

"Yes, I guess so. I'm just tired."

"Well, we are all going to bed early tonight, so why don't we go up now and you can take a hot bath and relax."

I was glad to see Sister Florence Jane. All of us younger sisters felt that we had to band together to survive Mother Mathilde's iron rule, especially because of her volatile and unpredictable nature.

I felt guilty over my attempt to run away, and inexplicably I did not want anyone to know, even my friends in the ranks, for fear that I might be considered an unworthy sister. I told her only that I had to "*get away a while*" and had taken a walk. Already I was feeling better; crying and talking about it had helped.

It was the summer of my twenty first birthday and from all external appearances I was the *"settled and happy one"* in the family. I smiled wryly to myself as I fell asleep with exhaustion.

Why didn't I leave? What kept me? I did consider leaving on the grounds that the life was too irrational and too emotionally strenuous for me. But then, I reasoned that things would get better. Mother Mathilde had a reputation for being a difficult superior; surely not all superiors were like her. Soon, I would be teaching, something I really looked forward to. Besides, these trials were part of my formation period. If I wanted to be a good religious, I had to suffer. As Mother Michael had said, "*As gold is tried by fire…*".

The second year with Mother Mathilde seemed calmer than the first. Perhaps it wasn't, but only seemed so since we had gotten used to Mother's ways. During these months, we often read circular letters describing events in the Belgian Congo. Several of our mission schools and clinics had been ravaged in the tribal warfare accompanying the struggle for independence. Four of our sisters had been killed and one of our American sisters, a woman in her early sixties, had been brutally assaulted and raped. She was eventually rescued and sent to the United States for treatment. She had stayed briefly with us en-route to Maine. She had appeared quite disoriented still.

Others in our congregation were in the wilds of New Guinea in the process of founding a Mission amidst reports that one of the priest founders, a member of our religious family, was missing. These were serious matters. How petty our little daily trials seemed by comparison. June approached and we were informed that instead of staying in Connecticut, we would attend summer school at St. John's University in New York. There we would attend two sessions enabling us to almost finish up our accumulation of credits. The rest we would pick up evenings and Saturdays during the year. I welcomed the news and looked forward to leaving Connecticut for my new community and my new life. Whatever might come to pass, Mother Mathilde had left her imprint on me.

TEACHING- OUR LADY OF WISDOM ACADEMY

We arrived in Ozone Park, a neighborhood in the borough of Queens before the end of the school year. It was a busy and bustling house, sisters arriving from north and south, sisters staying over for a few days while awaiting their departure for Europe, sisters scurrying about trying to get things tied up in school. I loved the hustle and bustle and the sense of excitement in the air. Summers for teaching sisters were always exciting times. No more school, papers to correct, kids, clubs; but more than that, summers were times of reunion. Since most of the sisters attended summer school in New York, they lived in Ozone Park because of the proximity to college campuses. This provided us an opportunity to see friends who had been teaching in faraway places such as Virginia or Maine - to exchange gossip and to renew old acquaintances and friendships.

Many of the Academy's regular teachers would leave, perhaps for Europe, others to study at Notre Dame, Catholic University, etc, or to go on a summer assignment such as helping out in a hospital, a school for the retarded, etc. Until they left, we were cramped, sleeping on cots in hallways, in study rooms and in the attic.

We arrived in June in the midst of festivities surrounding the feast of St. Anthony of Padua. Processions, bazaars, street singing went on into the night. Never before had I witnessed so much inebriation in the name of religion. I tried to sleep in the sweltering city heat. Planes rattled the convent every twenty minutes, using our neighboring Church steeple as a guide to landing into and departing from nearby Kennedy airport.. I thought over the first day's events and realized how relieved I was to be out of Connecticut and into the "real world."

I had arrived on a Saturday with six other young sisters in time to begin the first summer session. Sister Helen, Sr. Florence Jane, Sister Joan

Francis and I were directly from the College community. The others had been reassigned from another house. The superior had preregistered us at St. John's so that on Monday morning there would be no delay in beginning classes promptly at 8:00 a.m. She handed each of us our class cards, and with her characteristic no nonsense attitude, wished us well in our studies. I was registered into two courses, Economics and Geography. Mother explained briefly that I was to teach both History and French and would be applying for certification in Social Studies. For this reason, I had to take a certain sequence of courses. I was delighted that my first preference had not been forgotten. I would be teaching History at least part time. I looked forward to starting summer school, my first venture into the outside world since I had left home five years before.!

It was exciting to take a bus and to sit in class with people other than nuns. The economics classes, run by two high powered young economists, fascinated me and I devoured the readings. Geography, on the other hand, was taught by a middle-aged registrar from one of the city colleges. I've forgotten his name, but I do remember the old Bentley he spoke about with great pride and his youth spent camping in Maine. His intellectual growth had long since been arrested, but his class was relaxing and it put me back in touch with the world. In this class, I had my first taste of the restraint that I would have to exercise because of my status as a nun. He had cleverly devised a plan whereby we would work on projects and use class time to make oral reports on them. This eliminated all work on his part with few lectures to prepare and no papers to correct.

I started a project on soil analysis, getting specimens from different parts of Long Island and sending them for analysis. As it turned out the specimens had been too meager and I was told by the labs that I would have to gather more substantial ones to obtain results. It was three weeks into the six week session when I received the letter informing me of the error, not enough time to act.

My professor seemed unperturbed; in fact he had an immediate solution to my problem. I would take a field trip consisting of a visit to a steam liner and report on my trip to the class. It seemed an odd topic for a geography report and I told him so. He brushed aside my protest with an off-hand remark that this was human geography. He went on to say that he knew the captain of a certain ship, so he could arrange everything, picking me up on a Saturday morning, getting me a first class tour, having lunch together on the ship, and driving me home. I wondered why he was being so helpful and suspected his motives. I also felt uneasy about using this as a project for the class. I then remembered one of the girls in the class had reported on her visit to a gum factory. This professor was an oddball, why worry?

I told him I would ask permission and would let him know my

answer the next day. Once back in the convent, my doubts came back to me. It seemed like such a silly project. What would my new superior, Mother Daniel, think? This tall, stately, handsome woman of German descent was still a stranger to me. By reputation, she had conservative leanings and ruled with a firm hand. She was reserved and always in control of her emotions, but I detected a warmth, sincerity and rationality that beckoned me like an oasis after Mother Mary Ambrose and Mother Mathilde. She was young as superiors went, probably in her late thirties or early forties. Her rosy cheeks and clear smooth skin told me so. An excellent teacher, she had been principal of the Girls' academy prior to being named superior. I liked her and sensed that she liked me. I knew she would find this request strange, and I hesitated to approach her. Nevertheless, fresh out of training, I still felt I had to present all my problems to my superior.

Her reaction was predictable. "Outrageous!" she exclaimed. "You most certainly will not go!"

I suspected that she interpreted my professor's offer as a seductive advance. I found it amusing that she responded to it so strongly. I had been away from such advances for a long time, but I was correct in discerning that whatever his motive, sex played little if any part in it. Nevertheless, I had to refuse his offer.

He reacted with what seemed like genuine sorrow and told me to write whatever notes I had on the soil project. It was late September before his intentions became clear. He appeared at the school where I was teaching and introduced himself to the principal, as the registrar at City Community College and a friend of Sister Rachel's. Could he speak to the seniors about attending his college? He was using me as an entrée to the Academy, a valuable source of good students. Sister Mary Clare, my friend from high school days, was now the principal. Having heard about my crazy summer professor she immediately put two and two together. Nevertheless she did arrange a time for him to come to solicit candidates and we both had a good laugh over it.

The summer provided me and the other six new arrivals an opportunity to adjust to our surroundings. It was unusual for so many sisters to be moved into a community at once. Many sisters, previously assigned to Wisdom Academy, were being reassigned to staff a new diocesan school and we were to be their replacements.

Sometime in the summer, we learned that construction on the new diocesan high school was being delayed by a long steel strike. School would open on schedule by utilizing the empty classrooms of another new Catholic school. The sisters staffing the school would have to continue to live at Ozone Park. We would be sixty in a convent meant to house forty. It was disappointing news.

With the opening of the school year, we followed a tight schedule, fitting in our religious exercises mostly at the beginning and end of each day. Rising at 5:00A.M.was followed by prayers, meditation and Mass from 5:30 to 7:30. Breakfast was from 7:30 to 8:00. School followed from 8:00 to 3:30. After school, our time was our own to prepare classes, correct papers, or study, as most of us were enrolled in University classes on Saturdays. At 5:30 P.M., we were summoned by bell to the community room for fifteen minutes of spiritual reading followed by chapel exercises, i.e. meditation and recitation of the rosary. From 6:30 to 7:00, we had supper, followed by a half-hour study time, then recreation until 8:30. Lights out at 9:30 P.M.

Once a week, sisters with temporary vows were gathered together for a special instruction. At this time, new teachers were rigidly instructed in the proper decorum befitting a religious teacher. We were to maintain distance from our students. This policy was founded on experience; young teachers had to first prove themselves before they could become friendly. Despite the anxieties provoked by the numerous instructions on what to do, what to say and what not to do and not to say, I came to love teaching and found it a valuable source of learning about people.

I started the school year eagerly, even if a bit scared, as was the case with most new teachers. I had been assigned two history classes, two French classes and one religion class. I felt especially lucky to be given Sister Giorgio as my mentor in history. She was a dynamic, forceful and lucid teacher. Each Friday afternoon, we got together and planned what I would teach the next week, what I would assign the students, what books I could suggest they read and what I should read myself in preparation. I loved her style and tried to copy it in my classes.

Though teaching for the most part was routine, the high school ensured the students of good basic college preparation. The students were average or better. Students with serious problems were not admitted so teaching was pleasant. They were mostly from working class families. They worked hard, but had a limited view of the world. They served as my introduction to city provincialism.

It soon became obvious that though they were surrounded by famous people and places, in reach of cultural events of all kinds, and exposed to people from a wide variety of countries, ethnic groups and cultures, they remained untouched by it all. For the most part, these adolescents had learned to manage in the city by finding their way to school, perhaps to one or two shopping areas, and nowhere else. They rarely went into Manhattan and when they did, they considered it their big trip for the year. New York City was almost as mysterious and awesome to them as it was to their rural counterparts, hundreds of miles away.

This provincialism surprised me. At their age, I had been more exposed and more traveled than they were. It took me some time to understand the relationship of the provincialism of these city girls to the general danger and fear that urban living inspired. When I proposed field trips to them, I received answers like: "The Cloisters? What's that?"or "The United Nations? Can we visit there?"

Current political events may as well have been set on another planet as far as they were concerned. They had little knowledge of these nor did they display any interest in them. It was 1962 and political life had not yet caught the imagination and enthusiasm of the young. Kennedy's campaign and his inaugural of the Peace Corps had laid seeds for the future development of this interest, but the effects had yet to be felt..

The students generally respected and liked the sisters; they enjoyed playing adolescent pranks on them. One of the lessons to be learned that first year of teaching was to find the proper balance between an overly stern, unrelenting attitude and one of total laissez-faire. Slowly, I developed an ability to participate in and enjoy the fun while maintaining the controlling hand; then I could truly enjoy their pranks. Some of these gave me embarrassing moments, like the time I dropped my white flannel bloomers on the stairs.

We younger sisters slept in the attic of the school. This meant traversing the school in order to get to our sleeping quarters. One Friday evening, I was leaving the dormitory with an armful of soiled and torn clothes when I heard the girls in the yard. They had attended a basketball game which had finished earlier than usual. They would be coming into the school to get books out of their lockers before going home. I thought of how embarrassed I would be to meet my students with my arms full of soiled underwear, so I decided to make a dash for it and beat it into the convent before they saw me. I made it, breathing a sigh of relief.

On Monday, I found on my desk a small round package with my name on it. "Who put this here?" Silence answered me, then some vague noncommittal answers. I sensed a suspicious atmosphere of expectancy in the room. Deciding the package must be some sort of joke, I put it into my drawer for private inspection later on. As soon as I had dismissed the class for lunch, I gingerly removed the package from the drawer and opened it. Oh my God! I turned purple when I saw them, my long white flannel bloomers with my name sewn prominently on the front panels.

I quickly examined them to see if they were clean. Well, at least I dropped a clean pair on the stairs, realizing immediately how they happened to get to my desk. They had needed some mending and I was taking them to evening recreation to do just that.

A burst of giggles interrupted my thoughts, and I realized that I had been watched while I opened the package. I hurried to the door to see who it was, but they scurried away before I could get a hold of them. What to do? Well, I'd ignore the whole incident. I decided to act as if it had not taken place.

What a coincidence that the day's French lesson included the word for pants. In the middle of the lesson, I caught the class exchanging glances. There I stood explaining the meaning of pantalon when all they could think of was my white flannel bloomers. I smiled faintly and that was all they needed. The class burst into gales of laughter. It was funny, I had to admit, so I laughed with them and it was over.

I loved teaching. I gave myself to it wholeheartedly. It served as an escape from the problems I faced in the community. Between teaching, preparing classes, correcting papers, attending two university classes, and studying, I hardly had time to worry about my vocation.

As far as life in the convent was concerned, the situation was ridiculous. Some sixty sisters lived crammed into a sixty year old convent built to house forty. All things being equal, numbers alone would have created tension, In fact all things were not equal and life was further complicated by ideological difference. It was the era of Vatican Council II with hints of "radical change to come" appearing daily in the New York Times. The Catholic intellectual world had come alive after years of quiescence. Questions of ecumenism, papal authority, bureaucratic structure and decision-making ripped the Church apart. The community in which I found myself reflected these differences.

Sometime in the late fall and winter of this first year, we began receiving questionnaires from Rome. They were in the form of an agenda for community discussions. Topics ranged from prayer life and vows to externals such as the habit. In those early days, our protests for change were hardly what one would label revolutionary. But to the older nuns who had lived most of their lives in convents and had experienced almost no change, the demands appeared earthshaking.

The liberals in our community pressed for specific changes: change in the manner of dress, i.e. demanding that the habit be abandoned for modern dress; changes in the style of living generally, - wearing 1960's underwear instead of the 18th century garb, using regular china and utensils to eat rather than tin bowls and wooden ware; change in prayers, -.. adopting those rooted in the official psalms and the Divine Office of the church rather than the devotional prayers that the congregation had accumulated over the years. Most radical of all, they pressed for a voice in decision making.

The conservative tactic was to view the movement for change as a storm to be weathered. Their aim was to keep the liberals from making too many changes and causing too much damage. The Church, they reckoned, had lived through hard times before and had survived; it would live through these times and again remain triumphant. Most of the middle group, ages twenty-five through forty, belonged to the liberal camp. The older sisters, most of the superiors, and some young sisters formed the conservative camp.

Besides the fundamental differences in theological interpretations which underlay the disagreements, a backlog of personal grievances clouded the issues. The superiors' innocuous remarks seemed laced with double meaning to many of the liberal middle sisters. Heated discussions would be suppressed when some of the newer members walked into a room. Sisters who had not been selected as teachers for the new school envied those who had and harbored some feelings of resentment toward their superiors for being passed over. Others resented not being named superior.

We seven newly assigned nuns could not discern what was happening. We had been assigned to a convent racked with tension, rivalries and petty disputes. We chose to keep out of the politics of the situation; it was our only real alternative given the many other adjustments we had.

In addition to the pressures resulting from numbers and ideological differences, Ozone Park was also the administrative center of the American Province, and housed the Provincial Superior and her staff. Ordinarily, provincial superiors had separate quarters, i.e. they lived in a convent other than where the sisters engaged in active works such as teaching, nursing, or social work. In the United States, such quarters had never been set aside. Mother Michael, the Provincial Superior, had become, at least by reputation, the defender of conservatism. Her presence in the house was resented by the liberal sisters. The tension that existed because of it added to an already difficult situation.

Those days were incredible. We sat in rows of straight back chairs (we were not allowed any others) and spent our one hour of recreation mending our coiffes, kerchiefs, or stockings. The mending of the former consisted of laborious weaving, counting threads, and weaving in and out, two threads at a time. One would skip two rows of threads and repeat the process. It required an unusual amount of visual attention. As the superior often reminded us, "Words have no color" so there was no need to look at each other while speaking but should keep our eyes focused on our mending. If you were fortunate enough to arrive early, you could sit next to a sister you knew or cared about. As there were some sixty of us, most of them strangers to the new arrivals, it was hard to be natural, to relax and talk freely.

Often Mother Michael would interrupt the conversation to tell a story or a joke. I did not particularly resent this because I always thought Mother Michael an excellent story teller and some of her jokes quite good. The problem was the lack of opportunity to really let off steam from the day's labor and anxieties.

Despite this, life was more relaxed in the house than it had been during our days in training. We were so busy that the "little customs" were not emphasized. One never witnessed Mother Daniel publicly humiliating a sister because she had come down the stairs and allowed her skirt to trail behind her; this had been a usual occurrence in the Novitiate. No one made publically note that sisters sometimes walked without keeping their hands in their sleeves, a breach which had particularly aggravated Mother Mathilde and for which I had been publicly charged and made to kiss the floor on three different occasions one Easter Sunday.

Each sister was assigned housework and rotated duties for prayers, reading, dishes, and serving tables. Every few months the entire weekend would be devoted to starching and ironing our coiffes and kerchiefs. I noticed that some older and middle sisters signed up for as little as possible, expecting the younger sisters or house sisters to absorb the difference. I was energetic and cheerfully signed up for my share and a little more, puzzled that these sisters should be so reluctant to devote free hours to community activities. I did not resent these hours, be they for singing, mending, cleaning, or ironing. I fully accepted the personification and glorification of the *Community* above the individual. It was one of the most important principles of religious life, -acting for the common good, placing that good above one's own *individual* good. I gave myself to this belief wholeheartedly—the underlying principles of socialism/communism.

It was common for the superior to type, mimeograph and distribute various spiritual journals articles she found useful. One article distributed in the fall of 1962 made quite an impression on me. It was about the principle of the religious and the importance of acting for the common good, of placing that good above one's own individual good: I utilized these articles to meditate and reflect on the meaning of my life.

How religious are you? To be a religious is after all to live the life in common...I have inalienable rights, so the community too is such a person with such rights, all those things which go together to promote the common welfare. But this same common welfare, this same common good is MY GOOD swept full circle. .

The common good then is truly my good. The common good is cut to the figure of my happiness and my wholeness, my individuality.

Superiors and the rule mirror this moral person, this common life. If I am persistently troublesome to those persons placed over me with the blessings of God. If I am the veritable gall and wormwood of their offices, then there is something about "community" that I neither see nor practice clearly. I refuse to give it the right that belongs to it, namely the observance of the rule, that code of perfection whereby long ago I engaged myself to live in common for the glory of God and the good of souls. In doing this, in making this refusal, I fail the community, I fail every individual in it and most tragically of all, I fail myself.

In Ozone Park, it was customary on Sundays to attend one of the masses in the nearby Parish Church. We crossed paths with the parish priests in the Church yard on the way to Mass and to afternoon services. The sisters would bow reverently, but quickly, as they said good morning or good afternoon, and hurry by. The fathers responded in kind.

I was puzzled me that there was so little interaction. The priests belonged to a congregation of religious priests founded by the same French priest who founded our order and therefore shared our spirituality. I questioned Sister Mary Clare.

"Well, it started a long time ago, back in the thirties," she answered. "There was a sister, a very remarkable woman, who was a prominent musician and held a position in the parish. As a result of this she had a lot of dealings with the pastor. One day, the two of them disappeared. They had, it seemed, carried on a clandestine love affair, and decided that they could no longer continue in that manner, so they decided to leave together. The sisters never accepted the fact that both parties were to be held responsible. They blamed the priests for the loss of this gifted member and from that time on, they never spoke much to them."

It was an interesting and even quaint story. But why continue this feud some thirty years later when almost no one remembered the incident.? I found it childish laughed when I heard the explanation.

The priests, professors and the parents I came into contact with provided no sexual stimulation for me. I was concerned about other things. There was certainly some kind of sexual interaction at times, some of which I was aware of, , but much of it was in the nature of flirtatious nothings.

These days passed quickly, bringing us again to February and the renewal of vows. I had entered on August 2, 1957 and made first vows on February 2, 1959. This February, 1963 would mark my last year before final vows. In the coming October, in accordance with the custom in the Congregation, I would write to Mother General in Rome seeking permission not to make temporary vows, as I had done each October for the past four years, but to become a permanent member of the Congregation, to pronounce final vows.

I had never before hesitated renewing my vows. As it was a temporary engagement for one year, I pushed into the background a true confrontation with myself about making that irrevocable decision. This year, for the first time, I was hesitant. I still felt very much a novice in the religious life, even though I had already spent five and a half years in the convent. I felt that I understood better the true meaning of prayer. Religious practices such as kissing the floor no longer bothered me the way they had in the past. Still, there lingered deep within me doubts about my ability to maintain this commitment over time. I still hated to kneel to ask permission for things, and in fact, I would put off going to the bathroom rather than kneel to ask permission to go.

I hated to kneel to request a new bar of soap, or to bring my old underwear to have my superior examine it prior to deciding if it should be discarded. The practice of publicly declaring faults during the evening meal made my stomach tighten, even when it was not my turn to declare my faults - even though my repertoire of faults did not portray any extraordinary weakness. It was tremendously humiliating.

Despite my misgivings, I chose not to dwell on these but to go ahead. Perhaps it was because no real examination was possible, and not to proceed was to fail. Three days prior to the renewal of vows, Sister Constance Mary (Fiorella), the nurse who had been our doyenne arrived from Virginia with Mother Michael. Sister Constance Mary had been named to teach in the Nursing school run by our sisters in that state. She was on her way to a hospital in the New York area, and we were told that she was just staying overnight in our house. I was delighted, as were four other sisters. We would begin our two-day retreat in preparation for vows the next morning. As a special concession, we were allowed to spend the recreation hour together, talking over old time, laughing at the silly problems of our novitiate days. We had a lot to say as we had not seen each other since the fall of 1959 some three and a half years before.

The next day Sister Constance Mary left the order! I accidentally came upon her in the parlor hallway which was separated from the rest of the convent by swinging doors usually kept closed. I was startled because I recognized her parents and noticed her dressed in secular clothing. Without explanation, I knew that she was not renewing vows and that her trip to the Provincial house had been because of this. Our evening together had been an unspoken farewell. I turned and walked away, since it was not permitted in those days to say farewell to sisters leaving the congregation.

Why was she leaving? Why had she not given us any hint of her decision? Even as I wondered, I knew that the superiors had warned her not to discuss the matter for fear that it would adversely affect us.

Days later, Mother Daniel called us in one by one and told us that Sister Constance Mary had left the Congregation. No reason for her departure were given. We were merely asked to pray for her.

On the first of February, I awoke with a mouthful of open canker sores, making it impossible to open my mouth without severe pain. I never before had any such experience so I panicked, not knowing what it was. As soon as Mass was over, I went to the Superior to ask if I could see a nurse. I was convinced that I had some rare mouth disease.

Mother Daniel looked at my mouth and sent me to the nurse. Nurses who attended university also lived in our house , at the same time, served the sisters as nurses. As she peered into my barely open mouth, she asked, "Are you having any problems with your stomach?"

"Not any more than usual. You see since my postulate, I have been unable to digest my food properly,. After each meal, my food regurgitates and I have to chew it down a second time, and sometimes a third before it will stay in my stomach."

"Isn't it very acidic, or sour?"

"Yes, but I have gotten so used to it, I hardly notice it anymore."

She was disturbed by the news. Why had I never reported this to my Superior? I had, I told her, only to be told that it was usual for sisters to have nervous stomachs, that it would go away - that I should not worry about it.

"Well, I'll make an appointment for you to have a complete checkup. Meanwhile, I'll treat the sores with gentian violet."

What never occurred to me was the significance of developing a mouthful of canker sores the very day before I had to pronounce vows. The sores were so painful that I could barely talk. Still, I did not make the connection, which seems so obvious with hindsight. Though my symptoms had cleared, the nurse insisted that I to go one of our hospitals in Brooklyn for a G.I. series. The following week, I returned to hear the results. I sat in the cubicle waiting for the doctor, wondering if something was wrong. It was unlikely since as far as I knew I was in good health. I had never been sickly.

The curtain parted to admit a tall, lean, dark-haired doctor, accompanied by the sister/nurse.

"This is Doctor Rubio."

"Good morning, Doctor."

"Sister. What is bothering you my dear?"

"Nothing. Why? Were the tests negative?"

"You don't have to be afraid to talk to me if there is anything you are worried about."

"Well…."

I did not know what to say, and felt frightened by the intensity of his gaze. How does one explain to a total stranger that institutional living is strenuous and especially when one had been forbidden for years to speak about things of a deep personal nature. Besides, how could he even begin to understand?

Turning to the sister/nurse beside him, I pleaded: "Please tell him that it is not easy to be a nun. I feel very tense at times, but I don't think it's really anything to worry about. We are living in rather difficult times in the convent."

Sister smiled at the doctor who motioned her to leave.

"Is there something special you are worried about that you might like to discuss with me?"

For a moment I felt like crying. But I really did not have anything specific to discuss with him. I had hardly given my *"problem"* any thought. I shook my head and smiled shyly at him.

As he was unable to get me to talk, he proceeded to say that the tests were negative. He would give me pills to settle my stomach, but these would only remove the symptoms for a while. I would have to see about solving the real problems that were causing the stomach disorder.

He stepped out to get the pills and returned shortly:"These pills are green and black. You are to take one before each meal. Now repeat what I said."

"The pills are green and black and I'm to take one before each meal."

"These are multicolored. You are to take one each morning before breakfast."

I wondered why he was speaking so slowly, and having me repeat after him. Was it my imagination? Perhaps I was really sick and no one wanted to tell me.

I waited for Sister Louis Mary who had come to have her knees checked. They were swollen and painful. "Nun's knees" the doctors called it. All of us experienced some difficulty because of the long hours of kneeling. When I studied at night, I often picked at the scabs that formed on my knee caps and caused them to bleed more than necessary. But my knees had never really bothered me. I took the scabs for granted.

Sister Louis Mary emerged and we headed for the door. There we met my doctor. He smiled shyly as we said good morning and left.

"That's Doctor Rubio," Sister Louis Mary whispered, as the door shut behind us. "He's a psychiatrist from Chile and is learning English. It must be very hard for a well educated person to come to this country and to have to begin all over again."

I hardly heard. A psychiatrist? Maybe I was out of my mind, I thought. Why had I been sent to a psychiatrist and not told about it?

The sisters roared when I told them the story of the pills and the careful instructions. I told it as a good story, despite, or maybe because of, my fears about the situation.

My superior seemed to understand my plight. "Sister, you do not have to return to the clinic if you don't want to. (Doctor Rubio had scheduled a follow-up visit.) I did not know that you were to be seen by a psychiatrist. If you would feel better not going back then just say so."

"No, I want to go back. He'll think I'm not returning because I'm afraid of him, and I'm not."

It seems strange that I don't remember now what any of the other visits were like, or even if I ever returned to visit Doctor Rubio again. The incident had a rather marked impact on me however, and it was to come to mind many times in the future. February passed into May and the school year came to a close. I looked forward to the next year with confidence. I had learned a lot about teaching and had come out on top. My students were doing well, and I got along with them. I was generally satisfied with my performance as a teacher.

One Saturday, I held the door open for Mother Michael who had been but a few steps ahead of me leaving the refectory. "Come up with me."

It was such a routine remark that I thought little of its possible meaning and dutifully followed her up the stairs. Mother Michael was in the habit of asking sisters to carry boxes up or down the stairs as she had a bad heart.

"Take off your apron," she said as we reached the top of the stairs. My heart jumped. Removing one's apron was a signal for a scolding, a serious spiritual talk, an obedience; whatever, it was serious. I took off my apron, folded it over the banister, and followed her into her office.

"Kneel down, sister," she said gently. It wasn't going to be a scolding. I could tell by the tone.

"God wants you to serve him at Christ the King my child."

I was stunned. Christ the King. But I was just getting settled here, I thought. Tears flowed down my cheeks.

"Thank you, Mother."

After all, I had promised to go wherever I was sent, without warning, in the night if need be. Christ the King. That was the new school that had not been completed in time for the sisters to inhabit the previous fall. Christ the King. It was a widely acknowledged fact that the Congregation's superiors had wanted to impress the Bishop and staffed the school that first year with the very best teachers. In part, I was flattered to have been picked. I realized that they did not send just anyone to this school. Still, I had just established myself in Wisdom. I had made friends among the students. I sought out my friends Sister Helen and Sister Florence Jane so I could cry to my heart's content. There was no use dwelling on it. I would just have to get used to it

ASSIGNMENT TO CHRIST THE KING
Summer, 1963 - June, 1964

I had little time to mope over my Obedience. It was the end of the school year, a hectic time with numerous records to fill, kids to prepare for State exams, mounds of papers to correct, university classes of my own. Mother Michael announced that the teachers of Christ the King would move into their new convent by the end of June. We were not anxious to move. The landscaping had not been completed and the huge school with its convent on the fourth floor was surrounded by mounds of dust. Besides, we hated leaving our friends behind. Obediences were such heart wrenching times. Nevertheless, as planned, we moved in the last week of June. I had no way of knowing then that this summer would be a turning point in my religious life.

Having completed all my degree requirements by the end of the first summer session, Mother Daniel decreed that I should rest for the remaining six weeks. It was a much needed respite after a year of teaching and studying. I felt lightheaded and giddy coming home after the last exam that sweltering July day. My students had done excellently in their Regents exams, my own grades were good; for the first time, I had the luxury of a room of my own. Things were definitely improving.

That same day, Sister Theresa of Avila, the chairman of the religion department, accosted me in the hall: "Sister, the theology you learned in college is well, let's call it outdated. Here at Christ the King, we're teaching a new syllabus for which you need a lot of preparation. You can start by reading these."

Handing me a pile of books that she had tucked under her arm, she added, "If you have any problems or questions, just ask me or any of the sisters who were at Christ the King last year."

In the numerous debates that had divided our community the previous year, I had felt unable to participate intelligently, realizing that during my training, I had been sheltered from the thinking of radical theologians. My tendency had been to adopt a conservative position, while at the same time feeling uneasy about it. I had come to respect the radical middle sisters. They were reputedly the best teachers, respected by students and colleagues. More than that, they were cheerful and kind, down to earth and unpretentious. I seldom disagreed with them. Here, at Christ the King I had the valuable opportunity to catch up, to study the other side.

I took the books from her eagerly, went to my room, and began my education in the more radical theology of the day. I read through Bernard Haring, Congar, Karl Rahner, Bruce Vawter, Charles Davis, Johnson, Hans Kung and others. I was inspired and excited by what I read. It was a revelation - a liberation! During those six weeks, I discovered that the malaise I had felt, without fully being conscious of it, was not only felt by others, but was justifiable. My difficulties with religious life, my inability to understand or to perform weren't merely the result of my not being holy enough, or in control enough, as I had been led to believe. The present rules and regulations stood indicted independent of my performance. In the opinion of the Catholic left, the Church had become so engrossed in detail; that it was forgetting its essential goal.

It is difficult to describe the exalted feeling of inner liberation, especially to those who have never felt bound by the force of a religious belief. I felt a joy, coupled with uncertainty and yes, even a fear of freedom. I perceived for the first time that religious life, the life that I had tried so hard to live, was warped. Instead of beating my breast, and searching in my soul for the cause of my inability to be the perfect nun, I saw that the problem was with the ideal. It was inhuman, an impossible model.

These new insights gave me a sense of security and freedom as I had not felt since I had entered the convent. Secure in the belief that my judgment was sound, in agreement with that of major liberal theologians in the Church, I felt freer to act on my own beliefs and to express my own opinions, even when these did not agree with my superiors.

Through it all, I experienced profound uncertainty. It was not the uncertainty of the past. I was no longer always concerned with pleasing my superiors, a task made difficult by the volatile nature of Mother Mathilde and the harsh prejudgments of Mother Mary Ambrose. Now the uncertainty was of a different kind. Taught to suspect my judgment, to despise my pride, my arrogance and my self-centeredness, I wondered if I was now deceiving myself into believing what I wanted to believe. Was I interpreting theological thought to suit or vindicate myself? My newfound liberation led to the most profound inner conflicts.

This was my fifth year of temporary vows; time for me to write to Rome requesting permission of the Superior General and of the Congregation to be accepted for admission to perpetual vows. What to do? I experienced some vague doubts. It wasn't that I felt terribly unhappy, but I wasn't that happy either.

Did I really want this for my whole life? I discussed the matter briefly with Mother Daniel. "Sister, you've been a good subject, and you seem happy. I don't see why you should hesitate. Write to Rome. I'm sure it's the right thing."

I respected and trusted this stately woman. Without further thought, I sat down and composed the letter. Perhaps it was the fact that a nun's life was challenging and difficult appealed to me. Brought up in a totally Catholic milieu - nurtured in it - I was, on the whole, docile. I absorbed doctrine. I conformed. I tried deliberately to live focused not on this world, but on the next. I dreamt not of changing the world, but of saving it. I was innocent, messianic, insular, naive and full of good will. For me and hundreds of sisters like me, religious life appeared as inescapable destiny. We were singularly blessed by being *Called*. *To whom much is given, much is demanded*. *Noblesse oblige*. Looking back, I can almost say I drifted into perpetual vows.

With the coming of September, my second year of teaching began and our new superior was named. Mother Angelus was a thin wiry person with sharp features and dark penetrating eyes. She had been elected by the sisters to represent them at the coming General Chapter in Rome. For this reason, she was given no duties other than that of superior. Typically, superiors would also serve as principal of the school, or the hospital administrator. Known throughout the province for her radical views, the sisters welcomed her warmly as the superior of our community. She was a stranger to me, and I found myself less enthusiastic, reserving judgment. As time went by, I came to perceive her as authoritarian, despite her liberal views on the popular issues of the day; i.e. the habit, change in prayer life, the practices of poverty. She was not sensitive to the fears and insecurities of the younger sisters, insecurities that had been carefully nurtured in the training period. Instead of allaying these, helping the sisters to learn to form their own judgments, she encouraged the destructive dependency that had been fostered in the Novitiate and Juniorate. This was evident in the small daily events that were so carefully legislated by customary law.

Mother Angelus' inconsistency made her unpredictable, deepening the insecurity of her young subjects. In some ways, it was easier to deal with an archconservative- at least you always knew where you stood. In therapy, three years later, I blurted out "Superiors are destroyers of people,

I don't want to be a superior. People tell me that one day I'll be in charge. I'll be able to do what I want. But I don't want to be a superior; it frightens me."

Father Daly, the priest psychologist, seemed as surprised as I was at my outburst. He probed to discover what was so terrifying, forcing me to remember casual incidents seemingly long forgotten. One of these focused on Mother Angelus's treatment of one of the younger sisters.

It began with Sister Peter Mary coming to me for advice. "Sister, how do you clean your bedroom floor?"

"I just wash it with soap and water, using Ajax lightly on difficult spots and rinse thoroughly. Then, I apply wax using a clean rag."

"I see. But do you wax under your bed, or just in the aisle?"

"Well, it depends. For God's sake, Sister, it's just a floor."

She suddenly looked on the verge of tears and apologized profusely. "Well, Mother scolded me for the way I cleaned it the last time, and I just wanted to make sure that I did it right this time."

I was appalled. I looked at her for a minute and thought to myself, "Here is a very intelligent girl, who all consider one of the brightest and most promising young sisters. True, she is shy and lacking in self-confidence, but she shouldn't be this nervous over a silly floor. What is the matter with the Superior?"

I smiled reassuringly at Sister Peter Mary. "Well, I'm sure if you do what I just told you, it will be all right. Okay?"

"I guess so."

"Let's go get the mop and pail and I'll help you begin." And we went off to clean the floor.

This incident and many others made me wary of the tremendous power exercised by the superiors over the sisters in their care. Too few superiors understood their power and the effect it could have on their young subjects.

My new intellectual insights and sense of freedom allowed me to slowly reinterpret those miniscule customary rules which, by and large, I had learned to obey automatically. I remember standing outside the superior's room one day when a sister came along. "What are you waiting for?" Her question made me uncomfortable. She was inviting me to break the rule of silence. We were in a "regular" place, therefore doubly bound to silence and she was questioning me in a mocking tone. "I'm waiting for one of the sisters to come out of the superior's room because I want to ask the superior to read this book."

"My God, you're still asking permission to read books?"

"Aren't we supposed to?"

"Well, nobody does." With that, she walked away, leaving me to debate whether to go away and forget the permission or to wait for the superior. My training prevailed that last time, and I went in, but after more thought on the matter, I never went back.

So it was with each little rule and custom. Just as my learning and training had been a laborious process of adopting certain behaviors and responses, reinforced by theological interpretation, so now my *unlearning* was a slow process where each rule had to be reevaluated

While reformulating my own interpretation of religious life, I was constantly observing the behavior of my sisters and superior. These observations led me to note the inconsistencies displayed between what people said they believed and what they actually did. With the certainty and arrogance of youth, I believed that life was more clear-cut than that. Holding liberal views meant that all one's views were liberal, or so I thought.

I was amazed to discover that many adopt an idea because it is fashionable or convenient or persuasive, not because it fits in with their mode of thought. So a conservative could hold liberal opinions and a liberal could hold conservative views. Moreover, persons on both sides of an issue could be hopelessly intolerant of those who disagreed.

And while I took note of all these things, there still lurked some uneasiness in the back of my mind about my approaching final vows. Whatever I read, consciously or unconsciously I was looking for answers to an unasked question. *Do I belong in religious life?*

In November, I came across a moving passage in James Macgregor Burns' biography of Kennedy. In it he described the feeling of loss and lack of direction that plagued Kennedy after he got out of the Navy. Trying to decide what to do with his life, lonely without his older brother Joe who had been killed in the war and his sister Kathleen who had died accidentally shortly thereafter, he decided that he would go into public service. That would have been Joe's choice had he lived. From that moment on, he set aside all alternatives. He had made a choice and he would stick to it.

I felt exhilarated by the passage. That's it. Just look ahead. Make a choice and stick to it. I remember running out of my room to share my feelings with a friend. The solution to my uneasiness was not to look back, not to reflect on the decision, but to carry on.

November quickly passed into January. I got up one morning feeling dizzy and nauseous. After Mass, I went to Sister Joseph, the sister in charge in the absence of our superior, to ask for some medicine.

At the school doctor, Sister explained my symptoms to him. "Mmmmh," he said. "When was your last bowel movement?"

"I don't know. I never keep track of these things. Come to think of it, I haven't had one this week - nor last week. It must be at least fourteen days."

"Well, I think all you need is a good laxative."

"Are you nervous about your vows next week?" one of my friends questioned me.

"Nervous? I don't think so. I haven't thought much about it. Maybe I am."

"That could explain why your bowels are tied up."

"Really?" I had very little experience with illness and had never thought much about psychosomatic symptoms.

I took the laxatives as directed and put the matter out of my mind. The situation recurred and I learned to recognize the dizziness and discomfort. Sister Joseph, concerned that it was recurring, suggested that I visit a specialist. I remember climbing the dingy stairs in his office off Fulton Street in Brooklyn wondering what the examination would be like. I was surprised to find so luxurious an office in that old building.

His approach to the problem was quite philosophic: "It's modern man's disease. All this running around and tension. No one takes the time to just sit there and have a bowel movement." He had spoken with a certain indifference to the problem. He gave me instructions on how to relax muscles, kinds of oils to take and the like. I followed his directions to no avail. I progressed from oil to bulk producing additives to laxatives to enemas. Like my stomach disorder, I decided that it would always be with me, and I'd just have to get used to laxatives like I had gotten used to chewing down the food I regurgitated. There was no point wasting any more effort thinking about it. It was a fact of life.

Teaching and living conditions at Christ the King were ideal. For the first time in our religious lives, each of us had a private room complete with bed, desk, chair, a wardrobe and a sink. Quite a change from sleeping in the old wrought iron beds in the attic of the school building at Our Lady of Wisdom Academy, separated from each other by a curtain drawn hospital fashion around the bed and night stand. The bathroom facilities, like the rest, were new and modern. No wonder some sisters had been upset at being passed over when assignments were made to the new school.

It was a delight to teach with the sisters in this community several of whom would play key roles in my life. In them, I found reinforcement and support for the ideas that were germinating in my head about the way things should be. Having traversed the same intellectual journey a few years ahead of me, they saw me as a late convert to the *new way*.

There was Sister Theresa of Avila. By reputation one of the Congregation's brightest members, she had taught herself Greek and Hebrew, enough of the latter to qualify for an advanced course. Though she had started as a Chemistry teacher her distracted manner led her to forget she had Bunsen burners on or to break things. By the time I met her she was teaching French. She had a Master's Degree in religious education and had acquired through self teaching a thorough knowledge of the latest in theological and biblical studies. Though all the sisters were well versed, she definitely was the intellectual center of our group. She had a diminutive figure, with a round chubby face, and was of a temperament that made me often want to hug her.

Sister Mary Bridget- Rusty as we affectionately called her - was a master teacher, relating easily to the brightest and slowest, with each group acclaiming her as their best teacher. She earned their praise by lots of hard work coupled with creative experimentation. Rusty had enormous charm. There was something of an outrageous mischievous child about her, one whose natural habitat should have been country lanes, barns and little red schoolhouses. She had a homespun appearance with her flaming red hair, wide dancing eyes, and a broad ready smile. A most supportive friend, she had the knack of guessing when I most needed to hear that things would to okay. She would be the one to give me a big hug after an event saying, "Gee, you did a great job!" with the utmost sincerity.

Sister Dominic was the listener - a lusty, black-haired woman with deep set eyes that not even her smile flashing like a beacon could distract from. Her laugh came easily and was infectious. I always felt that of all of us she would have been the best administrator because she was not as opinionated or as sure of herself as the others. She had a great respect for people and a sincere belief that she could learn by listening to others. I remember being amazed to see her take notes as the youngest sister on the faculty gave in detail her ideas for getting a point across. It was not that she was incompetent, or even that she felt particularly inadequate, but primarily that she was in awe of other people. Never too busy to listen, she was the person with whom I felt most comfortable to share my "lows".

Sister Giorgio often acted as spokesman for the group. She was a short round Italian woman whose ability to grasp and summarize whatever the group had been discussing gave her authority. She was the dynamic and forceful teacher under whose direction I had spent my first year. She pressured me by her persistent questions about religious life, theology, and matters relating to community structure. What did I think of the habit? How did I view a change in living arrangements? Did I believe in poverty as it was currently practiced by the congregation? It was only later that I realized that her questions were not put to me as a mentor to her student, but as to a peer, as to another human being searching for answers. They reflected her own doubts. Because I misunderstood her intent, I felt confronted and often put on the spot by questions that I was not quite ready or willing to tackle. Later I realized that because of her, I had forced myself to evaluate and reassess many facets of theology and religious life and I had moved intellectually more quickly than I would otherwise have done.

Sister Mary Agnes was the bubbly optimist of the group. A bright creative woman, Sister Mary Agnes had also begun her career in chemistry but later had switched to Art and Music. She was a renaissance person, intellectually alive and well versed in several areas. She was a exuberant storyteller and an original and vital person.

These were the marvelous women who surrounded me and made my life joyous. It was to them that I turned when I began to discover theological approaches that differed from the Thomistic philosophy in which we had been trained.

With the opening of the school year, I continued to be absorbed by the demands of teaching. Despite my good first year, I experienced moments of uncertainty about my behavior as a religious teacher. This insecurity was fostered at times by my superior and at other times by some of the older sisters. Three incidents stand out sharply as examples of this. The first took place on November 22, 1963, that dreadful day of President Kennedy assassination. I had been teaching French to my last class when the announcement of the shooting and critical condition of President Kennedy came over the public address system. Understanding the need for order, I responded to the news stoically, reminding the class that we were not dismissed but that we would pause for a moment of prayer. Noting the tears and mounting hysteria on the part of the girls, I decided the best thing to do was to attempt some mechanical exercise that would keep us occupied until more news came. It wasn't long before the news of his death reached us and we were given instructions to return to home room for an early dismissal.

Freed from the burden of keeping a class going in a crisis, I took a deep breath as I walked down the long corridor toward my classroom. Is it possible, I thought to myself, feeling both dazed and fatigued by the strain of the last half hour. Tears slowly came down my cheeks.

I was stirred from my thoughts by a sharp voice. "Sister, control yourself." It was Sister Giorgio. "Don't you know that if the girls see you this way, you'll never be able to control them? Besides, tell them to take hold of themselves. They have to get home and many of them have an hour's ride on the subway or bus."

Why is she angry with me? I wondered. God, can't I even feel bad? What right does she have to speak to me this way? Still, maybe she is right. This is just a sign of my weakness again. How I wish I could be different.

I remember thinking of this with shame for a long time; shame that I had been so weak as to show emotion. I was not yet freed of domination by others' judgments of me.

A source of disagreement with my new superior was the question of how to relate to my students. Noting the visits of students from my former school, Mother Angelus suggested several times that I cut off these visits. It seemed a mean and pointless thing to do. How could I explain to these girls what I did not understand myself? What should I say? That they should stay at their own school? But why they would ask, in the manner of adolescents. And what could I answer? Fearful of hurting their tender feelings, I could not act uncaring and harsh so as to drive them away. Still loyalty to my superior kept me from telling them outright that I was being asked to stop seeing them. As I write these words, I can still recall Eileen's tearful face as she pleaded with me to let her continue her visits. She liked me, she felt comfortable talking things over with me. What was wrong with that?

There was a belief that to continue friendships with the students from a former school was somehow to trespass on the territory of the sisters at Wisdom Academy. But why should we look at life in this way? Wasn't our territory unbounded? Hadn't I given up the possibility of one love so as to open my heart to all? What were these petty boundaries all about?

Later, I understood that the Superior did not want to add to the sisters' potential for self-pity by depriving them of their students' friendships, as they had already been deprived of the opportunity to teach and live in the new school. I came to view it in time as a sign of jealousy and frustration. I continued to enjoy teaching and now that I felt more in control of my class and of myself, I was able to relax a bit. The kids responded to this treatment and were demonstrative in their appreciation. It was that fall that WNEW in New York initiated a *Good Guy* contest, instructing their listeners to send in petitions with fifty to hundred signatures nominating a certain person a *Good Guy*. At stated intervals, a petition would be picked at random and announced over the radio. If anyone of the signers was listening, they were to call the station and acknowledge it. In this way, the person who was the subject of the petition would be declared a good guy. They would be sent a bright yellow sweat shirt with the words *Good Guy* printed in large red letters across the front.

One school morning, as I stepped out of the elevator, I was greeted by a mob of screaming girls. "Sister Rachel, you're a good guy. You're a good guy." I quickly closed the elevator door feeling confused and panicked.

Good guy? What was that all about? I went to the administrative offices and asked the secretaries if they knew what was going on. They didn't. Afraid to go back upstairs and face the mob (the school would have

125

3,600 students when fully enrolled) I waited for the 8:20 silence bell to ring. Arriving in my classroom moments later, I felt the tension in the room. I looked at my students sharply and told them I did not want to hear any giggles. One of the girls raised her hand and asked if I wanted to learn about how I was a good guy. All around me were their innocent, mischievous, expectant faces.

"No, I answered," attempting to keep a straight face, I wasn't interested in learning anything about being a Good Guy I went on to explain, and furthermore I did not think it was funny. The class should study in silence, and I did not want to hear any more jokes. In truth, I was dying of curiosity, and had convent life been more normal, I would have felt free to ask the girls what it was all about, to laugh and to forget the incident. But I was not free, and I suspected that whatever it was my superior would be angry, and would consider it a fault on my part that the girls felt so free with me as to nominate me a *Good Guy*.

A few days later, I found the sweatshirt on my desk. I should have given it away to one of my more needy students. Instead, I dutifully brought it to my superior, as was our custom, anticipating an outburst of displeasure. I was right. She lectured me on keeping a distance from the students and informed me that she would send the shirt to one of our African Missions, seeing that we had no use for it.

Kids have a remarkable way of not learning things that they don't agree with. By the time Easter came round, they had another ingenious idea. Knowing that I was going away the coming summer, they had given me a beautiful suitcase for Christmas. I was surprised to find another huge box on my desk the day before Easter recess let out. It looked like another suitcase.

"No," they giggled. "Guess again."

"Gee, I have no idea of what it might be. May I open it?"

"Yes, open it, open it." Obviously it was something they felt very proud of. I was certain of that. I tore the wrapping with joyful expectancy. I always loved parties, gifts, surprises. Oh my God! What will Mother say? How will I tell her? There, before my eyes, was a huge Chocolate egg decorated in exquisite fashion into a candy house. I knew that they must have paid a fortune for it.

"Thanks, Girls. It's fantastic. You know that I won't be able to keep it, okay?"

"Well, at least you'll get a bite of it when the community gets to eat it."

I swallowed hard and knocked on the superior's door. I knew what her reaction would be. She would accuse me of being flighty to inspire such a gift in my student. I told her about the egg.

"Sister, this is terrible. How can you take a vow of poverty and

126

accept such a gift?" She went on for a bit about the unseemliness of the gift.

"They are only sophomores Mother, and they can't really understand why they should act as if they took the vow of poverty. They had no idea what to give me, so they decided to give me some candy, only they got carried away." I scrutinized her face as I spoke. I wanted to say that our practice of not allowing us to suggest appropriate gifts led to such fiascos.

"You will not accept this gift Sister. No, instead you will tell the class that you appreciate their show of affection, but that the vow of poverty does not allow you to keep such a luxurious item. We will raffle it and give the profit to the Missions."

I hated to break the news to the kids, knowing how they would react. Still, part of me agreed with the superior. Trying to appear calm, I told the class. They were disgruntled, but after sounding off a bit, those enthused lovable sophomores got to organize a raffle and made a hundred dollars profit on their chocolate egg.

Was it possible that the year had gone by so quickly? I had mixed feelings about the coming summer. My group, "the Candles" would be reunited for some two months, while we prepared in the manner of our novitiate to pronounce final vows. I looked forward to seeing old friends. As to pronouncing final vows, I thought of it as little as possible, remembering my promise to myself not to look back, but to look ahead with determination. And so closed my second year of teaching.

FINAL VOWS

For him who has responded to the Call of the Way of possibility,
loneliness may be obligatory. Such loneliness it is true may
lead to a closer communion closer deeper than any achieved
by the union of two bodies, but your body is not going to let itself
be rubbed off by a fluff; whatever you deny it in order to follow this Call, it
will claim back if you fail and claim back in forms which it will be no longer be
in your power to select.

It is not we who seek the way, but the way who seeks us. That is
why you are faithful to it, even while you stand awaiting so long as you are
prepared and act the moment you are confronted by its demands.

> Dag Hammarskjold
> Markings

It had been traditional in order to prepare for final vows to return to the mother house in France. The founder had expressed this wish and with the exception of the war years, it had been faithfully carried out for 260 years.

The secularization laws of early twentieth century France had driven the sisters from France into the far-flung corners of the world. Later, when they had established themselves in their new countries, and inspired local followers, they founded local novitiates to train future Daughters of the Spirit to carry out their work. In this "New World," the first novitiate was established in Canada to train both American and Canadian candidates.

Novitiates were never opened without serious consideration. Each time there was a fear that the bond of unity in the congregation might be broken. Many of the great orders, such as the Dominicans and Franciscans, had hopelessly splintered along national lines. Still, there was so much at stake in the forming of these young women to the religious life that sending them to France where they would face serious adjustments in language, climate, food habits and ways of life (the Mother House was not centrally heated, for example) would be adding unduly to the strains of the novitiate years.

Every effort was made to instill in each new sister a deep loyalty toward France and the Mother House. In those early years, French was strictly maintained as the official language of the Congregation, and was spoken regularly in community, a task made easier by the fact that many of the sisters themselves were French immigrants. The congregation's rule was written in French, prayers were recited either in French or Latin, and public reading at meals was conducted in French. After six and a half years of this way of life, sisters preparing for perpetual vows had sufficiently mastered the language to profit from spending two months at the Mother House. Moreover, they were hardened and disciplined enough to take the hardships imposed on them during their stay in France.

When the war intervened, the American sisters who would normally have gone to France for final vows went instead to Canada, where they had made their first novitiate. The Daughters of the Spirit were not spared the ravages of war and the immediate post war years were spent in restoring financial stability. Meanwhile in America, the congregation prospered. Indeed the number of vocations had increased sufficiently to warrant the establishment of an American novitiate which was opened in 1949.

Some things had been lost to those sisters who had never been to St. Laurent in the Vendee, the site of the impressive compound that formed the Mother House -the feeling of commonality with all the sisters who had come before them, the feeling of having touched the "Holy Places" where the founders had lived, the inspiration derived from meeting the old sisters now returned to the Mother House to spend their last days after fifty years of service to the congregation and to the church; intangible, but important, to a group whose ties were not of blood but of "spirit."

Because of this, plans were made to send these sisters to France. In the mid 1950's these sisters set out to make their *"third novitiate"* at the Mother House. They were given the opportunity to visit places of importance to the Congregation, such as Poitiers, where the Congregation had its beginnings, or places of importance to all of the Church's faithful such as Lourdes. They would have time to pray and reflect on their lives. They would meet sisters from the many countries where the Daughters of The Spirit were established. They would return with a livened sense of loyalty to the Mother House and all the retired sisters who depended on the financial contributions of the working sisters of the Congregation.

Besides the sisters who were sent to France for the Third Novitiate each year, there was the regular group sent for Final Vows. It was a costly venture and became more so as more sisters were sent, reflecting the steady growth in the number of vocations.

It was no longer a question of gathering at the Mother House from the far corners of France. The sisters were coming from the United States, Canada, South America, Africa, Indonesia, as well as from most of Europe. Given the difficulties of most of the sisters speaking French, the General chapter held in Rome in the winter of 1963-1964 re-assessed this practice. They opted to continue to allow final vows to be made in the various countries and to continue the practice of a Third Novitiate in France somewhat later. This experience seemed more meaningful to the Sisters; they were older, more proficient in French, and more relaxed as they were not preparing for final vows.

We were informed of the decision sometime in April. It has been rumored that this was a possibility but I had hoped that the decision would be to send to France only those fluent enough to profit from this trip. Most of the sisters in the group welcomed the decision. A stay at the Mother House would be considered an ordeal by most of them.

For me it was a great disappointment. Always fascinated by history, I longed to see the site of the order's humble beginnings. I wanted to participate in the glorious liturgical feasts celebrated with hundreds of Sisters at the Mother House. More than this, I wanted to see France, my ancestral home. I wanted the opportunity to meet my sisters from Colombia, Haiti, Madagascar, Holland, Italy, England, and Ireland, in short, to be in touch with the international links that had drawn me to the congregation.

We returned to Connecticut to prepare for our second novitiate in preparation for final vows. With the addition of the Juniorate and the college sisters, the Connecticut complex was filled to capacity. The sisters acquired the neighboring sixty acres of property to house the second novitiate. On it stood an old New England farmhouse built of natural stone in colonial style with a pillared entrance. It overlooked a vast expanse of field partly cultivated, partly wild, with an artificial pond in the center. To the right of the house was a magnificent sunken garden surrounded by hedges, to the left a hot house, a rose garden, and a small vineyard. Further along were the barns and stables. The house stood at the foot of a small wooded hill. A short climb to the top enabled us to take in a breathtaking view of the Connecticut Berkshires. It was a beautiful place to spend the summer.

Coming back to Connecticut was like coming home again! It was wonderful seeing old friends from novitiate days, especially those with whom we suffered during those college years. We laughed; we giggled, we hugged each other and told stories as we unpacked, made beds and settled in for our two-month respite. That evening we were introduced to Mother Thomas, the woman who would be in charge of the group for the summer, our mistress of second novitiate. Behind her plain Jane, even homely appearance, she projected a quiet serenity and warmth. She had twinkling lively eyes, a good sense of humor and a hearty laugh. In many ways she reminded me of Sister Mary Clare, one of the sisters I liked best in high school and the woman who had recruited me.

During our leisurely supper that first evening, Mother Thomas explained what our daily schedule would be. She would give us daily instruction in the vows and the rules. Similar in content to the eleven o'clock instruction in our first Novitiate; the format would be altered from lectures to discussions on major topics such as the practice of poverty, obedience and chastity.

Mother Thomas would monitor the discussions. Classes would be held in theology three times a week by Father Dykers a Dutch Montfortian priest. Father Daly, a priest psychologist, would give a series of lectures on the psychological stresses of religious life and discuss ways of coping with these. Sister Theresa of Avila would give lectures on scriptural interpretations. The rest of the time was ours to read, study, pray, and reflect.

I felt happy and at peace when I climbed into bed that night, cheered by my joy and the laughter with old friends. The night was filled with sounds of the country, sounds I had almost forgotten: crickets, frogs in the pond, insects, owls inhabiting the world finally left quiescent for a time by weary humans.

In the quiet of the night, the old poem that had haunted me since high school days came back to me: Thompson's <u>The Hound of Heaven</u>.

I fled Him down the Nights and down the Days
I fled Him down the arches of the years; I fled Him down the labyrinthine ways
of my own mind, and in the midst of tears,
I hid from Him.
(For tho I knew His love who followed, yet was I sore adread
Lest having Him I must have naught beside)

I was back in Connecticut where this chase had led me seven years before. I was different now, softer, less arrogant, and more capable of leadership than I had been. In my childhood, I had naively believed that intelligence and judgment were parceled out more or less equally at birth; that some chose to develop their share while others, either through lack of ambition, laziness, whatever, chose not to. Now I saw more clearly the inequality among us. I remembered well my moment of discovery, how I had cried the day I realized that my student Patricia, after two hours of unsuccessful tutoring, really *did not* understand any of what I had tried to teach her, and she had tried so hard to learn. Nothing that I could say enlightened her. Why was life so cruel and unfair? Some squandered their talents and others were so frustrated in their efforts for want of some small measure of intelligence.

I remembered the little girl of three that I had taken home when I was barely seven to scrub her clean and fit her with new clothes. The squalor of her home had so upset me and I wanted to do something to help her, not understanding how futile my efforts were.

Yes, it was fitting that I should devote myself to others, I who had been blessed with good health, intelligence, and a good temperament. The thought of my good fortune filled me with gratitude. And with these thoughts, I fell asleep.

The days dawned bright and clear, as would most of our days during this restful summer. It made me feel alive, energetic and vibrant, no classes to prepare, no papers to correct. I hurried to dress and ran outside for a brisk walk before morning prayers.

Father Dykers began his class that day by announcing that as long as it did not rain, he would hold sessions outside sitting under the trees. He was a tall muscular blond handsome man. I had met him on several occasions at Christ the King. A friend of the superior general, he had been sent to educate the clergy and the sisters of the order. As a young priest, Father Dykers had been assigned to Indonesia where he spent most of his adult life. Despite his remote geographic location, he was more intellectually alive than most of the clergy of my acquaintance. He had followed with interest the developments of radical theology on the continent. The new Bishop of Indonesia recognized his brilliance and had appointed him as an aide during Vatican Council II.

I thought him arrogant and suave, aware of his personal attractiveness. He spoke glibly of sacred traditions and disturbed the older Sisters and the clergy with his offhand manner. He seemed worldly and I wondered about his life in the wilds of Indonesia. His task was to instruct us in the new interpretations of the vows. In this he stressed the ministry of Christ and our role in continuing this ministry in our role as Christ's followers: to be prophets, witnesses to the existence of human Christianized love.

You must be women cultivated women. You cannot be asexual beings. The mentality that has been built up in the church through these last centuries about leading an angelic life is mistaken. We professed to be virgins not to live like angels.

I smiled as I remembered the Vatican debates on the meaning of the angelic life: More*over virginity is a sign of hope for Christians who live in faith* *and long for Resurrection. It is a promise to them of a life to come.*

This interpretation made more sense to me than all that nonsense about my being the bride of Christ.

Religious obedience calls for faith...His voice broke the pattern of my thoughts and I tried to focus on what he had been saying. "Faith in God's Word accepting it as God's will. Even the human error of superiors has to be accepted as in the plan of God."

"The human error," I repeated to myself. Why should I accept the human error? Doesn't that take away my motivation to bring about change? Isn't that the same kind of thinking as promising serfs eternal happiness as a reward for their miserable lives of drudgery on earth?

I realized as I listened to him lecture that I had come to final vows without resolving what had always proved a problem for me —my interpretation of religious obedience. Now was the time, I thought to myself. I have the leisure to read and study and grasp what had always eluded me.

I plunged into a study of the scriptures and scriptural interpretations hoping to find enlightenment. In F. X. Durrwell's <u>In the Redeeming Christ,</u> I settled on a definition that I understood:

The Greek ideal lay not in holiness in the biblical sense consecration union with God's Will, but in the autonomous development of all that is noble in man. The search for perfection achieved its goal more characteristically in the hero and the sage. The hero's heroism consisted in the affirmation of himself whereby he was superior to adversity, a lofty kind of egotism. The wisdom of the sage lay in grasping the great principles of life and living in conformity with them. In both cases the result was complete freedom; each obeyed only himself, his free will to be great, the truths learned from his own reason even when the Greek was obligate to carry his heroism as far as death. It remained always heroism of fidelity to himself.

That was me! That was my idea of obedience. That was how I had always understood it: to be faithful to oneself, which in essence was a fidelity to God, who had given me the power to govern my life. But I was wrong. What then was religious obedience? The author went on:

Obedience is the supreme law of Christian life. Therefore the criterion of our Christian conduct is not how admirable it appears to reason, nor how faithful to any given system of ideal but whether it accomplishes the will of God. The questions we must always ask ourselves are whether we are acting within God's will or obeying only ourselves.

Christianity is far from humanism, fulfillment of man's potential, it is a divinization a movement away from himself whereby man submits himself to God as the base of all Christian life in the redeeming Christ is submission to God. When you submit to the bishop as to Jesus Christ, I see you no longer living like men but like Jesus Christ who died for us.

I was immobilized by the impact of that passage-the will of God...

But how was I to know the will of God? Authority, the long respected interpreter of the will of God was being questioned. Isn't the will of God made known to man through reason? I asked myself, is a superior a better interpreter of the will of God than I am or than of the sisters in common? Ultimately if he is right, one had to sacrifice the judgment of man's reason. I wondered if I could conform to this.

I was shaken by this interpretation. I saw in it a condemnation of my point of view. If this was the true interpretation of religious obedience, then I was definitely going to have to change. But then the church was in flux, the interpretation was in flux; the true interpretation was not the certain thing it once had been. No one could give **the** answer. Though I wanted to believe there was a right way and a wrong way, a true and a false interpretation, in fact there were many varieties of each and being certain was no longer possible.

I debated these points on and off all summer long with myself and with those sisters closest to me, for I was not the only sister troubled by the authoritarian structure of the religious life. Among my friends it was a widely recognized problem. For all our study, reading and discussions, the best we could do was reach an uneasy compromise, reflecting as we did that being reared amidst democratic ideals made our ability to tolerate the religious structure more difficult.

Our discussions ran the gamut of religious topics. The other vows presented no major problems to me. If they did to the others preparing for final vows, they did not reveal them.. Poverty had always been strictly enforced in our congregation. We were proud of that as we dutifully darned our socks, turned the skirts of our habits from top to bottom, mended our coiffes, and used the backs of Christmas cards as scrap paper. Sometimes the order lacked common sense in its exercise; for example it was unfathomable to me why the congregation continued to import tin (pewter) bowls and wooden ware from France in order to maintain the 260 year old practice of eating the way the poor did in France in 1703. The poor in France had long since changed their ways but one never heard the sisters complaining about the sacrifice imposed by the vow of poverty, such as their lack of pocket money. Several orders of nuns in New York allowed their sisters to keep money gifts from their parents for pocket money. The Daughters of the Spirit forbade this practice.

We unanimously felt that it was non-egalitarian, a quality important in the exercise of poverty. Furthermore, as all our needs were taken care of, one had no use for pocket money except for frivolities and we were all too serious to indulge ourselves in this way.

Chastity was a personal matter to be discussed with one's confessor or perhaps with Father Daly. I had no difficulties that I recognized and if other sisters had any they did not confide in me.

Father Daly had quite a different task than Father Dykers. He was nearing his Ph.D. in Counseling Psychology and had been hired to serve as a sounding board for the Sisters who chose to discuss their individual problems with him. A big bruiser of a man, his theology was simple and unsophisticated. Leaning to a conservative position, he lectured us on the problems of communal living, problems of maturity, etc., He drilled into us the belief that to be psychologically healthy one had to order one's priorities, make choices according to those priorities, and finally suffer the consequences of our choices. Thus a choice to enter religious life meant submission of our needs and desires to this central mode of existence. Without this ability to order existence one could be hopelessly embroiled in inner turmoil.

I took copious notes and tried to measure myself against his concept of the mature person, for the most part deciding that I measured up. However, I lacked the ability to accept the limitations of others, a frequent failing among the brash arrogant young. I resolved to try to correct this.

Recreation afforded us the opportunity to renew old friendships and to compare notes on what our lives had been like for the last five and a half years. Most of us were still guarded in our conversations, still feeling some guilt over discussing personal matters. But we had relaxed enough to let each other know the anxieties and misgivings we had. We discovered that most of us had been forced to keep a notebook of personal thoughts to conquer our pride. We laughed now at the power Mother Mary Ambrose had held over us. For those of us who had known Mother Mathilde, we convulsed the others with laughter recounting her eccentricities (well known in the congregation). We discussed the future with a thin layer of enthusiasm, masking our uncertainties and our fears. With a few we spoke more openly.

In retrospect, I feel we were bound by our necessity to finish what we had begun, to go ahead with our commitment. None of us truly examined what we were doing -not the way we should have, not the way an outsider could have. We tried as best we could to learn the lessons of life but we were so sheltered, so lacking in breadth of experience. We were shielded from learning from life itself. We had to turn to books to deduce more. It was a slow process.

Despite my difficulties with obedience, despite my anxieties, I never seriously questioned whether I should go ahead with final vows. It was the old question of the decision basically being a function of the superior and not of the subject. If the superiors felt I had a vocation, then I had a vocation; if they felt I should go ahead then I should go ahead. Who was I to question? I was only beginning to question their authority in very small matters.

Sometime in the middle of the summer, we were visited by one of the superiors from Rome. Though the general chapter had ended in February, no official word of the changes enacted at the General Chapter had been forthcoming; we looked forward to her visit and welcomed any hint of the coming changes.

Mother Cecile joined us for dinner and in an extraordinary move permitted us to speak. After some moments, she took over the conversation, asking us, "What do **you** think of the structured way we have meditated?"

No one responded. By this time, we knew no one really wanted to hear our thoughts. What she obviously was fishing for was the **right** answer. What was **the** answer? The one we had been taught was passé. A new one had not yet emerged.

The silence was awkward. Mother Cecile looked around for someone who could interact with her. Finally she continued: "The old way had been stifling. Prayer, religious life must not be so constraining. We must shake off these old ways."

We chorused in agreement. There was an air of relief at what we had just heard, coupled with uncertainty. We wanted to believe, but we were unconvinced. Our training and our seven years of communal life had taught us to be cautious. She continued in this way, posing a question and without directly answering it indicating by her remarks that the thinking of our superiors General had definitely taken a more liberal turn.

It was at this time that we were told that Mother Michael was being removed from the office of Provincial superior, replaced by Sister Rosemary of the Sacred Heart. She would take over in the fall. The news surprised me. Provincial superiors were appointed for three years subject to renewal. Mother Michael has been in office for six years. I felt sad to see her go. I had always admired and liked her and felt secure with her.

The new Provincial Superior was an attractive blue-eyed blond. A bright energetic woman of 42, she had a whole new set of ideas on how to run the congregation. Trained as a psychiatric social worker, most of her religious life had been spent in communities of nurses. A promising young sister, she had been appointed superior at an early age. She was much admired by the sisters who had been her subjects. But for us in the teaching communities, she was unproven and most of us reserved judgment until we got to know her for ourselves.

The weeks had gone by quickly, but I looked forward to the end of our enforced leisure. I liked Mother Thomas and if the novitiate had taken place at a different time I might have been more relaxed, but as we were on pins and needles awaiting the decisions of the General Chapter, my own tension was reflected in my constricted bowels and nervous stomach.

The day of final vows was quite a festive occasion. Parents and families would be present and many sisters from the houses of the congregation. It was, after all, the first time the ceremony would be held in the United States. The ritual ceremony was a beautiful combination of Gregorian chants, antiphons, prayers and symbolic gestures. Each day we practiced the haunting chants. We not only had them memorized but we sang them perfectly.

I was eager to see my mother and sister. In the summer of 1963, while I was pondering over the writings of radical theologians, my sister had gone to Europe. Unable to decide what she wanted to do, she returned to France, ostensibly to study and to sort it all out. She rarely wrote but her letters were long and descriptive and I relished each one. However I no longer indulged in fantasy, imaging myself with her. Despite my uneasiness with religious life, I felt more certain of my place there and of my own goals. Now that my sister was back in the States, I was eager to see her and to hear stories of her travels.

The day of my perpetual vows, like the day of my admission to the Postulate, was a glorious summer day. I woke before the rising bell, sat up in bed and gave the hills and fields one long last look. How I loved Connecticut. I had forgotten how beautiful it was. As I had had to accustom myself to the crickets, now I knew I would have to re-adjust myself to the sounds of the city. I was sad to leave.

Despite the lavish public ceremony announcing our irrevocable commitment, the real taking of the vows was private, witnessed only by the Superior General's deputy and the sisters who had already taken final vows. No singing, no public prayer would attend us, only a reverent silence.

I felt numbness as I approached the altar. Finally the haunting indecision would be over. I was doing it at last. Now there truly was no turning back. I thought that I would be freed from doubts. Instead, as I was to discover later, the doubts would intensify.

Mother Marie Alexandre, our former mistress of Postulants, now an Assistant Superior General, presided over the taking of our vows. She had been elected Assistant to the Superior General as we ended our postulancy. She occasionally visited the United States and Canada to oversee the convents and to hear concerns of the superiors. It was a great joy for her to be the congregation's representative to receive us as perpetual members of the congregation she so loved, especially as she herself had admitted us as postulants in August 7 years before.

Like everything else we did in religious life, we pronounced our vows in doyenne order:

I, Rachel Marie Ethier, in religious life, Sister Rachel Mary of Jesus, in the presence of the most Holy Trinity, of the August Virgin Mary, Mother of Divine Wisdom, of our Father, St. Louis Marie de Montfort, and of the whole heavenly court, before the witnesses here present, I make into your hands Ma Chère Soeur, delegate of the mother general, FOREVER, freely and willingly the three simple vows of poverty, chastity and obedience, according to the constitution of the Daughters of the Spirit.

When the last sister had pronounced vows, Mother Marie Alexandre stood up and began the Magnificat, a gospel passage of the glorification of Mary the Mother of God, often used as a hymn of gratitude.

My soul magnifies the Lord and my spirit rejoices in God my Savior
for He Who is mighty has done great things to me and holy is his name.

Tears came to my eyes as I looked at my sisters. Of the twenty-three who had started out, seventeen stood before the altar, seventeen servants of Christ, seventeen women devoting their lives to the Church, seventeen fledglings each with the power to soar, voluntarily and irrevocably denying themselves this freedom for the love of Christ.

Each sister went to a room off the chapel to sign the contract which bound her to the Congregation, a contract which pledged her to work for no monetary compensation. Mass was then celebrated for the entire community, sisters, novices, postulants. We had a banquet breakfast, laughing and talking with abandon. It would be our last meal together as we would leave that evening to return to our respective assignments. We loved each other. We found strength in knowing of the existence, trials, joys and sufferings of the other.

Sometime in the morning we hurried off to the chapel to practice one last time the public celebration ritual of perpetual VOWS. We had prepared faithfully and lovingly each day for this impressive ceremony.

The choir began the ceremony by chanting an antiphon taken from the PSALMS:

Veni electa mea... come my chosen One and I shall establish my throne within thee for the King had greatly desired thy beauty...

After a brief exchange of antiphons between the celebrant, choir and final professed, the choir intoned in Gregorian chant the litany of the saints. a long list of supplications to the various major saints of the church. During this time we filed down the aisle, positioning ourselves in the form of a cross. On a signal, we prostrated ourselves on the floor of the chapel, completely covered by our black capes, symbolizing our complete renunciation of the world, our death.

It was impressive to see the black cross formed on the floor of the chapel by those human bodies. Every parent, relative or religious sister who has witnessed the ceremony can testify to its tremendous impact.

When the litany ended, we rose and returned to the altar to receive the holy cincture- the only piece of clothing that was added to our habit as result of final vows.

As a sign of the holy slavery to which you have bound yourself for the love of Jesus Christ, wear this blessed cincture your whole life long in remembrance of the bonds which he bore out of love for you.

In response to the celebrant's words, we rose in one body and chanted:

I am the slave of Christ, for this reason, I rejoice that my person is at his service.

The ceremony ended with a solemn word from the celebrant to the Mother General or her representative.

Receive in the name of the blessed virgin first superior whose place you hold these virgins consecrated to God, they are now confided to you in order that you may present them to him without stain. Remember that you will be held accountable for their souls before the judgment seat of their spouse when He will come to judge us.

These words of the celebrant were interpreted as a reminder to the Superior General of the gravity of her responsibilities in the spiritual and material welfare of the sisters. Now I realize how this speech and the meaning ascribed to it by our superiors in the congregation served to support the belief that the Sisters were as children in the care of their parents and that they did not have control of their own lives; without specifying it so precisely this belief underlay all the relationships of the sisters with the superiors in the religious congregation.

Haec requires mea in speculum specula: this is the place of my repose forever. I shall abide here for I have chosen it for my dwelling.

This was **my** congregation, the one **I** had chosen and in which I desired to remain all my days.

CHRIST THE KING 1964-1965

One day, just as simply, the whole formative period we find so painful will be behind us, and before us will be God in whom to lose ourselves.

Teilhard de Chardin
Letter to his cousin Marguerite

The ceremony for perpetual vows customarily ended with the celebrant reading the sister's new assignments. Formerly, it gave obedience a dramatic and solemn character. But during recent years the practice had become redundant because of increased job specialization and the need for planning when leaving one job for another; it was usually clear to a sister whether or not she would be reassigned to the same community. As I had expected, I returned to Christ the King. We had predicted the removal of Mother Angelus and in my summer absence we proved right. With her blend of tradition and radicalism Mother Angelus was too strong a proponent of the new order; too radical. Perhaps the superiors felt that she gave us too much freedom to speak our mind. In any case, Sister Joseph, the principal of the school, was named our new superior.

Mother Joseph was a brown haired, freckled faced shy woman in her late thirties, a pleasant person who could be lots of fun. The fly in the ointment was that she was very conservative. Not an independent thinker to begin with, she was comfortable with the way things were. She seemed to view herself as the protector of morality and religious spirit against the corrupting influence of radical theological thought popular among most of the sisters in the community. She was judgmental, and she felt it her right to be so.

Tradition guided her in these judgments. She was a defender of the old order. As long as she was in the ranks, her attitude did not matter. Elevated to the office of superior, however, we feared that she might make life difficult for those of us who disagreed. She was as opposed to change in school as she was in the convents. She seemed to view the school as if it were a huge complicated machine with herself as the principal operator. She had difficulty tolerating any deviation from tradition.

At first this did not present much of a problem. I too was concerned with maintaining the system in the best possible manner. However, as I matured, I saw the need to experiment. The self confidence that I had acquired in two years of teaching enabled me to make suggestions and voice my dissatisfaction in school matters, just as my radical theological education was doing in convent matters. This attitude did not endear me to Mother Joseph.

Our fears concerning Mother Joseph's conservatism materialized early. Shortly after becoming Superior, she gave away the blue and gold bedspreads which Mother Angelus had purchased, stating she believed the colored bedspreads were signs of worldliness. It was an outrageous lack of common sense, and a breach of poverty. Why were we darning our socks to death only to turn around and give away twenty-six good bedspreads? A small thing admittedly, but it served as a warning of the opposition and name calling we would be subjected to if we wished to change the established ways.

Despite Mother Joseph's self righteous attitude, she respected the individual sisters. A shy person, she must have found it painful to ask personal questions as was required during monthly interviews, (spiritual direction). Despite all the disagreements between us, I liked her. She was a well-meaning, not a phony. She sincerely believed that she stood for the truth and that we radicals were misguided. She felt responsible to God for all of us. She found strong support for her beliefs in Father Vitro the school Superintendent, a staunch defender of the old guard. A tall thin graceful man, carrying about his person that omniscient attitude characteristic of the old style clergy,. He belonged to a gentler age. He misrepresented liberal thinking as radical and portrayed himself as the defender of the Church against its attackers. His loyalty to tradition and to the church prevented him from listening to the experiences of the liberal opposition, prevented him from even considering their arguments.

Mother Joseph was distant and tense with me. She told me the friends I had made over the past year were unduly influencing me. She viewed many of the Sisters at Christ the King with suspicion because of their unabashed refusal to uphold tradition without question. These basic disagreements were kept in sharp relief because of the weekly community discussions – at that time mandated by Rome during Vatican Council II.

The delegates to the General Chapter had noted several areas needing exploration before decisions could be taken. Taking their cues from Vatican Council II, the delegates to the religious orders' general chapter (a governance council) asked their faithful religious to seek solutions to the problems posed to the religious orders because of changing times. The delegates had outlined the problems and soon we were receiving questionnaires to be answered by the community. Every facet of life was examined and scrutinized. What does it mean to be poor today? What does virginity mean? How should we live? What kind of cars should we drive? Should the sisters live like the rest of the world in apartments? And so on?

We broke up into small groups to discuss the topic of the week after which we would reassemble and the small group's recording secretary would report findings. Our sessions began with the reading of the final report of the previous week's discussion. The areas of general consensus were stated, giving reasons for positions held, after which minority opinions were listed, with brief reasons for these. Many of the groups' conclusions were contrary to Mother Joseph's stated opinions, which made her very tense.

Shortly after the chapter, we were told that the habit would be changed. We had in fact seen some experimental versions worn by one of the Assistant Superiors General. A few weeks after I returned to Christ the King, we were told that our new habits had been mailed from Belgium where they were being made. It was exciting news and we awaited their arrival with joy and expectancy.

The new habit was much simpler, a dress with a scapular front. It was to be worn with a white dickey and a veil. The whalebone corset was abandoned in favor of a bodice - a shapeless long-line bra - designed for religious sisters. We continued to wear the man's t-shirt we had always worn under the corset, but the loss of the whalebone corset made us feel remarkably light. The new habit was similar to the one adopted by many of the European religious orders at the time. All in all, the change was quite dramatic, and we suddenly appeared streamlined.

Post Vatican II Habit 1964

Mother Mathilde was reported to have declared, "I feel naked" when she appeared in the community for the first time in her new habit. It was not surprising after 50 years of wearing so many layers of clothing. For older sisters already in retirement, the new habit was not mandatory. Most of them chose to remain in their old habits for the rest of their lives. .

To those outside the religious structure, the change of the habit might have seemed a very superficial attempt to modernize. This was not so. Changing the habit liberated us from tradition!. Future changes would come more easily. The adoption of the new habit had a tremendous psychological influence on all the sisters in the Congregation.

For years the order was known among other religious sisters as a very strict French order. Most other religious sisters were allowed the use of pocket money; we were not. They were allowed a visit home once a year. We were not. Many of the other religious sisters were allowed to buy lunch in the college cafeteria on Saturdays; we were not. Most of the sisters could open gifts they were given; we could not. We were strict and we were proud of it.

The habit we wore was distinctive. It wasn't black and white, rather it was gray, and tightly fitted. We were proud of that.. It was a part of our uniqueness. Our Congregation, so we were told, was known for its discipline and the control exercised over its members. The Daughters of the Spirit were never to be found giggling in college corridors, exchanging local gossip. We were dignified. We had an aura of aloofness which we cultivated. I was proud to be a Daughter of the Spirit. I felt privileged.

Now this same order, due to its more progressive European members, was one of the first of the older religious orders to make dramatic changes. Instead of contradicting our faithful adherence to tradition, the Congregation saw it as a duty to follow the lead of the Church to be in the forefront of change, to make the church viable in the twentieth century.

The same discipline that enabled the Congregation to exact and maintain the most rigid code of behavior from its members was now marshaled for another cause, that of progress and change. In the letter of the Superior General accompanying the acts of the Chapter he wrote:

Up to the present time, we have perhaps been subjected to a way of life patterned too closely for its prescriptions, observances and traditions on the monastic style. For a long time, in the Religious Congregations the apostolate was considered as something accidental and at times even as a danger. This is why the formation of religious was almost exclusively directed toward a contemplative spirituality and a monastic form of life. ...And no thought was given, or at least too little to an apostolic formation.

And still, is it not true that the specific aim of your congregation is a total dedication to God for the evangelization of the world. Is it not true that your prayer, your meditation, your spiritual life must be the source of the fruit of your apostolate? Finally, is it not true that your communities must lead more and more an apostolic life in common? We have not dared yet to insist too much on the revision of the apostolic life. I encourage those communities who have such a desire to do so.

We took to heart these words of our superiors. The Church needed us. We read and re-read the Pastoral Constitutions of the Church, the other Vatican Council II documents and the new rules. We discussed in large and small groups the questions that faced us concerning the validity of our chosen way of life, and we prayed.

In truth, during those years, my prayer life was better that it had ever been. I reflected, read, prayed, pondered, and thirsted for more time to read and pray. It was exciting to be Catholic at this time. It was exciting to be a nun in a forward-looking community.

During the postulate, novitiate and juniorate, my ability to pray had been so structured that it was a chore- a contrived conversation with God rather than the spontaneous outpouring of my heart. First I had to "place myself in the presence of God," then read a preselected passage from the Gospel of the day, Epistle, or other spiritual work, and reflect on its meaning for my life. After some twenty minutes of these reflections, I had to draw a practical conclusion to apply to my daily life, attempting to tie it in with my general resolve to better a facet of my character, reflected in my particular examen. A resolution was drawn up and taken. Time to thank

God for this time with him and meditation was over.

I worked hard at this structured meditation. There were various methods to which we were introduced and I tried them all, attempting to discover what worked best for me.

When I was in the college community much of my meditation time was distracted by the irrational happenings in my daily life. How could I cope with all these things? Was I losing my mind? Did God demand this irrational suffering from his chosen ones? When I first began teaching my prayer life was often distracted by the event of the day, thoughts of my classes or fatigue. Now, finally, I was freed from this, my teaching was easy, my life was less fatiguing. I had made the commitment that had haunted me for so long; my final vows were behind me. I worked to deepen my commitment and make a worthwhile contribution to the Church and to the Congregation.

Shortly after we received the habit, we received the Acts of the Chapter. This was the name given to the decisions taken by the delegates to the General Chapter. The delegates had ruled on most of the Constitutions and their decisions formed a document of close to 100 pages. Characteristically, I gave myself wholeheartedly to the study of the new directives and to the questions raised by the delegates.

Only this time, unlike my earlier years, my approach was far more critical. I no longer accepted without question. I no longer read solely with an eye to conform. Now I had begun to doubt the validity of certain concepts and my doubts were reflected in the comments I wrote in the margin of the ACTS:

Obedience…is not weakness that yields to power. It is WANTING what God wants of us, and what he manifests to us through his instruments: the RULE, the SUPERIORS, HUMAN EVENTS, to which I wrote: "Is it?"

Personality results from the harmonious development of all the faculties. The superior who wishes to help her sisters form their personality must develop in them the natural virtues: loyalty, fidelity to the word given, frankness, and generosity. She must discover and promote the growth of their aptitudes and capabilities to which I wrote: "NO. The sisters develop themselves."

We would like a RULE that would be a CODE OF LIFE, containing only solid immutable principles, to which I wrote: "There are no solid immutable principles," a statement inconceivable just two years previous.

Even in the mysterious matters of spirituality I was beginning to exercise critical thinking:

"*The world belongs to him who loves it the most, who proves to it this love*, said the Curé d'Ars. *But he who loves the world with the heart of Mary knows that he loves it with the strongest love possible, and therefore, he has in his hands a power without limit.*"

Here I wrote: "This seems like a pious thought of the 19th century.

Why can't I love the world with my own heart? I can't love with any heart but my own. This thought is meaningless to me, except if taken in a poetic fashion. Solid devotion shouldn't be an exercise in literature - literary flourish I should say, or is it?

I was on more difficult territory. To try to enter into the thought of some saint, to do things as Saint So and So would have done was a widely accepted approach in spirituality. If these people had become saints, then their way of doing something was holy and right. This approach was unsuited to my nature. Up to this time, I had not allowed myself to exercise judgment in these matters. Throughout my training period, I had been taught to castigate myself for my failings - to suspect myself. Though I did not understand obedience, I felt committed to try harder. I felt that the deficiency was mine, that there was an explanation which in time I would understand, or which, if I could not understand, I simply had to accept on faith.

My firm commitment to an ideal: to be a nun, to be an apostle of Christ, to aid Man to achieve eternal happiness, enabled me to endure what seemed irrational to me. Over the years, I had noted some problems in religious life. For example, in the novitiate on cleaning days, I had found stores of candy in some of the refectory drawers of the older nuns. We were never given candy except on big occasions such as Christmas, Easter, the founder's feast day, the superior's feast day. On these occasions however, baskets, plates of candy would be left out to eat as much as we wanted. It was understood that the candy was for the duration of the holiday only. Hoarding was not permitted.

Now why did these sisters hoard candy? Perhaps they had suffered some unusual deprivation in their own lives which took away from them the capacity to deprive themselves further. If this explanation did not seem appropriate I would find some other. Whatever the explanation, it never was one that criticized the way of life. It was usually some psychological explanation for a particular nun's failing.

I wondered whether I would come to the same point after some years.

Hoarding candy was a minor failing, and I saw it as such. Later I became aware of a more serious problem, the bitterness that characterized the attitude of many older sisters. Not the majority, but enough so that it made me question whether it was an intrinsic part of the religious state. Reflecting on the sisters I had known, I saw a pervasive bitterness which underlay the hostility of Sister Catherine, the withdrawal of Sister Mary Francis, the self-indulgence of Sister Herman, and the cruel humor that the intellectual liberal sisters at Wisdom Academy used to caricature the failings of their conservative opponents in the community.

As the congregation relaxed its rules, the bitterness became more evident: in the way some older sisters demanded their rights to go to the Sisters' beach house on Saturdays, to have a vacation, to visit their families, to get the new privilege first. Prior to this time, no one was to be allowed anything. We were all equally denied. What caused this? I never spoke about it but I carefully noted these things and pondered them.

And there were other disturbing elements of community life. House Sisters, those assigned to cooking, laundering, and sewing, had to cope with the problem of physical and moral isolation. In the real world, a seamstress might work in a factory, a boutique or have her own small business. In these settings, she would be with others whose interests matched her own. Furthermore, she was paid for her work. There is a creative aspect to sewing akin to design, as well as the tremendous satisfaction of making something from nothing. In the convent, these nuns were made to do repetitive tasks, the same habit made over and over again - repaired, mended, washed, etc. In no way could the sisters exercise creativity-each aspect of the sewing of the habit was regulated. So too was the sewing of the aprons, the long white tunics we wore under the habit, the pockets, etc. Their lives were completely subjected to those of the teaching or nursing sisters who formed the majority.

At Christ the King, where most of us were teachers, everything revolved around us. If there was a school holiday, then the house sisters had a holiday. If it was state exam time and the sisters needed extra time to correct papers, evening recreation might be suppressed and so forth. Such organization had tremendous benefits for the teachers or nurses. All our washing, major mending, sewing and cooking was done for us. But it fostered a hierarchy among the sisters.

House sisters were allowed to read only books, which they specifically asked the superior to read, or publications that might be left out by the superior for general perusal, such as the diocesan newspaper. Teaching sisters, on the other hand, were permitted to read whatever pertained to their work. This meant access to the school library and most current periodicals and newspapers. Thus when some point about current events was mentioned in community, house sisters, always a small number in any community, must have felt quite left out of the general life of the other sisters. Though the Holy Rule stated that news and current events could not be discussed at community recreation, this was generally ignored.

Some of the house sisters managed their feelings quite well. Others used their small domain of power to display their authority, and to compensate for their generally humiliating position in the community. For example, when a sister was assigned to the house as a sewing or laundry sister she had full responsibility for the rooms and the equipment in those rooms. If another sister wished to use the sewing machine, she would have to ask the sister permission to use it. Often Sister Lucille (our seamstress sister at Christ the King) made this difficult. She would state that the sisters could not make use of the machine because she was using it, or if a sister asked to have something repaired quickly, she would keep it overly long repairing it. When a sister did work in the room, she would find reason to scold the sister for not threading the machine properly, for pressing too hard on the pedal, for leaving the room in disorder the last time she sewed. In this manner, she further alienated herself from the other sisters in the community.

I observed these things not only at Christ the King, but everywhere. Why did this exist? Was it that human relations had to be that way as a result of the authoritarian structure of religious life? Were sisters modeling their behavior on that of their superiors? Were they taking out their anger at being themselves scolded by the superior? Was it something even more general than that?

I came to believe that the structure was wrong. Despite the founder's early warning: "The Daughters of the Spirit comprise only one class...." there did exist a class system that was destructive to the human spirit, and made prisoners of the sisters caught up in it. Slowly I concluded that the religious structure imposed too many false hurdles, too many unnecessary sufferings, too many artificial domains of authority. After years of suffering, one could end up becoming not more holy but less holy, less joyful, less charitable, less generous, less capable of bearing minor discomforts, less capable of hoping for success for others. .

My vision of Christianity had been a simple one. It was to live a good moral life, to aid one's fellow man, to be cheerful and joyous because God had allowed me to exist and had given me health and intelligence. It was to be above all a compassionate person, to share with others the fruit of my talents. From my earliest years, I had tried to strip myself of such moral failings as selfishness, lying, greed, etc. I wanted my life to be governed by charity. Now I began to believe that the moral foundation of the government of the institution was twisted. It was not charity that was first in the moral order, but keeping the rule. Everything existed to safeguard this Holy Rule, instead of the rule being there to safeguard charity.

In general the sisters I lived with were well balanced, generous, cheerful and supportive. This generation of religious had grown up more comfortable than the generation of religious sisters who preceded them. But I did find the characteristics discussed above in some sisters, usually in the older ones, who had been deprived from living fuller lives because of

149

their assignments in the religious house.

School continued to be an escape and I devoted myself to it with relentless energy. Surprised as I had been with discovering that suburbanites rarely went into the city, I set about organizing trips to the United Nations and other Civic institutions. This proved to be my first major conflict with the principal, Mother Joseph.

Other conflicts with Mother Joseph were shared by my fellow teachers and often centered on petty details. Should the students have a regulation shoe? Should they wear a bow tie as part of their uniform? Each of these symbolized differences in educational philosophy. During the year, I completed the courses required for New York State teaching Certification. It was now time for me to select a graduate school major.. I had taken graduate courses in French. Mother Michael, our Provincial, had told me that her plan for me was to acquire two Masters' degrees - one in French and one in History. Since history was always my preference, I decided to start the Masters in that field immediately.

Sisters were usually sent to St. John's University for all their graduate work. Occasionally some sisters went to Fordham. Catholic universities were viewed as sanctuaries from the corrupting influence of a materialistic philosophy, and as a safe harbor against Marxism.

I wanted to attend Columbia, and decided to take it up with Mother Joseph. To my surprise, she gave me permission to apply. I filled out numerous forms and waited. It never occurred to me that she thought I would not be admitted and that this would resolve the problem for her. .

What a thrill it was for me to receive a preliminary acceptance and the possibility of a scholarship. I was excited by the news and approached Mother Joseph.

"I'm sorry, Sister, but you will not attend Columbia University."

"Why? Why won't you let me go? The constitution says that young sisters after final vows can go and I have already made final vows. Since this is the only specification, I can't understand what the reason is." I said this knowing full well that secular universities were considered a danger, persisting because I wanted to force the issue to the surface.

"We don't allow sisters to go to secular colleges unless there is a very special reason."

"Sister Mary Paul is attending the University of Chicago, and as far as I know there is no special reason except that she wanted to go."

"Sister Mary Paul is an older sister." Mother Joseph answered in a slightly exasperated fashion.

"Well, according to that criterion, by the time I am old enough to go, I'll be too old to learn anything. If you are afraid that I'll run away with some man, then you should be glad to have me go and run off. I wouldn't be much of a loss to the community."

My remarks provided comic relief and pointed to the absurdity of the rule. I knew that I was arguing in vain. Sister Mary Paul was a sister in her mid-forties at this time, and would be considered quite well formed intellectually and morally. I, on the other hand, was only 24.

Mother Joseph laughed at my remark, but volunteered no further comment. I left her office exhausted, crestfallen and. angry. I felt I was being stifled. I resented their protective attitude, which prevented sisters from growing up. I was upset too with Mother Joseph for being unable to break with tradition - to lift herself out of the pattern of "This is what we always do." If it had not been Mother Joseph, it would have been another Superior,. Their view of the world, of their vocation, of their place in society was narrow, hemmed in, carefully delineated. They did not see it as an exciting possibility for the Church to develop members who were professionally competent and competitive in every aspect of human endeavor.

For example, when I had first begun to teach French, I suggested setting up an exchange program for our third year students with some of our schools in France. How broadening it would be and how much easier to learn French in that setting. We had all the international contacts to do it. We could provide good homes, proper supervision. Instead, my idea was greeted with indulgent smiles-adults humoring the wide-eyed child.

The details of that year seem to have faded from my memory. It was a quiet year. I had achieved a new status: a sister with perpetual vows was a full-fledged member of the Congregation. The chance of leaving after final vows was very slim.

For Christmas my sister sent me Dag Hammarskjold's <u>Markings</u> which had recently appeared on the bookstands. Hammarskjold had been an idol of mine in high school, so I welcomed the gift. I was surprised to find so much that meshed with my own thinking. I was increasingly influenced by his interpretation of Christianity in social action terms. His words gave voice to my sentiments. Moreover, he saw obedience to God's Will as I did, as a faithfulness to oneself.

> *To love life and men as God loved them for the sake of their infinite*
> *possibilities*
> *To wait like Him*
> *To judge like Him*
> *without passing judgment*
> *To obey orders when it is given*
> *and never look back,*
> *Then he can use you, then perhaps He will use you*
> *And if he doesn't use you what matter. In His hand,*

Every moment has its meaning, its greatness, its glory,
its peace, its coherence.
From this perspective to "believe in God" is to believe
in yourself, as self-evident as "illogical" and as
impossible
To explain if I can be then God.

In view of the great commitment that I had just made and the daily difficulties that I was encountering, I read and reread with relish his comments:

The great commitment is so much easier than the ordinary and every day one and can all too easily shut our ears to the later. A willingness to make the ultimate sacrifice can be associated with and even produce a great hardness of heart.

Goodness to others, is something so simple, always never to seek one's own advantage

Life only demands from you the strength you possess
Only one feat is possible, not to have run away.

I drew from these passages the lesson that it was possible to survive through trials and obstacles; one had only to pluck up one's courage and go on.

In the spring I began again to worry about graduate school. Persisting with my desire to attend Columbia, I decided to try my luck with the Provincial Superior, Mother Rosemary, who came to our house for her mandatory annual visit. I did not know her very well despite some fleeting visits to our house over the months. Upon arrival, she had announced that we would have a community discussion on the changes in the Congregation and its future direction. We welcomed the opportunity to share our ideas, as well as to hear her point of view. I remember sitting in the community room waiting expectantly for her arrival.. I had not yet totally lost my awe of superiors. But instead of a discussion, it turned out to be a lecture, which we listened to critically. She and Mother Benedict, her assistant had just returned from a workshop for religious superiors in Cuernavaca, Mexico run by a controversial priest, Ivan Illich. She was bubbling with enthusiasm while she recounted some of Illich's ideas. She stated that if we were truly holy, this holiness would radiate and we would by that very fact be marvelous teachers.

What a simplistic attitude!. It sparked a lively disagreement on our part. One of the Sisters, one of the most charitable persons in the community, but a failure as a teacher, began crying during the lecture, feeling that her failure as a teacher was a condemnation of her whole life.

In the face of opposition, Mother Rosemary became intolerant and cutting. She seemed unable to listen to the "other side" and upset that the sisters had dared to disagree with her. Because of the numerous community discussions we had over the past year, and also because of our interaction as teachers, we were used to arguing, taking disagreements in stride. It was not, however, the traditional way of dealing with superiors, even when these discussions had in fact been initiated by the superiors. Mother Rosemary could not deal with an aggressive and intellectually alive audience. Her ideas were not greeted as insightful, ingenious, and messianic as she seemed to expect. She ended the discussion by walking out in a huff, without explanation.

Some weeks later, Mother Rosemary came to Christ the King to attend a series of Conferences. I did not relish the thought of approaching her with my request to attend Columbia but I viewed it as my only alternative. I left a note in her room stating that I wished to discuss something with her, without mentioning what it might be. I anticipated an evening appointment, but heard nothing.

The next day was unusually full. Lectures had been scheduled for most of the morning as well as part of the afternoon. I listened to the lecture half heartedly, wondering why Mother Rosemary had not acknowledged my note. Suddenly, during a five minute intermission, Mother Rosemary got up and called a friend of mine out of the room. Sister Joseph Mary was a younger sister who had decided not to renew her vows. She was leaving the congregation in a matter of weeks, and it would probably be Mother Rosemary's last opportunity to speak with her. After a few minutes she motioned to me. I was apprehensive because I foresaw the situation that might result from talking in a hallway during a brief intermission.

She started the conversation by telling me that she had received my note and as I opened my mouth to state my case, she stifled my comment: "Sister, I know what you want to ask and the answer is no."

I was taken aback and began to protest, "But the university to which I am being sent is inferior."

"Many other sisters have attended this university and no one has ever made this complaint before."

"It is common knowledge among the sisters, though they have not spoken to you."

"Sister, the answer is no. Do what you are told, and obey your superiors."

She had cut my sentence in half. She turned and went back into the conference room, letting the door swing behind her in my face. I was terribly upset. I ran upstairs to my room and burst into tears.

Looking back, I feel that I had set myself up for this rejection. I knew the attitude. I was fighting a losing battle, but I insisted on fighting it anyway, secreting hoping, to break through the closed minds of my superiors.

I wanted the institution to change.

.

CHRIST THE KING 1965-1966

True my taste for the earth is strong, and at first, most anti-
Christian, but it's precisely because I feel so intensely this basic
thing in the pagan soul that I feel in a stronger position to speak
with those who worship the universe. I certainly experience a
passion for the world and a passion for God. What I appreciate
in the earth is obviously not its lower part now
Outstripped and decrepit (although an instinctive charm still
leaves in our hearts a certain weakness, isn't that so for the age-
old abode of the past. For the "first earth and the first clay").
For me, the real earth is that chosen part of the universe
still almost universally distillations of knowledge of the beautiful
of the good life, are needed to achieve this task of life.

Teilhard de Chardin
Letter to his cousin, Marguerite

My third and last year at Christ the King was both my best and my
worst. Best because I had come to know and love the sisters I worked with
and this affection was mutual. Moreover, I was comfortable and confident
in teaching. Worst because it was marred by incredible hostility between
my superior and me. She was my principal as well as my superior, and I
found myself in conflict with her in both roles. I had no room to breathe.
At school I felt like the "rebellious nun" who teaches and in the convent
like the "rebellious teacher" who is a nun. There was no escape.

I wasn't that rebellious, or that radical. I spoke up more than most.
I thought that action followed ideas, so if I strongly believed in something,
I **had** to act on it.. I carried this with me into religious life. It was what
brought me to my superior's door so often with suggestions, reflections and

155

criticisms. It was why, at age 26, I often seemed spontaneous, carefree and unreflecting. I said things most people would have suppressed because I was attempting to be as completely honest as possible. Reflecting on it, this disposition seems self-destructive. It leads one to be very literal about things, wanting to clarify things to the utmost, more than is often possible, and it endows one with a false self-righteousness.

I was assigned a Junior Class for my homeroom.. They had been a problem the year before, enough for one student to have been expelled and for several others to have been suspended. I was a good teacher and had a reputation for being tough. My method of dealing with the class was an unexpected bone of contention between Mother Joseph and me. That year, for the first time, the students were allowed to nominate themselves as candidates for school offices and to let the class elect their officers from these self-appointed candidates. As it happened, the "school terror", Cynthia, presented herself as a candidate for class president. What's more, she gave a very clever and funny talk and I sensed that the class would probably elect her. First however, the field of candidates had to be approved by the faculty.

As soon as Mother Joseph saw Cynthia's name on the list she called me to her office."Sister, you must tell Cynthia that she cannot run for school president. It's impossible. It would make a mockery out of the office. She never keeps any of the school rules. What nerve!"

I replied that I thought she would respond to the challenge of being a school officer by obeying the rules. Moreover, I thought it would enable her to gain a bit of self-confidence, and deal with people in a more satisfactory manner.

"I think I can handle her and she should be allowed to run."

"I disagree, Sister."

I remember the tension that passed between us at that moment. "I disagree" was another form of "Do what you are told." She rarely chose to argue with me; closure was brought to a discussion with an imperative statement. "Well, then, I think you should allow the faculty to vote on it. This is the procedure we have agreed on." Having little choice, she agreed.

As anticipated, the faculty upheld my judgment. Cynthia stayed on the list, and was elected class president.

I wondered if I had made the right decision. Cynthia had her moods and was difficult to deal with. Nevertheless, I always felt that priority had to be given to the individual and not to the institution. Truthfully, I was wrong in that case. Cynthia proved to be troublesome and her misbehavior served as a reminder to both Mother Joseph and me of our disagreement.

During this year, I expanded my many projects. For the American

History classes, I organized a bus trip to Sturbridge Village, Massachusetts and a trip to the New York Supreme Court. For the World History classes, in addition to their United Nations adventure, I followed a lead and discovered that Colombia University gave out free tickets for high school students to attend theatrical groups from the Japanese Kabuki Theater performing under a grant sponsored by Colombia. These performances were given on school days in Greenwich Village. I managed to wrangle permission to take the students. I was the advisor to the Mission Club, a fundraising organization for the support of Catholic Missions in the underdeveloped countries of the world. In the spring, after I decided not to return to University for one semester, I had some free time. It occurred to me that a good way to make money and have fun was to organize a mission bazaar. My superior's response was predictable. No, we couldn't use the yard; it would be too much of a problem to set up. It would be a problem to get donations of gifts; it would be a problem to mobilize the students. "Well," I countered, "granted that all these are problems, still I feel that I can handle them. Can I have permission to try? "Mother grudgingly gave in.

Carrying out the proposal was like running an obstacle course. Everything had to be negotiated. If I wanted to make use of the school yard, I had to ask the superintendent myself. This would not have been a problem had it not been that Father Vitro was a close friend of Mother Joseph's and his office was adjacent to hers. I felt that she would prejudice his judgment against the idea before I went in and he would refuse the permission without really listening to me. As it turned out, I was wrong and he granted permission rather easily. I had to arrange to take tables from the cafeteria and to have the building and grounds staff carry them out to the yard. This also required a series of permissions and clearings.

Whenever Mother Joseph heard me discuss the bazaar, she would heave a great sigh and make it plain that it was all a waste of time. Her reaction was similar to the way one deals with an unruly child. I constantly struggled with myself: "Was I being stubborn? Was Mother right? Was I deliberately being obnoxious?" I decided I wasn't. My behavior was rational. But each conflict and remark would set me off into one of these moods of self-doubt and critical reflection. As it turned out, the bazaar was a huge success and I forgot all the aggravation I had experienced earlier.

What in a sense was the hardest year was in another sense the best because of the warmth and understanding of the sisters who surrounded me. One of these was Sister Dominic Mary, the head of the history department. She was forty-two years old, fragile, with large eyes and a small fine head. She had a s shy smile, and a soft voice. Everybody felt she was one of the gentlest persons in our convent, kind and sweet. One of the unfortunate things about the institution was that individuals like Sister Dominic Mary were placed in positions of authority. Though virtuous and good, they found it difficult to bear the weight of decision making for a group. Their inability to cope with the job, often led to chaos in the community.

As was to be expected, Sister Dominic Mary, being the most virtuous and the oldest of the history teachers, was made chairman of the department. I worried about the appointment. As a teacher, she was hardly the daring, risk-taking type. In fact, she was so paralyzed by the details of history that she found it difficult to make simple decisions, like what was important to teach and what wasn't and attempted to include all significant events in the chronology. This made the class boring, repetitious and a seemingly meaningless presentation of individual points. Sister Dominic Mary had not wanted to be a teacher. For a number of years, she had requested permission to become a librarian, a career more suited to her gentle nature. The Congregation, set on providing service through its traditional careers of teaching and nursing, denied her this request. In Mother Joseph's view, Sister Dominic Mary was reliable, not the kind to do anything wild and foolish. This image was important, for as an educator Mother Joseph was conservative; it was not that she was unwilling to change, categorically, but things had to be proven right before they were tried. In her view of the world, one didn't try out "wild or foolish" ideas but if change had to take place then it would be in the direction of the tried and tested. In my view, this was a ridiculous bind to be in because creative teaching is often a response to a situation or need. It's spontaneous and as such cannot be tested except in its execution.

Ironically Mother Joseph's choice of Sister Dominic Mary, worked out well for me. Though not a leader, organizer or an ideas person, Sister could recognize these qualities in others and had the humility and intelligence to make use of them. She could catch the glimmer of hope for a new and stimulating educational experience. Unable to execute it herself, she would say to me: "I'll ask permission, you organize it, and we'll do it together." Moreover, she lent me support by getting excited by some of my ideas and encouraging my enthusiasm, as well as sometimes restraining me when she felt I was unrealistic about a project. We formed a good partnership.

During this year, some decisions taken by the General Chapter were put into practice. For the first time a petty cash box was set out for the sisters to use. No longer would we be required to go to the superiors, kneel and ask permission for thirty cents fare to college. Rather, we were expected to take it from the petty cash box and log it as expenditures for transportation. Eight years had passed since I had had the use of money. For Sister Dominic Mary, it was over twenty years. It seemed such a minor change but it liberated me from one of the more humiliating and inefficient practices of the past.

For Sister Dominic Mary, the change was overwhelming. "I can't do these things," she declared one day, and began crying softly. "I can't do these things. Here I am 42 years old, and I've never made a decision in my life. I can't start now. It's too late. I entered the convent at the age of eighteen and up to that time, I had been completely under my parents' domination. All of my religious life, I've been forbidden to make decisions and have been told to obey without thinking. All of a sudden, when I am forty-two, they decide that now I have to make my own decisions. Well, I just can't do it," she sobbed.

It tore my heart to witness this, she who had given me the gift of believing in me and supporting me despite her own fears and insecurity.

"I really feel bad, but I don't know what to say. It must be very hard for you and I wish I could help you." It seemed like such a lame response on my part.

Later, when I had left the school for Maine, I wrote her thanking her for her love and encouragement while we were together in Christ the King.

I cried when I read her response, so touched by the sincerity and suffering of this wonderful person:

Your letter made me cry. I don't doubt your sincerity but that you found me encouraging and relied on my good example and that I had a good effect on you is more than I can take - all at once. No need to tell you that we are very different. Sometimes, Mother loses patience with me - or nearly - because she thinks there is no reason not to be 'confident'. But it is another to face things inside of oneself. I really am not being falsely humble, or at least not intentionally when I hesitate over things and lose heart. Before God, I just don't feel I have the 'over and above' physically, emotionally or intellectually that I think a profession like ours takes, especially today. And sincerely, if it were a question of making final vows today, in view of all I know and feel, I don't think I would do it. No matter what I do, I don't feel I will ever rise above this deep-rooted insecurity. The only comfort that has come to me lately is a beautiful sentence apropos Osee's vocation (married to his unfaithful wife) 'God seems to call some people to make what humanly speaking are the mistakes of a lifetime in order that the sufferings resulting from such decisions may constitute the essence of a deeper vocation altogether.'

The changes wrought by Vatican II were continuing to affect our daily lives. There was an openness to change that had never existed before in the congregation. We continued to receive questionnaires from Rome about once a month. Each centered on one topic, such as teaching, nursing, social work, prayer, penance, and the concept of community.

As before, a secretary was appointed at each meeting to take the minutes. When the hour was nearly over, she was expected to read the minutes to the group to check their accuracy. If everyone agreed, she would reduce them to a summary statement or short position paper on the topic. The overarching concern in all of these discussions was the relevancy of the vows and monastic practices in the modern world. They provided us with a forum to discuss current convent practices as well as to present alternatives for the future.

The intellectual leader of the liberal wing, Sister Theresa of Avila, cut a quiet and reserved public image. She spoke sparingly in large group discussions. Sister Dominic was the cautious one, concerned that no one should feel hurt or upset. Sister Giorgio, the most outspoken member of the group, had been reassigned to a small community in Maine.

In commenting on her departure Mother Joseph had said that she thought it would be good for me to be separated from Sister Giorgio, adding, "She's like a bulldozer. She'll run down anybody she finds in her way." It was an unfair comment to say the least. As a result, publically supporting the liberal position primarily fell into the hands of Sister Mary Agnes, Sister Mary Bridget and me. The same urgency that prompted me to say what I thought in school governed my behavior in the convent. Moreover, now that I was more certain of my ideas, feeling duty-bound to take an active role for change, I spoke vigorously.

One night, while we were discussing dining room practices, I commented that if anyone looked at pictures of medieval dining halls, she would see that these were organized much like a religious refectory- the raised estrade which had been for the noblemen and his court was now for the superior and her assistants and the long tables placed perpendicular to the estrade were for the serfs who were invited to join in the major festivities.

"We are the serfs. This bowing to the superior as she walks up the aisle is another relic from medieval days."

I said it half jokingly, but it had been a serious consideration of mine since I had first noted the remarkable similarity of physical layout. My instinct for saying things with the right inflections at the right time, in an offhand and understated manner, served me well. Everybody laughed, but got the point, including Mother Joseph who did not think it was funny. I did not want to make light of the point. I deplored the artificial distance created between the superior and the sisters by these archaic customs.

What did it have to do with religious life anyway? So what if I had to joke about our similarity to serfs to get a point across!

On the occasion of my next monthly interview, Mother Joseph quite seriously said to me that I should not discuss my ideas with the younger sisters in the community. (I was surely one of the ten youngest in a community of about forty-two sisters). "Many of them are disturbed by your ideas." I was stunned and hurt but also flattered that she thought I had so much power.

Although I knew my case was lost before I began, I defended myself by saying that my ideas were not so radical and that they were not even original.

"You may be sincere in presenting your beliefs, Sister, but many other sisters have not read as much as you have, or the things that you have and they do not understand the points that you are trying to make. All it does is to disquiet them."

Frustrated that I was unable to attend Columbia University I returned to St. John's in the fall, enrolling in the Masters program at the Asian Institute. I chose Asian studies because of the excellent reputation of one of the professors, Father Thomas Berry. He was a scholarly man. I was amused by the way he'd come into class, take his raincoat off, wrinkle it up in a little heap and then rather carefully place it in the corner of the window casement. He thoroughly prepared, and despite his monotone delivery, I enjoyed them. He demonstrated a dry wit, a wry humor and thought provoking ideas. He spoke of his vision of compiling a world scripture out of the truth as revealed to Buddha, to Christ, Confucius, Mencius and so forth. He saw this body of revealed truth as something above and beyond one organized religion. There was no reason, he thought, why God could not have revealed himself to mankind in more than one way. Christians could believe both in the divinity of Christ and in God's Will to reveal himself to others through holy men at various times in history. The idea held me. I was already beginning to break out of the confines of a narrow Christianity, and I saw him as an ally, a guide to help me develop myself along these lines. I made it a point to walk with him after class to discuss these things.

One night he turned to me and said: "You absolutely have to read Teilhard de Chardin."

"Well, you might say it's one of those things I've been wanting to do for a long time, but I just haven't gotten around to it. I don't seem to have the time.

"You have to **make** time," he answered. "Tell you what, I'll bring you what I consider to be some basic books that put his thought in a philosophic context and you can go on from there to his own works"

The next week, as promised, he brought three books to class. He handed them to me after the lecture, and mumbled something to the effect that we could discuss their contents the following week. I remember feeling panicked because with teaching five classes daily, being responsible for one of the school clubs, and having college homework, I didn't know where I was going to fit in the reading. Not wanting to appear uninterested, I began rising at 4:30 instead of 5:00 in order to get some reading done. This was the beginning of my exposure to de Chardin's thoughts. Teilhard de Chardin was a French Jesuit priest and a respected archeologist/anthropologist who had participated in the Peking man discovery. He had worked in the scientific forefront, supporting Darwin's evolutionary theory, maintaining at the same time his belief in God, in the church, and in his priesthood. He was a powerful model for me. From studying him, I concluded that if theological thought was rooted in history, if it could be "reinterpreted", how much more subject to change was the structure of religious life, as embodied in the Constitution.

Teilhard de Chardin's writings had a profound effect on me, not specifically because of what he said, but because his approach to solving problems was suited to mine. He did not attempt to justify the old traditional answers, to find reasons for them, to accommodate. He merely grappled with the world as it was, not as Catholic theological dogma said it was. Through reading his works, I became aware of the controversy over polygenesis, the implications of this for the Catholic dogma of original sin, and the Church's defensive attitude toward the scientific community. I was not completely convinced by his attempt in the <u>Phenomenon of Man</u> and the <u>Divine Milieu</u> to develop a larger scheme into which to fit scientific findings. But what his writings did make me realize in a way nothing else had that being Catholic did not mean accepting scholastic philosophy and Thomistic theology in their entirety. Other avenues of thought were possible, such as integrating a body of revealed truths with scientific findings. His writings restored reason as a criterion of judgment. It made plain what I had felt all along: if something had to be swallowed, accepted ON FAITH- especially if that something conflicted with established scientific findings- then tradition was probably historically rooted, man-made and subject to change.

De Chardin's spirituality touched me directly. When I read the introduction to The Divine Milieu I immediately felt at home.

This book is not specifically addressed to Christians who are firmly established in their faith and have nothing more to learn about its beliefs. It is written for waverers,

162

both inside and outside, that is to say, for those who instead of giving themselves wholly to the Church, either hesitate on its threshold, or turn away in the hope of going beyond it.

It wasn't that I was on the verge of leaving the Church, far from it, but the doubt which he spoke about was mine and I recognized myself.

Teilhard goes on to describe the answers given a man seeking spiritual advice. Most likely he would be counseled to try to live in the world, "without being of the world," as work is encumbering and involvement in this world distracts one from spiritual realities. But these two ideas, Teilhard argues, are false. The world has been given us in order that we might participate with God in the act of creation. By virtue of the creation, and still more, by the Incarnation, nothing here below was to be considered profane for those who knew how to see. He discussed how man can be sanctified through involvement in the world, the very attractiveness of God, who is in all creation. He argued that there should be men:

Vowed to the task of exemplifying by their lives the general sanctification of human endeavor. Men whose common religious ideal would be to give full and conscious explanation of the Divine possibilities or demands which any worldly occupation implies, men in a word who would devote themselves to the basic tasks which form the very bonework of human society.

He thought natural progress was too often left to the children of the world, that is, to agnostics or the irreligious. I was exhilarated when I read him, very happy, joyful. I would no longer have to turn my back on the world.. I could love the world, and I could be a good Christian at the same time. His approach to orthodoxy was compatible with mine. If a conflict was evident between an orthodox theological position, and scientific findings, he grappled with it head on. He attempted to understand why the Church had adopted its historic position. He pointed out the man made quality of theological doctrine - that it was after all only an interpretation. He showed me how scientific discoveries could be integrated with a belief in the Church. I also read other Catholic Liberal theologians who influenced my development.

The Ecumenical movement and the theological discussions that surfaced from Vatican II were moving in the same direction. Most prominent of all the documents that articulated this point of view was the Pastoral Constitution on the Church. It wasn't just one man, nor one thinker, it was liberal Christian thought that I had become caught up with. I could have rejected this new interpretation of Christianity, but when I came upon it, it was as if I had known all along that this was where I was going. I had a feeling of "at last I am home," with a definition of

Christianity I understood.

Teilhard de Chardin, Father Berry, reading new theology, all three happened together, and fed on each other. Further, they coincided with certain experiences which invited me to go further.

One of these resulted from a school trip I organized to the United Nations. To make history come alive for my students, I arranged for meetings with delegates at various United Nations Mission houses. I felt that by actually meeting delegates from various countries, they would better understand current events. I felt myself getting excited as I thought about it. I set about organizing it, drew up a master plan with the information gathered, and assigned students to the various mission houses. My students were thrilled. I armed them with maps of the city, addresses to the mission houses, their appointment hours and directions. I had arranged each student's schedule to include three visits: to a socialist country, to a Western European one, and to a developing nation. Thus, they would come away with a wider world view.

I was so absorbed that I did not reflect that one normally did not set out with two hundred high school students to wander around New York City. I knew that Mother Joseph would not approve, so I delayed informing her until the last possible moment.

When I finally did, she was alarmed: What if the students were hurt, seduced, attacked? Did I realize I was responsible?

"But these kids are New Yorkers," I replied. " They're fourteen and fifteen years old. My God, they're old enough to travel on the subway. Besides, they're in groups and each group has a parent chaperone."

In exasperation, Mother Joseph capitulated but only because I had already made the appointments at the mission houses. If she had it her way, she reminded me, she would call the whole thing off. I felt a twinge of triumph when I left her office.

The day of our adventure proved to be exhausting but rewarding. The kids "discovered" Europe, Africa and the world. They were alive with enthusiasm and questions when I next met them in class. Did I know how resources were allocated in a socialist system? Had I ever been made aware of Lenin's humanist writings and qualities? Hungary had been part of a huge empire and some of her land was unjustly taken after World War II. The Czech nation was really made up of two national groups...etc. When I listened to my students, I knew I had been right. They had learned more in those few hours than from several months of reading history texts.

I had another reason for feeling satisfied with my day. Like the students, I had limited time and had to choose only three Mission houses to visit. Among my choices was the Hungarian Mission House. The account of it in my diary conveys better than anything I could write now, years later, and the spirit of my discovery:

Today was one of the most wonderful experiences that I have ever had. We went to the United Nations with a group of about one hundred and fifty girls. Each then went to a different Embassy. I had expected that my greatest pleasure and enjoyment would be at the Ukrainian and Soviet Embassy, but the highlight of the day was meeting with Dr. Prandler, the deputy permanent resident of the United Nations Mission, representing Hungary. The appointment was for 11:30. I arrived very embarrassed to be so late, at twelve noon. Expecting the girls who were meeting at another embassy to be already there, I rang the bell and went in to find myself alone. Dr. Prandler very graciously received me into the large parlor beautifully decorated in red, gold, and green. The wall was light green, the wood walnut, the rug dark green, the drapes gold and the furniture, carved Hungarian furniture upholstered in red and gold leaf. The atmosphere was very warm, friendly - one might almost say casual.

We sat down and I apologized for arriving late and inconveniencing him, but he graciously denied the inconvenience. He had a luncheon appointment at the United Nations for 1:00 P.M., so he had to leave at 12:30, but said he would arrange for someone to replace him if the girls finally arrived. He then asked me the purpose of our visit, and I explained that I wanted the girls to be international in their thinking, etc. He thought it was a marvelous idea. After exchanging these "business" remarks, I dared ask him if he was a member of the Communist party(what a naïve question) and what the state of the Church was in Hungary. He very frankly explained about the abuses of the Church prior to World War II in that many bishops owned large tracts of land, and had kept what he termed the "latifundia" system, but which we more commonly refer to as the feudal system. The church, he said, was rich and unconcerned about the lot of the peasants. Most of what he said, I was already familiar with because I once had to prepare a talk on Hungary in the "interwar" period, so I was grateful that I could affirm that this was generally accepted as fact at that time.

All of this set the stage for more "real talk" so he then proceeded to tell me about himself. He had been baptized and was a practicing Catholic until the age of 15. We were interrupted to say the girls had arrived. He quickly finished up by saying that being a communist, he could say that communism does not encourage religion, but does not necessarily forbid it either.

Excerpts from my diary:

Those were the words of a deeply committed man, committed to his country, to his fellow men and to, I believe, a sincere search for truth. I sensed, not regret, but a question formulating, or formulated. He is still searching. This experience helped me to understand so much better the concern in Europe about Dialogue with the Marxists, and I came home and reread the article that had appeared in <u>America</u> a year ago on the talks that took place in Austria with Cardinal König and top Marxists. The basic question, the first article began, *is to determine whether atheism is basic to Marxism, or whether you can still be a Marxist and believe in God. It is on the answer to his question that the prospect of a dialogue between Marxists and Christians depend"*

Before Dr. Prandler left, he invited me back to visit the mission at any time, and said that he would be most willing to receive any group. On the whole it was a deep and very meaningful spiritual experience and it revived my hope in man and his ability to cope with the problems of the day.

If I had not recorded in my diary my impressions of the visit, I think I would today deny its importance.. Despite the masked attempt to proselytize, I made an important discovery - that atheists can be good men, that one doesn't have to believe in God to lead a moral life. I had taught this in religion classes, that morality and religion can be separated, but this was the first time I understood it. Here, before me, was a man whom I felt to be a good living person, a communist, who in the daily exercise of his life, would probably maintain the same moral code that a Christian would. I was overwhelmed. I was even obsessed with the thought for several days. I remember walking down the long convent corridors repeating the idea to myself over and over again.

The trip to the United Nations was successful beyond my hopes. However, in my enthusiasm, I had invited the wife of one of the secretaries at the Russian Mission house to visit our school. Much to my surprise, she accepted without hesitation. I was not prepared to have her agree to my proposal. Now I had to tell my superior what I had done. I prepared myself for the outburst, and walked into her office.

I blurted out all at once, "Mother, I invited the wife of the fourth secretary of the Russian Mission to visit the school, never thinking that she would accept, and she said yes."

"You what?!"

I repeated the sentence. I'm sure she wanted to close her eyes and hope that when she opened them again, I would have disappeared. We argued but in the end, she permitted me to proceed.

Mrs. Loshinskaya arrived in a mini-motorcade. I gulped when I noted the arrival of the flag bearing limousines. I had tried to play down the significance of the visit and arranged for her to attend ongoing classes to see the school in action. I felt the students would profit most by her visit if they saw her as part of their regular history classes. That way, they would feel free to ask questions, and not be embarrassed by the presence of a large group of people. They bombarded her with questions. There were a large number of first generation Americans in the school - Lithuanians, Latvians, and other refugees whose parents did not look kindly on Soviet Russia. At one point, an East German refugee got up and hurled abuses at Russia for political repression. But in general, there was a fruitful interchange between the students and the gracious Mrs. Loshinskaya. I invited her to have lunch with the faculty in the cafeteria and friends of mine engaged her in a lively conversation. I remember Sister Mary Agnes initiating an interesting comparison of Russian and American music and the French ballet as opposed to the Russian and American styles. I was grateful that the sisters I lived with were so intelligent, well-read, open and aware of international affairs.

After she had visited the last class, she turned to me and asked, "Could I possibly speak with you alone?"

"Of course," I responded and led her down to the parlor. I was curious, not knowing what to expect. We passed some sisters in the hall and I arranged with one of my friends for her to come down and serve tea. One of the great features of community living was this ability to call on each other for help at any time.

Natalia opened the conversation by saying that she had been surprised to find the sisters so well educated, bright and alert. To her, Sisters had always been odd people who lived in dark convents. Certainly, she had never imagined them to be the way she had found them. I quickly recalled how we had discussed Russian and French novels and music. It certainly was not the conversation of dull backward people.

"Do you really believe in God?" she asked finally, almost apologetically. And then, as if to prevent my taking offense, she rephrased the question into:"That is, how can you reconcile the latest scientific findings, for example, the proofs of evolution, with a belief in God the creator?"

In response, I explained that Catholics integrated scientific findings with Catholic dogma by positing that God was responsible for the soul of man. The Church did not necessarily deny the natural progression of animals from one state to another. The liberal theological position, I explained, held that nothing that man could reason to be true could possibly be in conflict with the teachings of the Church. God would not create man with a reason only to contradict the laws of logic. As a result of recent discoveries, the Church had to rethink some of its explanation.

She listened to all this and said, "Well, I suppose it is a little like communist theory. The early theoreticians claimed that there was a peak in

167

the distance to be reached, you know, a certain form of government, a certain state of life, and we had to struggle to reach it. Having had a revolution and achieved that peak, it became clear that this is not THE peak, that there are many peaks, that having reached one goal is only a step toward a second goal, and that in turn, is only a step toward a third goal, and so on."

Thus, communist ideology was constantly being revised to fit new findings and to fit reality. This position, she said, was much more acceptable to her than dogmatic older theory. We noted our similarities both coming from backgrounds of authoritarian institutions and observing these institutions adapting in order to maintain themselves. Both of our conceptualizations of history were similar - we agreed that history was not cyclical, but linear, that there was progression in history, not just a repetition of patterns.

"Well, there is one thing that puzzles me," I said, "and that is, how can the state motivate people to work for the future? Man works for the here and now, and man doesn't work for the future. In a Catholic ideology you can always say to the people, 'You will be rewarded in heaven,' but if you don't believe in an afterlife, what can possibly entice people to sacrifice present satisfaction for the future?"

She looked at me with a quizzical smile on her face and replied," Why, one works for man! One works for the betterment of the race, or for progress, that's all the motivation that we need."

Though I found the answer simplistic, even unbelievable, she seemed sincere. We parted with good wishes.

When the visit was over, Mother Joseph recovered her usual good sense of humor. The next day, she came to my class and called me into the hallway.

"Sister," she said, "Two men from the FBI are downstairs. They have asked to talk to you."

My heart jumped! I was flabbergasted. What! You mean because I went to the Soviet Mission House?"

She shrugged her shoulders. "I guess so," she answered. With a look of dead seriousness, she added, "They are waiting for you in my office."

"My God, they really are sick. Why for heaven's sake investigate me" I hurried down to the office. "I'm Sister Rachel Mary," I said as I entered the room.

The two men jumped up politely and each shook my hand with that supercilious politeness that people often have with nuns.

"Sister," one of them began, "Your name has been given us as a reference for Cynthia P. She has applied for a job with us. We understand that you know her quite well."

I felt the tension leave my body and I broke out in a big smile as I pictured Mother Joseph's mischievous and hearty laugh at my expense.

"Yes, I do," I answered, "What would you like to know?"

* * * * * * *

The experience with Mrs. Loshinskaya and Dr. Prandler motivated me to delve into Marxism. Honest people had found in Marxism a solution to social ills. What was it? What, I asked myself, was in my education, that had enabled me to deny the validity of a Marxist solution when so many people found it acceptable? I began paging through journals in my spare time, reading about the varieties of communist parties - the Italian communists, as opposed to the French, the two as opposed to the East Germans, the Russians, the Hungarians, and so on. I never read the great theoreticians, such as Lukas, but I became sufficiently fascinated with Marxism to read the more popular explanations. I found Roger Garaudy's (a leading French Communist) book **Dialogue** very congenial to leftist Catholic intellectual thought.

I read about the priest-worker movement in France and saw in the idealism of its heroes, the Marxist influence. Henri Perrin, one such priest-worker, discussed the social ills of Europe prior to the War, the smug clergy of Hungary, and the appeal of the Communist party. I began to collect articles about the Communist-Christian intellectual movements.

I was gradually pulling away from traditional Catholic thought. I could not have fully believed all the truths of the Catholic Church with absolute certainty one day and suddenly leave the religious institution the next. There was a slow progression in my thought, with each incident enabling me to redefine what I felt to be true and what I believed.

Further, though all these personal experiences were powerful, they would not have had the same impact on me if there hadn't also been a strong atmosphere of openness in the Church. The Church as a whole was experiencing a redefinition of itself. It was asking itself the questions: "Who am I?", "What do I represent?" "Where am I going?" In this atmosphere of intellectual and honest searching, it became possible to question myself concerning the validity of fundamental Catholic teachings.

Coinciding with these developments was an inner struggle with personal belief. Only one thing was clear: I was in doubt that I still believed in God, in doubt that the modern world could find the religious life a necessary and meaningful service, in doubt about the mission of the Catholic Church. I questioned the Divinity of Christ and the whole resurrection theology. My doubts motivated me to steep myself in reading the writings of liberal European theologians. I continued to discipline myself to rise at four thirty instead of five o'clock so that I could fit in an extra half-hour of reading. For several months, I had read Teilhard de Chardin's <u>Phenomenon of Man</u>. Now I avidly read other books but with some anxiety. I was reading to recapture my faith. I wanted to convince myself that my life was not meaningless. But the more I read, the less convinced I became. All the intellectual arguments that I absorbed were not restoring my faith. My whole life seemed disordered.

By December, I was in such bad shape that I came down with a cold that I couldn't shake off. My sinuses became infected and I lost my voice. I was forced to stay in bed for the first time since I had begun teaching four years before. I worried about the cold being psychosomatic while the pressure from the infected sinuses increased. I felt at times that I would go out of my mind with the pain and heaviness. I found it hard to bear the slight discomforts of illness. Despite the changes that had taken place within me, I still felt obligated not to ask to see a doctor, but wait for it to be recommended by the Superior!

When Mother Joseph did not send me to a doctor, I indulged my fantasies with the belief that she was allowing me to suffer as a punishment. One night I sat in my bed sobbing with the pain when she surprised me with a visit. I was not a whiner and my complete exhaustion and crying must have frightened her because she decided then and there to send me to the emergency room of one of the hospitals that the sisters staffed in Brooklyn. I felt so relieved that I cried tears of joy. The hospital attendant drained my sinuses and the doctor prescribed medication that curtailed the effect of the bacteria in my sinuses. The pressure was suddenly gone from my ears, forehead and nose. For the first time in several days, I slept peacefully and through the night.

The experience left me quite shaken. I had already observed many sisters who had psychosomatic illnesses, and I feared that I was following the same path. Shortly after this, I happened upon Victor Frankel's book - <u>Man's Search for Meaning,</u> a book which had a profound effect. We had no recreation hour on Saturday evenings. Instead, the sisters used the time to launder personal effects, clean their rooms, prepare coiffes for the following week, and make other personal preparations for the upcoming week. I was usually quick at these matters and Saturday nights gave me extra time to read. Often I spent them browsing in the library, reading articles here and there, catching up on the news after a busy week. It was on one such Saturday night that I ran across Victor Frankel's book. The title caught my attention and a quick glance through it assured me that it would interest me. I took it up to my room. I desperately needed to believe that one need not be disfigured by excessive suffering. I saw many who were neurotic, hostile, bitter, frightened, broken, who, in one way or another, showed the marks of the years of sacrifice.

From Teilhard de Chardin, I had become hopeful that change would ultimately come. Now I wondered if change would come in time. If institutional change had to be wrought at the sacrifice of our youth, our joy and our sanity, was it worth it? I suspected that I was exaggerating our suffering - that because we were so isolated, things looked worse than they were. Frankel's book deals with his experience in the Nazi concentration camps. He detailed how the ability to bear untold sufferings was beyond human understanding. The book is a powerful document. And because of my own particular needs, I read it with more than usual interest.

We who lived in concentration camps can remember the men who walked through the huts comforting others, giving away their last piece of bread. They may have been few in number, but they offer sufficient proof that everything can be taken from a man but one thing: the last of human freedoms, to choose one's attitude in any set of circumstances - to choose one's own way.

Even though conditions such as lack of sleep, insufficient food and various mental stresses may suggest that the inmates were bound to react in certain ways, in the final analysis, it becomes clear that the sort of person the prisoner became was the result of an inner decision and not the result of camp influences alone.

Dostoyevsky once said: "There is only one thing I dread, not to be worthy of my sufferings." These words frequently came to my mind after I became acquainted with those martyrs whose behavior in camp, whose suffering and death bore witness to the fact that the last inner freedom cannot be lost. It can be said that they were worthy of their sufferings; the way they bore their suffering was a genuine inner achievement. It is this spiritual freedom which cannot be taken away that makes life meaningful.

And with these words, I reinvested my life with meaning. I interpreted "*Christian freedom*" as the ability to shape my life, to rise above the mistrust, the suspicion, and the traditions that bound me. I cried because it seemed too difficult, and yet I convinced myself that it was my "*assignment.*"

As I mentioned earlier, in the fall, I had enrolled in the Asian Institute at St John's In addition to Father Berry, there were two other people in the course with whom I became close, Mrs. Desai, an Indian woman a few years older, who was getting her Ph.D. in Asian History, and , Mike O'Shea, a few years younger, who was getting his Masters.

In a short space of time, the four of us formed a mutual admiration society. We compared class notes and impressions of books assigned by Father Berry. We dabbled in university politics and shared jokes. Mike was a burly Irishman, big, tall, red-haired and freckled, with a beautiful smile and dancing blue eyes. He was witty and vivacious, but yet a serious and sensitive person.

Mrs. Desai was a quiet serene woman, shy and reserved. She found Mike unruly at times and would scold him for his loud behavior or his inappropriate remarks. Nevertheless, we liked each other. Though the difference in our ages was slight, I viewed Mrs. Desai as much older and wiser, perhaps because she had a family.

Suddenly, in December, 1965, Father Berry was fired!. Several 1 other faculty members were dismissed as well. The news was shocking and the move unprecedented. Mike organized a petition to protest the purges. The reason for Father's dismissal was a speech he had given on university grounds arguing for a more liberal theology department. Catholic universities had to truly become "Catholic" and include in their curricula the spiritual teachings of the great religious groups in the world, such as the Hindu, Buddhist, or Confucian religions. It seemed ridiculously out-of-date to demand that only Thomistic theology be taught at a Catholic University.

What surprised me most of all was the way Father was dismissed. Without knowing what charges had been brought against him, without even knowing that he was being charged, a trial was held in Rome in absentia. ,Subsequently, he was notified that he had been found guilty. He would no longer be allowed to teach in any Catholic university. Father Berry was no heretic. Even the most rigid theologians of the Church would have to admit that. And besides, even if he were, what right did the Church have to try a man without his knowledge.

The incident awakened me to the issues of authority and hierarchy in the Church. It was clear that a man like Father Berry was a threat to the established. I knew that if I were to participate more actively in the Congregation for its reform, and through the congregation for reform in the Church, I too might have to face unjust accusations.

Due to my severe winter cold, I had missed a few classes. It seemed natural that Mike would call me to keep me informed about protesting Father's firing. I was vaguely conscious through it all that there was a mutual attraction, but I wasn't consciously aware of it. While I was sick, I had decided that it would be best to eliminate one source of pressure in my life and discontinue graduate courses for the spring semester. It was always busier in the spring and I felt that I would run myself down. I came to school on the day of the final exam.

The exam was given by a substitute teacher as Father Berry was forbidden to appear on the grounds of the university.

When I arrived, I spotted Mike and Mrs. Desai in one corner of the room and naturally went over to them. "I won't be returning next

172

semester," I began, "I feel that I have too much to do at school and that I've been so run down this winter that I should take it easy. I will continue in the summer."

Mike responded with a rather distraught "What?" Then he added: "I have something to tell you, wait for me after the exam.'

"All right," I said, surprised at his response. I finished my exam, handed it in and went into the hall to wait for Mike.

I waited and waited and waited. I glanced at my watch. It was only fifteen minutes but I knew that I could not wait much longer as I would have to meet the sisters taking other exams so that we could drive home together.

Mike did not seem to be coming out, so I tiptoed back into the exam room and went over to his desk. I whispered in his ear that I really had to go and that I probably would be coming to school on occasion so I would see him then."No," he said, "I'm coming right out."

He signed his name to the exam paper and handed it in. I was puzzled by the whole thing. As we started to walk he began telling about an article he had read in the Harvard Asian Review on the Emperor Han Wu Ti and the salt tax and the significance of the fact for the proof or disproof of Wittfogel's theory. I was only half listening because I was wondering why he had made me wait that whole time to tell me about this article. I did not recall having shown any extraordinary interest in the Emperor Han Wu Ti or in Wittfogel's theories.

By this time we had gone down the three flights of stairs and we were outside. It was a terribly cold January and I began to shiver. I decided to break into his monologue.

"Mike, is this you wanted to talk to me about?"

"No."

I forget now how he started but the next thing I knew he was telling me about how he graduated from Brooklyn College and not knowing what he wanted to do joined the Peace Corps. He had studied engineering and as a result, the Peace Corps sent him to Africa to build a rather complex bridge. He recounted that he felt unprepared for this job. He said to me "You don't really learn how to build a bridge in engineering school. You have to work with an experienced engineer to build a bridge" He told the Peace Corps Director as much and after some time he came home in angry protest. I listened attentively, bewildered by the conversation.

A very strange and incomprehensible thing was happening and I wasn't really sure that I knew what it was."Mike, what are you trying to say? Why are you telling me all this?"

173

"He turned to me and with a dead serious expression on his face he said:

"*When are you going to leave the convent?*"

I was so taken aback that I just said: "*But I'm not going to leave the convent.*"

"*Don't give me that, you know that you are thinking of leaving the convent. And if you're not, you should be.*"

We stared at each other for a few minutes and he continued. "*Look at Sister Michael. She's so out of it. That's what you're going to become if you remain in the convent!. You're a normal loving person. You shouldn't be wasting your*self in a convent. *You're much too lively and dynamic.*"

"*Mike, that's precisely the reason why I'm not going to leave the convent. The Church needs people who are lively and dynamic. If only people like Sister Michael stay in the convent, then what will the Church become?*"

Despite my response, Mike had touched on some of my own concerns of growing old in the convent. I had seen so many Sister Michaels. Perhaps he was right.

"*How old are you?*" Mike asked suddenly.

"*Well, I've been in the convent nine years.*" It was only eight and a half but I figured it wouldn't harm to round it off to the nearest number and besides, by answering in this way, it would make me appear older than my twenty-five years. I wanted Mike to think that I was much older than he was. Mike was twenty-three.

Mike's response was typical. Feeling bad and awkward in the situation, and at the same time wanting to express his feelings about me he broke into a big grin and joked: "Well, what kind of soap do you nuns wash with, is it Lux or Ivory? You have such beautiful skin!"

It was the tension breaker that we both needed and we cracked up laughing about it. Mike was delicate and sweet. We talked for a while and he told me how comfortable he felt with me. How I laughed at his jokes, how I never found him rude like other people did, while at the same time, I was myself very refined and polite, which made him feel acceptable.

"It's wonderful to meet a girl with whom you can share your ideas and you're the first girl I know who is like that for me."

I thanked him for his compliments, and assured him I was pleased, but his hopes were unfounded. He should forget the whole thing.

I wanted to laugh, I felt so nervous. When I got back to the convent that night I told some of my friends about it, making light of it. I did not fully understand what had happened and I was not sure what I felt about it. I wouldn't allow myself to know because only one reaction was possible for the faithful nun- to deny any responsibility for Mike's feelings. I desperately had to believe that I wasn't a bad nun.

174

Instead of leading me to nonchalance and laxity, my doubts led to a more scrupulous adherence to the rule. I had promised in a vow to God not to do anything to provoke this kind of male attention. I had to deal with my feelings of guilt that were awakened in me as a result of Mike's revelations. Though, I was flattered, still it frightened me. The door had been opened ever so slightly to the possibility of an alternative life style.

I did not allow myself to reflect much on this experience during the ensuing months. I buried myself in my work and became absorbed by it as well as by my conflicts with Mother Joseph.

I was easily irritated and impatient. I found a passage in Ignatius Lepp's writings at the time which seemed to characterize me so well that I copied it and made a book mark out of it. It read:

The irritableness of her character, her laziness, her passivity and finally her loss of joy in living were the consequence of the exhausting battle she was waging in order to safeguard her illusion.

Looking back, I don't think I was as irritable and joyless as I thought of myself at the time I copied out the passage. But I was so taken up with my inner struggle while attempting to maintain a happy front that I felt exhausted and irritated by it all.

I saw my cross clearly: each time that I considered the thought of leaving, I was tortured by the thought that this would be a selfish and non courageous thing to do, to run away from my cross.

When I recently viewed the film L'Aveu (The Confession), I understood very well the dilemma of Arthur London. "Admit What?" London asks repeatedly in the film. After a time one of the investigators says to him, "But it isn't important whether it is true or not true. What is important is that you acknowledge as true the judgment of the Party- that's what's important."

In a flashback in the film he remembers what he learned when he became a member of the Party- that one must put party interests above one's own; that if the Party asks something difficult or incomprehensible, one must submit, for the good of the whole.

I knew instinctively what kind of bind such a philosophy puts one in. It makes one suspect one's judgment as weak, fallible and selfish (which it certainly can be).The tragedy is that the collective judgment fares no better.

.

MAY TO AUGUST 1966

The end of the school year! It was a hectic time as school exams and NY State Regents' exams coincided with the beginning of university summer sessions. It had become the practice in recent years for "obediences" to be given on June 8th, the feast of our Lady of Divine Wisdom. On the evening of June 7th, Mother Joseph announced that she would replace the usual half-hour of evening meditation with her weekly spiritual conference. We filed into the community room and sat in a circle.

"The Congregation is going through many changes," Mother began, "there will be many obediences in our community. One must not interpret obedience as a measure taken against people who are in disagreement with the superior," she continued. "You might be a good teacher, an outstanding teacher even, and as we all learned when we took our first vows, one must be ready to use one's talents for the Congregation, wherever that might be. There are schools which perhaps need good teachers, more than we do here. Do not be surprised if you are sent there."

We looked at each other half smiling.. So there would be a purge! Mother's lasted a half-hour. When it ended the sisters exchanged whispered comments as they filed down to chapel.

"Guess we'd better pack our bags."

177

"Wonder if we'll be separated North and South?"

Our fears of dispersion were totally justified. When Christ the King opened in 1963, the Bishop of Brooklyn had entrusted it to the Daughters of the Spirit. Of the five high schools that he had constructed, he considered this his biggest and best. The Congregation had been honored to have been favored and saw in the choice an indication of the reputation of the sisters as good educators. The superiors did not wish to jeopardize this belief. Consequently, they staffed the school with their most experienced and most promising young teachers. Now, with the end of the fourth year of the school's operation, it would be easier to shift teachers

There was another reason why changes could be expected. The Sisters of Christ the King formed a tightly knit community and were known for cheerfulness and community spirit. These qualities strengthened their intellectual positions. Because of their *"radical"* ideas, their reputation as a happy, peaceful, dynamic community threatened their superiors.

When I walked into the Chapel the next day, I remember thinking: "There's going to be a note in my bench." I genuflected, raised the cover over my books, and saw the note. The worst had happened. I genuflected, walked out and went to the Superior's room to receive my new obedience.

As was the custom, she handed me an envelope and I ripped it open amidst freely flowing tears. It read: "Sister Rachel Mary of Jesus, God wants you at St. Agatha, Maine."

St. Agatha! My God! That was Siberia! St. Agatha was the location of a small rural school over six hundred miles away, far from my friends in New York, far from the center of activity in the Congregation.

"Didn't you expect it Sister?" Mother Joseph asked. She seemed to be truly solicitous.

"No, Mother I had no idea."

"I'm sorry; I thought Mother Benedict had told you when she spoke with you earlier this month."

"Mother, why did you ask to have me changed?"

"Sister why would I ask to have you changed?"

"I just feel that you did - that you asked to have me changed and I don't understand why."

"No, I did not ask Sister."

I did not believe her. But why should she lie? Still, I felt uncomfortable. I left the room and returned to the chapel. I had not noticed any other teaching sisters leave the chapel, only one older sister and one very young sister beside myself. These two sisters had currently finished a year of study and were expecting an assignment. I felt a sudden surge of sobs and tried to muffle it in my handkerchief. I did not want to leave. It seemed significant that I was the only one of the entire teaching community to receive a change. "What had I done wrong?" I asked myself. "I do the best I can. I work hard at teaching. I know I'm a good community member. I work hard and do more than my share. I give generously of my time and energies. Why was I being sent away?"

I was really upset! I decided to ask the Assistant Provincial Superior for an explanation. If I at least understood why, I would feel better . But Mother Benedict's answer was that Mother Joseph had not asked to have me removed from the community. The Provincial Superior, Mother Rosemary, said she was aware of the conflict between Mother Joseph and me, and since they needed a social studies teacher in St. Agatha, everything would work out for the best. I would go to St. Agatha to fulfill a need and Mother Joseph and I would be separated by the move. The explanation made sense. I accepted it, but I had lingering doubts.

I told my classes that I would not be returning in the fall. Consequently I would need their help to prepare my desk, closets and the storage room so that the next teacher could easily step into my place I knew that once I was fully engaged in correcting exams and preparing report cards, nothing else would seem important. I threw myself into my work with characteristic energy.

I eagerly awaited the beginning of summer school. But before summer school got underway, there was another disturbing incident.. , Mother Rosemary called for a general meeting of the sisters attending summer school. These sisters would normally live in convents in New York, Washington, Maine, Virginia, and St. Louis. The meeting would be held at Christ the King. What could it be about? Summer time was time to gossip - during these few short months, one could learn which superiors were conservative, which liberal, which books were currently on the "best seller" list in the convents, which sisters had had a hard year, which had enjoyed theirs. We ignored the superior's warnings against this type of gossip.. We suspected Mother Rosemary would deliver another "warning."

Instead, Mother Rosemary stressed the danger of relationships, and the fact that some sisters believed themselves to be "intellectual" because they read books that they did not understand. She chose Teilhard de Chardin as her example. I slipped the copy of Teilhard's <u>The Divine Milieu</u> under the folds of my skirt as she talked.

"Furthermore," she continued, "you are not supposed to talk to a man, including priests. A confessor is appointed by the Bishop to serve the needs of the sisters and the sisters are forbidden to talk to any priest except the one thus appointed by the Bishop. And then the sisters are allowed to speak to this priest, only at specified times…. For any other contact you must ask permission, not only of your local superior, but of me."

I was appalled. What right did she have to curtail our rights? Moreover, according to canon law, each sister had the freedom to see a priest. She did not need to ask for permission from her own superior or her Provincial Superior. The only requirement was to inform her own superior that she was leaving the house. In fact, a sister who might be out of the convent for some other reason could obtain spiritual counsel from a priest. These new restrictions were monumental!

I had to talk with someone who was detached from the politics of the community. How was I going to do this? I was not allowed to speak to a priest outside the community? Who would understand? And who did I have access to? If another Sister had presented the problem to me, my unhesitating advice would have been: "Sister you are free to find a priest or anyone with whom you feel you can sincerely discuss your problems and you are not bound by this nonsense. Mother Provincial cannot control your conscience." And I believed that. But for me, things were different. I could not grant myself the liberties I would have easily granted someone else. I was prideful. I did not want my superiors ever to find anything reprehensible in me. And since there was a chance that they would find this behavior incorrect, I would not risk it.

Still. confusion plagued me. Could I continue in religious life? Was my interpretation of it wrong? Should I accept things as they were and attempt to conform my thinking as well as my behavior? The more I thought, the more confused I became, and the more I felt the need to talk to someone other than a fellow sister, who frequently was also confused.

One alternative was to write to the Father General. I had met him several times and he had seemed eminently reasonable. Moreover, he knew the congregation in a way that no outsider could possibly know. That's what I would do, so I set about composing my letter. I had to laugh when I reread the letter a few years later. I was so intense, so involved in the petty details of convent life. Looking back forty years later), it seems hard to believe that I was this person.

"Religious life is a heavy weight - all the laws and regulations upset me." These words spoken recently indicate a general feeling in many quarters. I hope you will not misunderstand Father, I love the congregation and I am happy basically — as does the Sister who spoke thus love the congregation - The practice and interpretation of the vows is upsetting to me. For example, three years ago, when we moved into Christ the King, our new superior, a delegate to the General Chapter, Sister Angelus, bought blue and gold bedspreads for our rooms. Historically dyes were for the rich, thus the old practice of having white linens etc. One year later, Sister Joseph who disliked our first superior, and disagreed with the colored bedspreads on the grounds that it was not "religious" became the superior and the next thing we heard was that Mother Provincial felt it against poverty to have color bedspreads so we gave them away! One of the women who works for us took them home and made an entire bedroom set for her daughter-in-law out of some of them.

Who is right? The one who makes the decision because she bears the title of Provincial or the one who bought them? And what does a colored bedspread have to do with poverty and religious spirit? Could it not have been poorer to use them instead of buying new ones? And what of the $70. habit that we wore EVERYDAY from August to May to teach, scrub floors, clean classrooms, go to the parlor, because we had no other. Is that poverty? Could we not have made some simple dress to wear around in order to preserve our good and expensive habit, which is now worn to shreds? And what of the swimming pool that we "hear" is now being built in Connecticut...identified with the BETTER MIDDLE CLASS...IS THAT POVERTY? "Religious life is not a democracy", this we hear often. We never hear "Religious Life is an absolute monarchy". But isn't it just that? Isn't it still the noble superior who makes the decision for us serfs? At least on the lower levels? And why isn't religious life a democracy? I don't believe that God reveals himself to the majority, because they are the majority - I *don't believe that majority rule is the best answer. Even our American forefathers did not believe that. But does God really reveal his will to the superior.*

Why? How do we know? It seems to me that the best any man can do is apply his human reason, prayerfully, and then make a decision. In most cases, the reasons of many combined are closer to the truth than one because good old scholastic philosophy tells us that every man sees only one aspect of the truth. Well, should the superior in religious life suddenly become the authority, the bearer of truth? Obedience is definitely my major problem. The more I go, the more I believe that obedience should govern only the VERY BIG THINGS. Really Father, you should see our guidelines for vacation. We started a few years ago saying a new wave of freedom had set in - no more minute regulations - Well, everything is spelled out up to a sentence which literally reads, "Walking. . . will be permitted on the beach." and it goes on to say, not beyond property boundaries.

We teach religion to girls of thirteen and fourteen years of age and we tell them that they must judge in the light of their Christian conscience the particular circumstances, etc. General guidelines are given out they are very broad. However for us, between the ages of 20-80, a detailed outline is provided. Another regulation is that we may not watch TV in our nightwear. Now the background to this obviously is that in one house, the Sisters had a party in their nightwear. As a result, if a sister or group of sisters ask and obtain permission to watch a program for cultural purposes, they must stay fully dressed, sometimes until, 10: PM, 11: PM or 12:PM., and of course rising is the same as usual. Even a good atheist, trained in scholastic terminology and logic knows the axiom that To Rule for Abuse is a Fallacy. (There's a Latin phrase for this, which I forget). Despite this fact, ruling for abuse seems to be a guiding principle. Is religious life made for weaklings? We have two types of shoes to choose from - Why not say a simple black shoe, and leave it at that? We have been told how long our hair should be, what type of eye glasses are favorable to authority, what type of apron we should wear to do dishes, etc. Regarding Chastity, we now need permission to see a priest, permission from the Provincial. I understand that this is a safeguard, but from who did your married sister, if you have one Father, or ours, get permission to speak to men other than her husband? I know that there have been abuses. Mother Provincial has been very clear on that - A sister and priest were fondly holding hands, and we imagined the rest . . . Still, do you think that our counterparts, our sisters in the world have not fallen in love with men other than their husbands? Or at least, have been strongly attracted by other men? I think so - yet . . . I know that we are not all Herculean, and that human weakness exists but the point is, SHOULD ADVICE BE MADE INTO LAW - as is

182

OFTEN *the case. If the sister is a mature adult, she will seek advice and will be honest enough to see the danger she faces, as they present themselves. If she isn't, then* NO AMOUNT OF LAW *is going to help her,* FATHER, *may I repeat that I love the Congregation, but I don't understand the inconsistency between what we say and what we do. We speak of adapting to modern life. We speak of religious life as a life for others, for the apostolate, yet, my superior questions me each time a young girl comes to see me at seven in the evening, whether she could not come at some other time. It just so happens that they work and are not free any other time. Mother* RELUCTANTLY *gives the permission, and she feels a heavy weight on her conscience for our lack of "community spirit". Father, what are we here for, to lift up to the conscience of the individuals where these are unselfish and enlightened Christians, because the Church has never urged blind obedience to doubtful knowledge - (This is simplified to get a point across). In this age, when Christian women our own age are making such major decisions, we have to ask permission to write a letter, and our mail is censored, and we are corrected if the particular superior does not like what we have written - or a remark is made if too many letters are received from your students. (Of course, you are also encouraged to let your students feel at ease with you!) My mother* NEVER *censored my mail, and I'm sure that I did nothing to disgrace her - Now, at the age of twenty-six, am I supposed to have regressed? What of clothing? Why aren't the sisters allowed to wear regular bathing attire or perhaps you do not know that we wear gym suits. And why can't we wear gym suits to play in the gym instead of playing in our one habit? And why can't the sisters wear slacks of some kind in the cold north when they go out? Must we wait for a general chapter to make these major decisions? Another point is attendance at Secular colleges. Last May, when you were there, Father, I was the sister who asked you about the sentence in the Acts that says, "A sister needs the permission of the superior general to attend a secular university?" I wondered and still do, why this was emphasized. It was typed in* CAPITALS *and underlined. If I understood you correctly you replied that it was a danger to the sisters - exposing them to Marxist philosophy.*

Well, I thought a lot about it, and I tried to read up on it. By chance, or was it Providence, I read Henri Perrin's autobiography Priest-worker, *that summer and I also had the unique opportunity to meet two communists (Since the party is outlawed here it is unusual). The two people in question were a Mrs. Lozinskaya, wife of the second secretary of the USSR mission to the UN, and Dr. Arpad Prandler, deputy ambassador of the Hungarian People's Republic to the UN. Dr. Prandler with whom I had the opportunity for a half-hour talk spoke about the conditions in Hungary prior to the WW II and the land-power of the Church. It is true that the Church often used her land for the benefit of the poor, but first, I wasn't sure of specific information about Hungary, and secondly, even if this were true, the Church did identify with the upper classes, and did not promote social and economic reform so she certainly could not have been looked upon by the young intellectuals of the day as the salvation of their country. Well, anyway, he was a Catholic, and turned to Communism, he said, because at that time, he felt that it provided the only solution to his country's problem. I sensed (or perhaps I imagined) a tinge of regret in his tone. He spoke about Cardinal Mindszenty as a reactionary who wished to recapture the power previously exercised by the Church. I think his view was somewhat exaggerated, but at the same time, I believe it was partly true because that's what I would expect of an old man whose suffering probably confirmed his fears and views so as to make him inflexible. Mrs. Lozinskaya spoke to the students about the USSR and I invited her to come to the school, which she did. When the day was over, she very hesitantly asked me if she could question me on a few things. It was the same cautious approach that I would have used toward her. She began by asking if I believed in Darwin's origin of Species and the theory of evolution. We went from there to a discussion of religion. I found her a sincere well-intentioned person. Your remark, these two experiences, and Henri Perrin's book made me curious about Marxism, and after much searching, I found two good articles on the meetings of the Christians, and Marxists that have taken place under the sponsorship of the Paulist Society. All in all, I was introduced to the real concern in Europe for the plight of the working class, the slowness of the Church to adapt to the needs of a revitalized apostolate, and the appeal of communism as a solution to economic and social problems. The whole question of Marxism has become one of real interest to me. However, I also think that what is of great concern and interest to Europe and has become of interest to me is not typical of American feeling. I could count on one hand the Sisters whom I could possibly interest in this subject. In other words, Father, I have examined to the extent possible, with the time permitted, and I don't think that Marxism is the problem the Sisters would encounter in the US while attending a secular university. There are many reasons for this, and I'm sure that many books have been written that pinpoint these reason, but I think a prime factor is the relatively comfortable position of the laboring class. First of all, very few among the rich in the US do nothing. Everyone works - almost - and there is no ancient gap between the labor and nobility - Also, land was not controlled by a few rich. Up until 1890, with the closing of the frontier, we had plenty of land for sale, cheap. So the appeal that Marxism has to developing nations and to nations with*

184

land-aristocracies does not apply here. Now the question still remains, are secular universities dangerous? Isn't all life dangerous? I think there is a danger of comfortable materialistic philosophy and/or of an atheistic humanism on a higher level, but these permeate our entire society, the catholic as well as the secular campus. Besides, Catholic Colleges are far too numerous in the US and many are mediocre or worse (I'm not against Catholic colleges, just feel that we have overextended ourselves and we would be better off with fewer, but better colleges!) Other reflections on the apostolate bring up the question of an exchange program among the teachers of different countries. What a great benefit to the Sisters, to the educational system, if we could rotate one or two teachers, France-USA, or Holland_ -USA, etc. Couldn't this be worked out, or at least discussed? Why can't official channels of communication be opened up so we could discuss ideas like these? What about service to Mission areas on the model of the Peace Corps? It would seem feasible. Had you heard that Sergeant Shriver had suggested recruiting seminarians, young priests and religious into the Peace Corps? I believe the possibility is open, but whether this would be desirable is still an open question. Perhaps arrangements could be made to use their training facilities? So many possibilities are open to us...I hope this letter doesn't sound like one long list of complaints. It isn't meant to be. It stems from a real concern for the future of religious life. I know Father that were I to leave the congregation, I would not be giving more of myself to the Church, because right now I practically give 99% of my time and effort, and the 99% of other sisters' time and efforts is often exhausted over non essentials but I firmly believe that the Cross will come, I don't have to plant it in my path, or in the path of those who live with me. Am I mistaken? Have I really a wrong notion of religious life? Is it really supposed to be like this? And if it is, do I really belong in it, does God really implant desires, thoughts, and insights only to frustrate their development? I am writing to you Father, because I hope that you will understand. May I count on your prayers and advice?

Not surprisingly, he never answered me.

Toward the end of this school year, one of the best known moral theologians of the Church, Dr. Bernard Haring, came to New York to deliver a lecture. There had been a series of conferences among major world theologians at Notre Dame University. Some from other countries took advantage of being in this country to lecture at Catholic universities in the United States. At St. John's, Father Haring's topic was the freedom of the Sons of God. I was captivated.. He was immensely humane and compassionate. Like many of his generation, he had lived through war experiences that would prevent him from ever again returning to the smug security that was possible before. In the face of war, mankind soon lost its enthusiasm with categorizing sins.

I have often wondered where Catholic theology would be if there had been no European Front in World War II. Much of Father Haring's lecture was devoted to moral questions surrounding birth control. He directed his remarks to the clergy who would have the task of advising Catholics in the Confessional, although as teachers, we also advisors. He stressed that the ultimate responsibility belonged to the couple. As he talked, he went off into a discussion of St. Paul's letter to the Romans, and the concept of law.

The attitude of placing the law above the individual was Old Testament morality. The big message of the New Testament was that the law was to be found within oneself. The criteria of judgment were to be found within the individual. Man was above the law. Thus, God did not demand irrationality. This contradicted the interpretation of Christian obedience that I had read in Durwell's In the Redeeming Christ the summer of my final vows. He had stated: "*Christianity was not a humanism, but a divinization, a movement away from himself whereby man submits himself to God at the base of all Christian life is the Redeeming Christ, is submission to God.*" This interpretation, taken in conjunction with the fundamental principles of religious life, that the superior's will represents the will of God, made the religious superior a blind force to be obeyed, not to be reasoned with.

I now saw this reasoning in the light of Haring's interpretation as Old Testament morality. If my superiors opposed change, if they wished to continue practices that had been in effect in the Congregation for some 250 years, these wishes did not necessarily mean that God so willed it. In fact, each practice must be examined on rational grounds to see if it was suitable.. Though the Church had always opposed Marxism on the grounds that it systematically denied human freedom, there were some truths to be learned from Marxist philosophy. One had to see in what way it was responding to true social needs, and in what ways it was not. In this way, the Church would be able to reformulate its own social thinking.

I was bursting with excitement as I left the lecture hall. I felt another infusion of enthusiasm and support, giving me energy and conviction to carry on.

That spring browsing in the library, I discovered another important book-the diary of Henri Perrin. The Worker Priest consisted of his letters as well as notes collected from his diary. Perrin was one of the founders of the priest-worker movement in France during World War II. When the Germans occupied France, they shipped French workers to Germany to work in German munitions factories. A group of young priests, Perrin, foremost among them, asked the Bishop of Paris if they could join the French workers in Germany to support them. Because of those extraordinary times, the Bishop granted permission.. In the fifties, Perrin became a construction worker, building passages through the Alps. It was an experiment for the French Clergy which had become isolated from its parishioners. I was tremendously impressed with Perrin's closeness to the real world. I was now aware that my life was different from the life I had anticipated when I entered the convent. I was cut off from the real world. Furthermore, I did not see how religious consecration could help people. I needed reassurance that the life I was leading could be meaningful. Perrin had encountered many of the problems I had been grappling with in the last year.. He had confronted these not in a polemical sense, not even intellectually but by meeting living representatives of opposing points of view. He had not dismissed them with name calling or apriori categorization, as was often the case with the clergy. He had attempted to integrate these new perspectives into his own frame of reference, becoming more compassionate and tolerant as a result. In his letters, he discussed at length Christianity's relationship to the War, and referred to Cardinal Mindszenty's lordship over the Hungarian peasantry as an example of abuse of power – not how a Bishop or priest should care for his flock . I felt excited as I read his letters. I read and reread his book seeking answers to my own questions.

When the school year ended, I began summer school. I had put the experience with Mike out of my mind, but my return to campus brought me face to face with him and forced the issues back to the surface. In the intervening months, Mike had obviously decided to try to push me a little. He took a casual attitude toward me, calling me his girlfriend to his friends, waving to me across campus and generally embarrassing me.

I asked him to stop his behavior but he merely smiled and responded, "We'll get you to leave yet." I didn't need that extra pressure. I had just received my obedience and I was leaving for Northern Maine in a matter of weeks.

For the first time in my religious life, I had begun asking myself the question: Should I leave the convent? Maybe I don't belong in religious life? It was not that I had never thought about it before, but I had never faced it so directly. I was ripe for being confused by Mike. He had brought up the fact that Sister Michael, a classmate, a sister from another religious order, was a misfit. I had argued with him that if I wasn't one now, I wasn't going to become one. Sister Michael's problems had begun long before she entered the convent.

Still, I had seen enough sisters who, though initially stable, healthy people, had, through a series of experiences, become twisted, hard and I might even say cruel.. I feared that eventually I too would be affected, no matter how aware I was of the danger. I thought of Sister Lucille who terrorized everyone who wanted to use the sewing machines, and of Mother Mathilde who had us engage in community chores to the detriment of our studies. Mike's comparison rekindled all those fears accumulated over the years. It was impossible for me to deny them any longer. I had to confront them. I avoided Mike as much as possible, taking refuge in the library. But whether I saw him or not, his words were constantly in my thoughts.

* * * * * *

I made another discovery about people that summer. During the spring semester, while I had some free time, I had read Harvey Cox's, The Secular City, a book that had been "hot" on campus the previous fall. Now I was ready to discuss it and I sought out those persons who had mentioned it to me some months earlier. It had raised questions for me, and I was curious about the effect of Cox's new view of the urban community on those persons. To my great amazement, most confessed they had never really read the book, only skimmed it, and they were unsure both of his views and of their reactions to it. Why the enthusiasm over something they knew nothing about? It puzzled and shocked me.

I had hoped that my studies would push aside my inner conflicts but I found myself growing more introspective and tense as the summer progressed.   Sister Helen, my friend from college and Ozone Park days, had started therapy in the spring, and was herself in the throes of deciding whether to continue her religious commitment.   Unable to articulate my own turmoil, I listened to her enunciate the list of problems that I had already encountered and struggled with.   But, I reasoned that her family situation had been difficult - so unlike mine.   I could not in any way allow her decision to influence mine.

When summer school ended, several of us went to Connecticut for our annual retreat.   Each year, the sisters spent a week in prayer and meditation.   A priest was assigned to give a series of lectures.   As it turned out, Father Terstroet, the elderly Dutch priest sent by the Superior General to give the retreat, was a wonderful compassionate man.   He had been a member of the Dutch resistance during the war and had the ability to dismiss meaningless tradition and to cut through the guise of holiness in which these traditions were often shrouded.   What's more, he shared my love for De Chardin and gave a retreat based on the latest scriptural scholarship, rather than one based primarily on moral exhortations.

I spoke to him about my conflicts and doubts.   He pointed out how all change is painful, how much more so for institutions with long traditions.   As Teilhard had been faithful to his priesthood, as he had suffered and offered up his sufferings for the conversions of others to this new way of viewing Christianity, so should I accept my vocation as one in the forefront, one who has the ability to see the future, to dream, to plan and one who has, as a result, to suffer the consequences of living in the present with the mind and heart of a future person.   It was flattering to be viewed in this way.   And he meant it.   He believed it.   He believed in me. We spoke of the Church's backwardness on many fronts and the necessity to press for change.   I felt renewed.   I had a place.   I had a role.   There was a meaning to my life.

When the retreat ended, I said good-bye to the sisters I had learned to love and left for Maine, fully resolved to try again to be a successful nun.

ASSIGNMENT TO MAINE

Yes, even if contrary to all expectations, the War should end badly, not only for us, but also for the real progress of the world (though God knows how much I believe in the ultimate success of the world and of the progress, in spite of everything of life. I have faith in life) even then I would feel like repeating over all these seeming victories of evil, the ancient cry of the Greek festivals Io Triumpe. And yet, I love beautiful things, science, progress almost ingenuously. I am a man as much and more than anyone else. But there it is; we believers have the strength and the glory of having a faith in God more profound than our faith in the world, and that faith in God reemerges and persists even if our faith in the world should be crushed by the impact of events.

Teilhard de Chardin
Letters to Marguerite

My family drove me the full day's journey to my new assignment in St. Agatha. I was going home, back to the rural valley where I had been born and raised. Nine years had passed since that summer of 1957 when my mother, sister and I last traveled together before they had dropped me off in Connecticut to begin my life as a nun. It seemed much longer than that. I was only 26 years old, but I felt much older- worn and anxious. I

191

discussed my transfer with bitter humor, only to be countered by my sister's insistence that I had freely chosen to become a nun, so I should live with the consequences.

We ran out of chitchat as we drove the several hundred miles and I sat back in the car mulling over the events of the past few months. I felt relieved that I had been removed from a situation which was increasingly distressing, while at the same time I felt punished and unappreciated. My ambivalence was supported by the knowledge that I was a creative and exciting teacher with excellent credentials to teach in the rural bilingual town so similar to the one I had been raised in, and the knowledge that although far more challenging to my skills as a teacher, the rewards of teaching would not be forthcoming, as they had been over the past four years. I thought with sadness of friends I had left behind and of my many students. Well, I reasoned, here I could begin again.

The school to which I had been assigned was a small rural public school with grades seven through twelve. It had recently been slated for federal funds to develop a bicultural, bilingual curriculum. My natural drive, coupled with my commitment to students, made this aspect of the move exciting. I arrived fairly late on a Saturday night, just in time for bed. I was greeted warmly by the sisters, especially by Sister Giorgio, my friend and mentor from Ozone Park, and Christ the King; Sister Florence Jane, my friend from Connecticut days and Ozone Park,, and Sister Mary Joy, my colleague from Christ the King High School and the new superior of the convent. She had been appointed superior at the time of my transfer to Maine but it had been kept secret. She had arrived in Maine about one month ago and was glad to greet an old friend from the "South."

The next day, Sunday, I unpacked my suitcase and was shown my classroom. School was to begin with three days of workshop. I planned to spend most of the time looking over textbooks and prepare classes. In my view, workshops were boring, time consuming and usually unproductive. Sister Giorgio informed me that this was not going to be an ordinary workshop. This was going to be an "encounter group" and I would be left too emotionally exhausted at the end of the day to care about classes.

"Just relax," she advised, "we'll have time over the next weekend to prepare classes."

I was skeptical that I could become as engrossed as she seemed to believe. Encounter groups, I had no idea what these could be, and I didn't give it much thought. I spent some time listening to my friends telling me what life in Maine had been like their two years, and reacquainting myself with some of the older sisters.

Monday at 9:00 a.m., all teachers from the district gathered in the school gym. There, Mr. Brennick, the Superintendent, informed us that the district had received a federal grant to develop a new bilingual curriculum. The administration felt that before committees could be set up to work on a new curriculum some attempt had to be made to deal with the conflicts between the administration and the faculty. They suggested it would be helpful if we first discussed these problems.

I felt uninvolved because I was too new to be familiar with the problems, let alone contribute to their solutions. I had my own ideas about teaching and the needs of schools in Northern Maine, It was the same school district from which I had graduated nine years before. I eyed the superintendent carefully as he spoke. Mr. Brennick showed the effect of the years that had elapsed. Instead of the boyish, shy young man I remembered, he cut a rounding figure, looking much older than his years.

The leader of the outside team of consultants then spoke, interrupting my thoughts. He hoped the teachers would not regard the workshop as a move on the part of the administration to manipulate them. The team had no such intention. After this brief introduction, he divided us into groups of twelve, assigning us to various classrooms. By this time, I was curious and gladly went to my assigned room. Once we had settled into our seats, a quiet unassuming man at the head of the circle began explaining the purpose of the group. He spoke so softly that I remember straining to hear what he was saying. He insisted that we should feel free to discuss whatever we wanted.

It all seemed pretty silly. What did he mean, "What we wanted?" I wondered why the leader did not give us some kind of problem to focus our discussion on. You just don't get a group of strangers into a room together and ask them to discuss whatever they want.

I grew impatient. "What are we doing here anyway," I finally said. "This is a waste of time."

Paul, the leader, responded that we were supposed to discuss whatever we felt like discussing.

Larry, one of the men in the group shouted: "Well, I have something to discuss," and he immediately launched into an attack against nuns teaching in the public schools. There were two sisters in the room, but because I had already spoken and was aggressive he directed his remarks toward me. Others cautiously joined him.

What emerged from the discussion that followed was the hostility of the staff towards the principal of one of the high schools in the district. The man they criticized was a conservative, insecure, threatened individual, and a religious brother. It became apparent that the teachers considered him ineffective as an administrator, inept as an educator and a failure as a human being.

What had started as an attack on the Church ended as an attack on this man. The fact that he was a religious brother made it difficult for this community of French-American Catholics to separate an attack on his personal shortcomings from an attack on the institutional church.

Larry, had real hostility towards the Church and told of his experiences with nuns in his early schooling. In third grade, he was told that urinating against the school building was a mortal sin, punishable by eternal damnation in hell. I had never heard anything so ridiculous! I did not take it as a personal affront or attack. That Larry generalized his anger to all nuns was understandable. I sympathized, knowing full well the strong impression that teachers make on young sensitive children. I told him I agreed that if this truly had happened, the nun was at fault, but that I had never met a nun like this. I felt sorry that a religion to which I had committed my life had been so damaging to a young child.

Larry declared that I was obviously very different. "I've never met anyone in the Church who is so open to criticism of the institution. If I try to talk to a priest about my criticism they just give me some sort of sermon and point out my own inadequacies."

Though he may have been exaggerating for effect, I was all too familiar with the behavior to which he referred. The institution is above mistakes. It always had to be the individual who fell short and who had to search his soul. I did not wish to seem critical of the clergy so I kept these thoughts to myself. Instead, I pointed out that persons often misuse

194

religion for their own ends, such as his teacher had done in order to enforce a rule of conduct she felt she could not enforce in any other way. And we went on to discuss how the religious brother in question also hid behind the "authority" of the Church to justify his positions, to end debate.

Participants admitted that their hostility was not really toward the Church, but toward this particular principal and the hierarchical structure in the school, which did not permit them any voice.

We had dinner break followed by a gathering of all the faculty at which we discussed self-actualization and self-fulfillment. Our group leader, Paul, made the presentation. We were requested to return to our respective rooms to discuss the points of the general presentation.

Larry came into the room and sat down next to me, putting his arm around me with a great flourish. "I'm infatuated with you," he said, with a big grin on his face.

"Well, you mustn't worry about it," I answered laughingly, "these things pass with time." The feelings that Mike had been aroused in me were coming back. Only this time I recognized them. I was attractive to men, I was desirable, a warm, sympathetic person, and a good companion. Up to now my sexual feelings had been successfully repressed. It is not all that difficult to imagine because I had had almost no contact with men..

The others in the group took their seats while Paul greeted us and sat down. "Can a person be fulfilled in an autocratic structure?" he asked.

Because of my own experiences, I took the question more broadly and felt myself come to attention, listening to hear what the other members of the group would answer. Could it be, I thought to myself, that other people had problems similar to mine?

Nobody picked up on the question. Instead we found ourselves discussing the meaning of self-fulfillment.

After a time, Paul said, "I think we should try a different exercise. Rachel, would you role-play with Eldon?"

"Sure," I answered, not knowing exactly what I was supposed to do. Paul explained that I was to act as counselor and Eldon as counselee. I forget how it began but we got into a discussion about Eldon's self-concept.

A frightened individual with very little self-esteem, Eldon placed all self-importance on his roles as father and husband. He dodged my every effort to face the fact that he was more than that. His wife and children could be accidentally killed tomorrow and life would have to go on. What would he do? He answered that he would return to his father's house but denied any importance to his own life.

Larry came over to me when the session broke, put his arm around me and suggested, "Hey, Rocky, (a nickname he continued to use) why don't we go to Black Joe's and discuss some more over a glass of beer."

"That's all I need, to be seen drinking with you in the local bar at midnight. I'd be tarred and feathered tomorrow and run out of town. Besides, I hardly think my superiors would find it amusing."

Paul interrupted, saying that I had shown a lot of natural skill in role-playing and that he was impressed with my ability to diagnose people's problems. I thanked him for the compliment and we continued to talk together until we got to the door. I said good night and started toward the convent. Was it my imagination, I wondered? I knew by the remark and I also knew by the warmth of Paul's glance that there was a lot of feeling for me. I couldn't very well discuss this with anybody. Besides, what was there to discuss? I hardly dared think about it. But I experienced a warm satisfying feeling as I walked back to the convent that night. I remember thinking that I didn't want to stop and talk with the other sisters who were also on their way home. I wanted to be quiet so as not to break my mood. I already felt eager to begin the next day.

*　*　*　*　*

At the next day's session,, but just before lunch, Paul said, "This group has expressed so many negative feelings that I think it might be a good exercise for the group to express some positive feelings for one another to set things in perspective. So we'll start at this end of the group," motioning to his right, "and if you feel like saying something positive to each person as we go around the circle, speak up. You don't have to say something to each person."

Simone, one of the first in our group, was an attractive young woman about to begin her first year of teaching. "I think you're very sweet, sincere, and that you have a lot of feeling and concern for other people, Simone." I said. "Besides, you're very beautiful and feminine and I

196

appreciate those qualities in you. Especially, I think I like your sincerity the best."

As I spoke to Simone, I felt a tremendous sense of exhilaration, even of freedom. I was not bound by the pettiness women so often exhibit toward one another. I could tell another woman in the presence of a group, that she was beautiful and attractive, and that I did not feel diminished. I caught Paul glancing at me. His glance seemed to express those exact sentiments about me.

Most of our group were self-conscious about expressing their feelings. The comments I recorded had to do with others' perceptions of me. Eldon, said he found me warm - that I had demonstrated an ability to pry. He explained, "you can make people look into themselves." Others commented that I was frank, sincere, open and demonstrated a strong concern for others. This had helped the group because I had insisted on treating people with respect.

One of the men said that he felt something strong for me, which he did not know how to express. As we left the room, he said, "I think you are very sweet." Sweet was not an adjective I would use to describe myself. Even now, as I write this, I never have fully believed it. I was the tomboy, the adventurer, the daredevil, the prankster; myself-image had no room for "sweet". I was beginning to formulate a new self-image, and I welcomed comments these on my behavior and personality.

The session ended abruptly as we had gone overtime. I felt sorry that Paul had cut off the session without allowing us to express our feelings toward him. As usual, people were milling around him, as we emptied the room. I stood to his right, a bit behind him. I knew he was aware of my presence. I remember feeling that he would turn and talk to me when the others had finished.

We walked toward the cafeteria in close proximity. Just as we were about to turn the last bend, he turned to me and said, "Would you join me for lunch?" I nodded affirmatively, feeling as if I had known all along that this would happen.

"I really appreciate your ability to deal with the group in a non authoritarian manner," I started. It was an issue to which I was especially

197

sensitive, as my dealings with superiors had been so disastrous in the past..
I suddenly became conscious of a general good feeling in my body - a
comfortable secure feeling.

I smiled at Paul shyly. Someone interrupted us and Paul turned to
answer whoever it was. "I feel very warm toward you," he said as he faced
me again.

I was confused. Was it a response to my expression of his role in
the group? Was he saying to me that since he felt warm toward me, it was
likely that I would feel positively about him? Or was he just taking the
opportunity to express something he was feeling regardless of my remark?

"Do you think that's why I feel positively toward you?" I asked.

"I think you have demonstrated a very rare ability to diagnose
people's problems and that you have a great sympathy for others. You
should try to do something with this talent, professionally, I mean."

"Many of my students come to me for advice and present their
problems to me, so that I actually have a lot of practice acting as a
counselor. Still, I often feel inadequate in helping them reach solutions."

"Maybe we could discuss this in one of the sessions." We walked
into the already filled cafeteria.

"Who are you?" I asked, breaking the momentary silence. "Where
are you from, and what do you do?"

"Well, I'm from Boston, and I belong to a professional group that
does this sort of thing."

"Are you religious?" I was still discovering that there were good
people who weren't religious. I felt tremendous warmth for Paul and
recognized in him a real empathy for people.

Paul ignored my question, so I rephrased it to a less threatening
one, "Have you ever dealt with religious people before?" I certainly don't
remember being interested in whether he knew nuns. There were a lot of
confusing thoughts swirling in my head. I wanted to know what he
thought of nuns, and of the whole idea of a life set apart. I was curious
about whether religion had in any way influenced his development.

"Well, yes, I conducted a workshop at St. Catherine's College in
Minnesota, and dealt with religious there."

"But you didn't have the sisters in the workshop?"

"No."

"Would you describe yourself as a religious person? Have you believed in any kind of a religious system before? Have you ever practiced any kind of organized religion?"

"I was baptized a Catholic, but I no longer practice." His eyes searched my face as he spoke.

"Since when?" We had reached the food and were scooping it onto our plates.

"For a long time, I rationalized that the commandment 'Thou shalt not Kill' was a farce when in World War II I killed people. I felt a crying within myself. Now I often ask myself whether this was really the reason why I gave up my religion, and the question has bothered me."

As I sat there and listened to him, I thought, my God, what a sensitive man. It wasn't an overwhelming romantic feeling - rather a calm awareness that this was the kind of man I would want to be the father of my children, the kind of man I might want as a friend and companion for life. I was surprised at my feelings.

Children! I had never once imagined myself a mother or thought of having children, and I was certainly in no position to think of having them.

"Are you married?"

He shook his head. "Divorced three or four months" It was as if that was what I had expected to hear and I nodded my head knowingly and asked,

"Do you have children?"

"Yes, five." He went on to say that he didn't really know what had gone wrong in his marriage, that he couldn't fully explain it to himself, that he had a tendency to blame it on his wife, whereas, he thought perhaps that there was some fault on his own part.

"When did you get married?"

"After the War."

"How long had you known your wife?" He recounted they had met shortly before the war and had corresponded while he was away. He had married her because of previous protestations of love, intimacies and plans for the future.

199

"Besides, my parents were opposed to the marriage and I felt that I had to assert my independence. I wasn't a boy anymore, that sort of thing."

"Why did you leave her?"

"I was afraid that violence would result."

"You mean that you would have been violent toward her, or that she would be toward you?"

"She toward me."

They had consulted marriage counselors, priests, psychiatrists, but nothing had seemed to work. He felt guilty about the marriage and he didn't understand why he was unable to cope with the problem, but it seemed impossible to continue in that way. He worried a lot about the children, his four girls and boy. He felt that they resented and blamed him.

"Do you get this kind of feedback from them?"

"No, but they live with their mother." He figured that was how they felt. Perhaps when they grew up, they would be able to have a better relationship with him . Problems with his marriage had gone on for a long time, but there had been many constraints on his decision to separate. He feared his divorce would affect his children and his work. He hoped to find a solution to his own problems through his work.

"Well, who are you and why are you here?" Paul asked, smiling gently at me.

I felt scared. I didn't know what to say. I was not used to revealing myself. "I'm the one who usually does the probing. I'm not sure what to answer."

"Do you think religious life is an escape for many people?"I asked after a short pause.

"Yes," Paul answered. "I had the opportunity to work among the Navajos for a number of years, and there I met many missionaries with varied motivations. Many of them, I felt, were working off guilt for the white man's treatment of Indians. And in the process of trying to help, they came to hate the Indians and took it out on them in subtle ways. It was at this time," he added, "that I became interested in Navajo religion and began to ask myself why it was that I had left my own."

The short digression had provided me with enough release of tension to feel free to talk about myself. "As for myself, I graduated from high school and I wanted to help others. I was living in this area, in the days before the Peace Corps, and I felt that the most effective way of helping people was by becoming a nun."

"Why didn't you go into social work, or nursing?"

"Well, I had high ideals at the time, and I thought that I would never be able to find anyone with whom I could share my life in marriage. I thought that instead of becoming a spinster I might as well join a religious order."

"Do you still feel that way?"

"No," I answered a bit hesitantly. "I see now that there are alternatives. That one doesn't have to be a religious to help other people, but well, there's a whole other area, that of faith here. Somehow I feel bound that God wants me to be a religious."

"Could you leave?"

"Yes, but I don't know if I will. I'm in the process of reevaluating my initial decision."

I looked into the eyes of this individual I had known for less than a day. For the first time in years, I felt someone was truly interested in my· interests, my· needs, my· future. I trusted this stranger more than my superiors. I felt that my superiors would advise me to stay.. Even my friends in the convent had a vested interested in advising me to stay. But Paul did not threaten or pressure me.

"Do you want me to leave? I suddenly asked Paul. He was very clever inanswering..

"No, the important thing for you is to be happy. If I felt that you could be happy in religious life, if you can find fulfillment, then maybe you should stay. If not, then you should certainly think of leaving. In any case, it's your decision."

"There's another problem," I said, only half hearing what he was saying. My thoughts were racing. "Religious look upon suffering as having value in itself. I certainly believe that suffering is a valuable experience for a person, that it enables one to grow, to become tolerant and understanding of others, but nevertheless, I can't internalize suffering as a value in itself."

"Do you want to suffer?"

"No," I answered firmly, surprised by the question. We sat there

201

and looked at each other for a few minutes.

"What do you think?"

"At first, I felt what a waste of a beautiful woman. She could make some man happy and be made happy by that man. Yet, I feel if you can be happy in this life, then perhaps you should stay."

As Paul spoke, I recalled a scene from The Inn of the Sixth Happiness: "you are very beautiful," Robert Donat said to Ingrid Bergman, "Thank you", she replied "every woman should hear that at least once in her life." I remembered thinking when I saw the film that I had entered the convent at seventeen thereby cutting myself off from the possibility of any relationship. I regretted it.

Now I was feeling very calm, happy and peaceful.

"You're obviously suffering from a great deal of conflict involved in decision making," Paul continued, "Some people resolve that conflict by waiting so long that the alternatives disappear."

"You mean, if I wait long enough, I wouldn't be able to get married anyway?" Paul nodded.

"Well," I said, "there's another problem, I'm a very warm person and if I made this conflict known, it would be very difficult for me to come to a decision." I meant that I was well liked and I felt that because of this, aside from other considerations, the sisters would not want to see me go. On the other hand, friends outside the convent would wish to see me leave.

"You mean many pressures would be brought to bear on you?"

"Yes, for and against staying," I answered, thinking of Mike and of the sisters who would object.

"Maybe it would help if you could talk with Roger. (He was one of the team of five consultants). He was a Catholic Priest, and maybe you could discuss some of the problems you face with him since he had some similar problems to face in making his decision to leave." I was surprised by the news of Roger's priesthood and though the possibility of speaking with him vaguely intrigued me, I felt that I would not be comfortable in discussing my conflicts with a former priests or an ex-nun.

"Thank you for telling me," I answered, "I'll think about whether I want to talk to him about it."

It was only then that I looked around and realized that the full two-hour lunch break had ended. The room had emptied and we barely had time to return to the group to begin the afternoon session. We carried our trays over to the serving counter and hurried down the hallway to our room.

Paul began the afternoon session by suggesting that we could break up into groups of three with one playing the role of counselor, one playing the role of counselee, and the third observing. The three could during the course of the two-hour session switch roles. The exercise, he explained, would sharpen our skills in handling advice giving. He was responding to my need. I smiled contentedly to myself. Moreover, I knew instinctively that Paul and I would form the nucleus of a group of three. We ended up together with Simone.

The session was stimulating and passed quickly. Afterwards, I walked to the convent with measured step. I can't remember what it was we did that evening.. I remember thinking that I didn't want to talk about my feelings. It wasn't clear what it was I was feeling anyway. If anything, I felt a bit dazed. Everyone around me was keyed up. Each teacher had become very involved in her own group. All were busy discussing their afternoon sessions.

The next morning I awoke with a strong feeling of loneliness. The last day, I thought to myself. Who could have thought that a few days could leave me in such turmoil? At 9:00, we met in the gym. We were informed that we would begin in general session. The hour was interesting enough, but I found it hard to concentrate. One hour before lunch, we were instructed to return to our assigned rooms for small group sessions. We all seemed relieved to be together again.

We had barely settled into our seats when Eldon turned to Paul and asked, "You look so serene, so calm, Paul. Are you happy?"

There was a long silence. To break the silence, I interjected that people often appear happy by their control over situations, but this may not necessarily mean that they are. I knew that I was being overprotective of Paul. I might have been so even if we had not shared our feelings. I tended to be protective in any case. But I felt guilty about having broken in and not allowing the discussion to take its normal course.

I can't remember now what the rest of the session was like. The

203

next thing I recalled was my superior running over to grab my arm and invite me to join her and her group leader for lunch. It seemed like a good idea, so I joined them. But, I kept an eye on the door until Paul came in. I was pleased that he joined us at our table.. I wanted to talk to him before we returned for the last session. I waited a moment for him to approach me when we got up from lunch. My anxiety didn't permit me to wait very long however, and I found myself walking toward him.

"How did you feel when Eldon asked you if you were happy?"

"I would have spontaneously answered yes, but then I kept asking myself the question, ' Am I happy? Or am I just content? I decided that there were some things that give contentment, but that I don't think that I'm really happy. I was asking myself the question, what is happiness? Where can I find happiness? when you interrupted. I realized that you wanted to protect me, but I felt some resentment that I didn't have a chance to tell the group what I was feeling. At the same time, I felt relieved."

"I thought that I didn't want you to feel obliged to expose yourself to the group and that was part of my motivation. I also felt that Eldon had no right to pry because of your position as leader. I'm not sure. I think I would have answered for you even if I had not known you." We continued to walk for a time in silence.

"I feel worse leaving this workshop, Rachel, than any other. I never let people get too close to me, and in these two days, I got closer to you than anyone else in my entire life. On the other hand, though I like the feeling of closeness, I am relieved that the workshop will be over soon."

"Because you are afraid that you will get too close and reveal too much?" I broke in.

"No, I've more or less revealed the kinds of things I have to say. No, I'm relieved because I could easily become emotionally involved with you and I don't know if I could handle it."

We stopped and looked at each other.

"And you, where do you go from here? Where are you?"

"What do you mean, emotionally involved? I said. "In a relationship between a man and a woman, emotional involvement tends to be expressed physically, is that what you mean?"

"Do you mean, do I desire you sexually? No, not yet. Not now, but if I stayed around here long enough it would probably come to that. If I could never see how this desire could be consummated I don't know whether I could live with it.."

I sighed and continued walking in an effort to relieve the tension."Well," I said, " I guess my feelings are similar. I'm sorry to see you go, and at the same time, it will relieve some of the pressure."

"You're going to have to do some sorting out of your values."

"What do you mean by that? You mean the advantages of marriage over non- marriage?"

"Yes, and what it is you really want."

"I thought I had sorted out my values. Don't you think I have?" I turned my face up inquiringly at Paul, aware that my reaction was a bit that of a frightened child.

"I don't know, I was just asking."

"I'm confused. You know, the religious dimension complicates things," I continued. "I don't know whether I really believe any more. It seems ridiculous for a person in my position to say such a thing."

"I think you do believe, but you have doubts, and it will probably reinforce your faith."

We were already in the doorway of the meeting room. I hurried to take a seat. It was another large group session and I sat next to one of the men in my group. I was indifferent to the summary and conclusions that were presented. I did not feel romantically involved with Paul at that moment. I wasn't sure what it was I was feeling- perhaps a bit confused and tense - wishing the workshop didn't have to end so soon. I stole a glance in Paul's direction. His glance met mine. The session was finally over and typical of endings, some were crying, some were swearing eternal allegiance to their new acquaintances and others were hurrying out resenting that they had been kept so long. I watched members of our groups go up to Paul and wondered what to do.

I didn't want to say goodbye, yet I didn't want to just walk away. So I took a place in line. "Goodbye," I said, as I extended my hand.

"Rachel." The moment was charged with emotion. I had barely turned away when my superior came bustling over to tell me that the

Assistant Provincial Superior was coming to visit us and we had to go to the airport to meet her.

"That's probably the best thing for me to do right now," I thought to myself. So I jumped into the waiting car and we drove off.

We were standing in the lobby waiting for the plane when Mother suddenly yelled out, "There's the team" and got very excited. "That's terrific, they can meet Mother Provincial." My heart jumped and I turned to see if Paul was there. He was. I don't remember saying anything to him, but I slipped my hand onto his arm for a moment as the circle closed in and I felt my gesture wouldn't be noticed. Paul smiled at me. There was a lot of bustle, activity, greetings and pleasant exchanges. The plane landed and Paul turned to take his place on line to board it. I felt terribly alone and needy. I wanted to run to Paul, throw my arms around him and rest there. He made me feel so safe. Instead, I continued to chat amiably and found my way to the car. I turned to see if Paul was looking. He had not turned back. I climbed into the car and we drove away. What would I do?

MAINE FALL 1966

.

It's strange how on the one hand it all seems so long ago, yet sitting down to record it I remember my feelings of immense weariness. This weariness had become quite familiar. I was greeted each morning by the thought that I had "another day to get through." I had lost my wide-eyed wonder. I felt disillusioned. I was tired of being misrepresented and misunderstood, tired of making an effort for nothing. I frequently wiped away the tears that fell for no apparent reason.

I was confused by the events of the past few days. What would I do indeed? What had happened to me? Should I leave? Was I happy? Could I be happy? Images of Paul and a life together crowded my imagination. I sat in the car and listened to the superior's account of her trip to Maine. It was not Mother Rosemary that had come to visit us but her Assistant, Mother Benedict. I was happy to see her. I had always liked her. She had taught me in high school, and was not only a competent teacher but also exciting. Now, however, I found her too much in the shadow of the more dominating Mother Rosemary. She no longer seemed to have a mind of her own, always in perfect accord with her superior. I now distrusted her. I wondered if she was just being loyal or truly agreed with her.

Mother Benedict suggested that we recite community prayers in the car so that we would be freed of community obligations once we arrived at the convent, about an hour's ride away. I was grateful for the silence. I had found it difficult to participate in the conversation and feigned interest, something I could not do well.

We had a big celebration dinner in honor of Mother Benedict's arrival that night. She surprised us all by apologizing on Mother Rosemary's behalf for Mother's hysterical talk in the earlier part of the summer. Her apology allowed us to release a lot of suppressed anger over being treated as children. It was our first opportunity to discuss issues as a community. I was pleased to discover an atmosphere of openness despite the wide age spread among us. We were a small convent, there were twenty-two of us. Fourteen were teachers, while the others were retired or sick. The old did not suspect the young, nor did the young attempt to argue with the older sisters. It was delightful; I could be happy in this community. I was used to having some of the older sisters accuse us of having "poor religious spirit" whenever we disagreed with the superior. Here, the sisters seemed willing to listen to the other side's perspective. The older sisters did not seem shocked or upset by the views of the younger sisters; sometimes, they even agreed.

I wondered how the sisters were reacting to Sister Mary Joy. She was an unusual choice for a superior. Most superiors were characterized by their calm demeanor, (although Mother Mathilde had been an exception). Instead, Mother Mary Joy was a high strung woman always on the verge of tears. The years of sacrifice and deprivation in the convent had not erased the effect of being a beloved only child - viewing all events, remarks, incidents as applying to her personally. Despite this, she was warm and outgoing, desperate to please, and to do what was best for the sisters in her care.

After clearing the dishes, we went outside for a walk. I was moved by the positive attitude of the sisters to chip in and do the dishes together. This was the first convent where I had witnessed this demonstration of family spirit.

The sisters had once operated a farm and still owned a large acreage, partially wooded, partially pastured, and partially rented to local farmers for planting. The rolling hills behind the house overlooked a large lake. It was a magnificent setting. The evening was warm and pleasant. I was at t peace.

Mother Benedict walked up to me as we were leaving the dining room. I had been thinking about her again, remembering what a competent teacher she had been. She was highly respected, with a forthright manner, giving the class a sense of confidence about learning. Moreover, she had a good sense of humor and came through as a real person who could appreciate a good joke, without ever letting the class get out of hand.

Even when I was in high school, I had noticed a tendency for her to set others up as a model to which she became attached.. Such was her relationship with Mother Alexandre, the superior of the convent when I had been a student. It appeared to me that she had developed this same fawning relationship with Mother Rosemary. What a shame that she never exhibited her independence. Perhaps years of subordination in religion eventually robbed her of the ability to take initiative.

"How are you?"

Mother Benedict's question jolted me out of my reverie. I don't remember what I answered. Probably that I was fine that I was looking forward to starting the new school year. I intended to work hard, I knew the people, I knew the language, and I knew the problems. I was eager to settle in.

"Good," she said, "I'm glad. I know you'll be happy here. You know Mother Joseph is so much more relaxed since you left. I think it was wise for her ask to have you changed."

I was stunned - Mother Joseph had lied to me!

Why didn't they tell me? At the time, I sensed she had asked to have me changed. Why couldn't they simply have told me that when I had asked? Why did they have to lie? Why is it that people shun the truth? It was so much more painful to have so much unexpressed hostility.

I don't remember the rest of the conversation. But I do remember that the whole evening, this admission kept coming back to me. That night, I tossed and turned and couldn't sleep. I was so confused. I thought over all the problems of the previous year, the intensity of my winter cold and its psychosomatic aspects, the doubts about God's existence, the pull exerted by Mike's expressed feelings for me, the experience with Paul, and now this.

Taken together, the various events proved that religious life was no place for me. I was too forthright. I was too insistent on understanding things. I couldn't simply obey without question.

I had never been able to submit to all the little rules. In the Novitiate, Juniorate and College, I couldn't walk right, always swinging my arms to my sides instead of keeping them in my sleeves, looking into people's eyes when I spoke to them instead of looking down, gesturing too much, tossing my head from side to side instead of holding it still.

I reflected on why I had stopped asking for permission to read books. I thought of how I rolled up my bath towel-placing it on the floor next to my door at Christ the King to hide the light so that Mother Joseph would not know that I was staying up late reading. There was a litany of small deviations from the customary practices.

I couldn't go on like this. It seemed hopeless. What was I doing this for anyway? Why was I a nun? Why had I become a nun? I had been filled with glorious ideals and I was going to accomplish great things - that had been my dream -but life was slipping by while I became mired in petty details and nuns became a fringe group in society. How was I being useful to anyone? By prayer? I did not believe; I had always doubted the effectiveness of a life of sacrifice, denial and seclusion such as cloistered nuns lived. Now I was even more skeptical that it was of any use except to themselves - if they found satisfaction to live this way. Certainly it was a witness to the world that these sisters believed that there was a higher power who governed their lives. And it was a powerful witness. But it touched so few people. Who knew and who cared?

This constant inner conversation was driving me mad. I had been in turmoil all summer. The retreat had helped me sort out my feelings and, I thought, renewed my belief in myself, my belief in religious life and confirmed in my mind, my place in it. My retreat was not even a week behind me. If it all could be undone so easily, perhaps my problems were more deeply rooted.

I resolved to talk to Mother Benedict. W met the next day. I told her about Mike and briefly about Paul. However what concerned me most was the superiors' unwillingness to accept me as I was. If I wasn't acceptable as I was, what was I to do? God knows, I had tried to change. People outside the convent found me acceptable, my professors, my students, and my fellow teachers. My superiors however only saw me as a rebel, a rabble-rouser, and a promoter of wild ideas. I wasn't sure I believed in God anymore. I had gone through a terrible winter. I didn't think that I could continue. Furthermore, I didn't believe that suffering was a value in itself. I didn't think we should seek it out and it seemed to me that I was being asked to believe this. Perhaps I should see a psychiatrist.

She didn't seem surprised. She advised me to consult Father Daly, who would be coming north soon. I knew him from second novitiate days in Connecticut. Despite my low opinion of Mother Rosemary, I recognized that because of her training as a psychiatric social worker, she was attuned to the psychological needs of the sisters. She encouraged sisters who needed professional help to seek it. Furthermore, sisters could now speak to Father Daly without "asking permission." Mother Rosemary recognized that not all problems were problems of faith, that there were also human problems and that sometimes it takes human means to find solutions.

Father Daly struck me as very conservative. I knew he was conservative theologically. I felt he would be judgmental. "I don't want to talk to Father Daly," I answered. "I realize that the Congregation is paying him a lot of money to serve the community, but I feel he will be too conservative. He'll probably tell me to 'grin and bear it, God will reward you.' I don't want to hear that. I'm tired of it. It just doesn't help me. I really think I would like to talk to someone outside the religious community."

She shook her head and said, "Well, there isn't really very much to offer you up here in Northern Maine, but if you find someone, you can tell Mother Mary Joy and we'll make the arrangements."

I really thought that she didn't want me to look for a psychiatrist. At this point, however, I didn't care. I felt too pressured. I came out of her office resolved to find someone. As it turned out, the one psychiatrist in the area was known for entertaining his guests at local cocktail parties by telling stories of his patients. That clearly wasn't for me. So for the time being, I buried myself in my work and tried to forget my problems. Things would have to change drastically. Either I would have to change, or I would have to make some decisions that would change my situation. I had no clear vision of the future. I didn't know where I was going, but I vowed that I wasn't going to be in the same situation when next year rolled around.

*   *   *   *   *   *

I was used to teaching New York City college bound kids who were highly motivated and highly competitive. If you dropped a hint that a certain book would be helpful, they would go out and read it, or barring that, they'd skim it or at the very least, they'd remember the title and what you said about it. Motivating the kids had never been a problem, even when teaching classes of between forty and fifty students. The challenge had been trying to keep up with the mammoth task of correcting two hundred assignments, projects, essays, term papers, and exams.

What a difference Maine was. Motivation was low in almost all classes. Bright kids were not sufficiently challenged. Many of the teachers had the attitude that the kids did not need a demanding program since most would not go to college or if they did, they wouldn't attend very competitive ones. When I arrived in Northern Maine I had resolved to work the kids hard - "whip them into shape". I would prove that they were capable of superior work, and that the reason they weren't performing well was that no one had demanded it of them.

I went into class with great enthusiasm. I had a few bright classes, a few average classes and one simply indescribable class of 23 boys. These were freshmen who ranged between the ages of 13-19. Some were bright but lazy. There were at least two seriously retarded and the remainder was a mixed bag. I always expected a submissive class. I was teaching them geography. It only took a few days for problems to develop.

One of the boys got up and began strolling around the room.

"Darryl," I said, "Please be seated."

"Me, I don wanna learn dat me." The class laughed. "Me, I run a tractor. This is not important."

"Young man," I said, "Kindly be seated." The class laughed again.

I didn't know what to do. I just looked at them. What was going on?

"Look at the cows, sister." I turned to the window; there were some 10 to 15 cows almost within stroking distance of the windows. A nearby farmer had forgotten to lock his fence.

For the class, this was clearly a ruse to distract me and to avoid studying. The entire class got up and went to the windows, talking loudly as they went, making jokes before I could even bat an eyelash.

"Gentlemen," I said, "Would you please return to your seats?"

"Gentlemen, you heard what I said," I tried again. They continued to talk.

"Sit down!" I yelled finally, slamming my hand down hard on the desk for emphasis.

I was surprised at the sound of my own screaming voice. They didn't exactly jump to attention, but meandered back to their seats. It was the beginning of my education in learning how to teach these kids. I soon discovered that their boredom had multiple sources. One was the language barrier. *I don't understand that, me,* wasn't a prank. They actually didn't understand my vocabulary. I learned to think carefully before I spoke; to phrase concepts in simple words, not to choose analogies beyond their experience. The few bright kids in this class had gotten by without working. They had no reason to change, or to want to work. How could I motivate them?

It was my most challenging assignment as a teacher.

Honors students also were used to doing well without working. They had never been asked to read four books a semester in addition to their textbook, *and* work on a research paper. They indignantly objected.

I ignored them. Here I was on sure ground. I knew how to help bright kids achieve success. Some years after I left the school, the federal government evaluated recent graduates because of the large amount of federal assistance given to these rural schools. I was thrilled to learn that my students almost unanimously put me down as the high school teacher who in their opinion had best prepared them for college by helping them develop the kinds of skills they were to need later on.

My relations with the administration weren't wonderful. The principal was an insecure middle-aged man who had taught grammar school most of his life. His appointment was political. Once in power, he ran the school as if it were a military academy. Class discussions, according to him, were merely the teacher's way of not doing their jobs. His concept of a good teacher was one who could maintain a quiet classroom, discipline, rules and the like. It did teach me that convent superiors were not the only threatened and insecure individuals who misused their power. Administrators in all institutions had to resolve the question of authority. The problems I faced as a member of a religious institution were no different than the problems of any other institution. It was rare to find an administrator secure enough to allow members in the ranks some freedom.

It was a good lesson. Despite all our conflicts, Mother Joseph respected me as a good teacher. Our concepts of education were not as disparate as I found mine to be with this new principal. She had not been able to accept bringing two hundred students into the city, scheduling them for interviews and being responsible for their punctuality. She had made things extremely difficult for me. But she did recognize that it was a good thing.

This man was different. His concept of learning was sitting quietly and memorizing. I don't think he could acknowledge that one could learn from life, from experiences such as meeting people. He had no respect for the self-educated wise man. He could not at all understand the value of exposing students to experiences which would bring them into contact with the realities of the world outside rural life. It was strange to find myself comparing Mother Joseph favorably with my new principal. I wondered if I had judged her too harshly. Perhaps religious life was not as bad as I had thought.

Northern Maine was giving me a new perspective on religious life and on teaching. I was happy to have this opportunity. I saw that despite the stern hierarchical structure of the religious community, the schools I had taught in previously were run more democratically and allowed for more teacher initiative than this one.

My stay in Northern Maine had other rewarding aspects. Removal from New York, the center of activity, was not a thing that I had relished. I liked being in the turmoil of new ideas. I had grown by leaps and bounds during my last four years; I had grown intellectually, in my appreciation of group living and in the acquisition of the skills necessary for success in dealing with other people.

Nevertheless, several factors made New York a difficult place to live and an almost impossible site for true experimentation. First of all, one was always under the nose of the authorities. Even if a superior held liberal views and would have liked to experiment with a different style of life, it was difficult to deviate from the "established way." At any moment, the provincial superior could "drop in." If superiors had been trained or encouraged to develop their initiative and creativity, the commanding presence of the provincial superior would not have been an obstacle, but superiors were viewed as guardians of the rule. If a superior deviated from orthodoxy, she would most likely be reprimanded or removed.

In Northern Maine, a superior could allow more freedom to the sisters, as there could be no impromptu visit. The provincial superior paid a formal visit to each convent in Maine once a year. During this time, she checked financial records and reviewed major problems facing the local superior. For example, she might opt for a new furnace, decide whether to buy a new car, determine pay for lay help. As was required by canon law, she saw each sister privately. She had little time to observe how the rule was being implemented in that house. Living in remote Northern Maine have us all more freedom. And since the local superior was not under pressure, she put less pressure on us.

In New York, convent life had been was tense for another reason. At Christ the King, every superior who was en-route to Haiti, Colombia, Peru, Canada, the Midwest, or from these points to Europe would stop over. It was a new school. a large convent with several private rooms and easy access to the airports. Since it was reputedly one of the best schools in the area the American Province wanted to show it off. With all these visitors we always had to be on our best behavior.

The presence of nearby convents was another source of stress especially for the superior. When asked to permit the sisters an extraordinary outing, a superior always contended with what superior so and so was going to do in this case? The thinking went: "If I say yes, and she says no, it will appear that I'm lax in interpreting the rule, I guess I'd better say no." Thus, even moderate superiors who might otherwise have tried to experiment felt compelled to maintain tradition.

The separation of work from the rest of life made our lives less stressful. In Maine, the sisters taught in the public schools. School decisions were not religious community decisions. Here school concerns did not serve to divide the community. Far from university centers, the sisters did not attend graduate school part time, as was the case in New York. Thus we had much more leisure time. We read, listen to music, and relax in a way most of us had never experienced in our previous convents.

Finally, the convent had been in this rural town for over fifty years. Many families had relatives among the sisters. The sisters were viewed as a part of the village community and their participation in the political life of the town was natural.

But for the first time in my life, I felt listless. We started school in early August to accommodate the fact that school would recess for three weeks in late August and early September for the harvesting of the potato crop. For teachers, this was the golden opportunity to readjust plans for the year. Usually my mind raced with ideas of what to do, new projects, a new book to assign, a point to make in class discussions, a pertinent current event. I should have been breathless with enthusiasm and energy.

Instead I prepared classes with effort. I found myself daydreaming, reliving the three-day workshop until I had memorized every minute detail of it. What did it mean for me? Did I secretly desire male attention, such as to draw Mike and now Paul in this way? Why did I feel so listless?

An hour would elapse when I would find myself staring at the same page. I sat up nights reading Steinbeck, Hemingway and filling in the gaps of my reading of Camus - all in an effort to keep my mind occupied.

Camus, another one of those religious men without religion.... I read his speech to the monastery of Discalced Carmelites with avid curiosity. I sought to know if it was necessary to be religious to be a good man. And everywhere the answer was the same, no!

Feeling confused and cut off from my friends, I began corresponding with former students, friends and sisters in other convents. I remember receiving a buoyant and vibrant letter from Father Berry and feeling uplifted by his joy, his confidence in me and the assurance of warmth from my friends.

Work, the letters, the novels all staved off my depression, but only for a time. Nothing was resolved and I knew it. I grimly weighed the prospect of speaking with Father Daly. His visit was approaching and I had to make a decision soon whether to see him or not. I viewed him as a close ally of Mother Rosemary and believed that he would verbalize her disapproval of me - that he would say: "You must be patient. Changes take time. You are too demanding." It would be the same old story. Still, I needed to speak to someone, so I decided to go ahead with it.

I can't recall now when I first talked to Father Daly, but it must have been some time before Christmas. I had worked out pretty well in my mind what I wanted to talk about - my trouble with superiors, the false accusations, the feeling of not being trusted.

I was tense when I turned the knob and entered the room. I smiled at Father. It was a forced smile. I could feel my lips tremble. I sat down on the edge of the easy chair that was placed before his. I opened my mouth to begin and instead of speaking, I let out a loud anguished cry and heard myself shouting: I *hate religious life, I hate it, I hate it, and I hate it.* I burst into tears.

I was shocked. What was I saying? I couldn't stop crying. My body was shaking as I sobbed. I can't remember when I cried so much and so long. I used up all his handkerchiefs and most of the Kleenex box. I never got another word out except to say, "I'm sorry" between the tears, "I can't stop."

It was well over an hour before the sobs subsided to a whimpering. My face was swollen and itchy. My body ached. I felt exhausted and spent.

Father Daly had said nothing except to reassure me quietly that it was all right to cry.

Now he glanced at his watch and advised me. "Sister, I think that you should go to bed and rest. Maybe you could come back tomorrow if you feel like it." I was grateful for the easy dismissal.

Though my face was still swollen the next day, I felt calm, expecting that with the outburst over, I would be able to discuss more easily.

This time, I didn't scream. No words at all. I just began to cry and spent the entire hour crying. I was confused and embarrassed. I had been so totally unaware of my hurt and hostility. Should I try speaking to him a third time? I mistrusted myself, but I decided to go ahead with it because Father Daly would not be available for at least two months.

It was better this time. I cried softly and talked through the tears. Why had I been sent to Maine? I had tried to be a good religious. Why was I being punished? Was religious life only fit for those who bowed their heads submissively to everything whether they thought it was reasonable or not? What did they expect of me? I had entered the order with the intention of devoting my talents to it and to the Church. Instead I was being stifled. I found myself recounting story after story giving details that I believed I had forgotten.

"Now people tell me that I'll be a superior someday," I said. "I don't want to be a superior. Superiors are destroyers of people." I gave examples of how superiors managed to undermine the self-confidence of the Sisters.

Father Daly said, "I feel like I've been watching a flower attempting to grow in barren soil and each time it sprouts, someone comes along and moves a stone to cover it. It must be very frustrating for you."

His analogy was painful. As he spoke I felt like a heavy stone was being placed on me. I felt struck down, punished, and reprimanded all at once, for no clear reason. It sent me into another fit of sobbing.

Father Daly merely listened as I spoke.. He occasionally put questions to me to help me clarify my thoughts. I was surprised and happy to find him so sympathetic.

It would be at least six to seven weeks before his next visit. We discussed what I should think about until I saw him again. I had described my listlessness and laziness and exposed my feelings of guilt over not working as hard as I used to.

"Do you prepare your classes, Sister?"

"Of course," I answered.

"Then, why do you feel guilty?"

"Well, I could be better prepared. There are several projects I could undertake."

"Yes, Well, I think it would be good for you not to be so compulsive about your work. Try not preparing occasionally. You've taught four years now. Surely you know most of the material. I 'm sure your students will not suffer from it. In fact, it might remove some of the pressure you feel and make you more relaxed with them."

We discussed the daily schedule and decided that I should make use of the half hour of free time allowed us from 4 to 4:30 to relax in the common room, listen to music and force myself not to bring a textbook to read or papers to correct.

I knew what he said was reasonable but I wondered if I was able to accomplish it. I remember sitting stiffly in our newly acquired easy chairs (we were now permitted to use them), closing my eyes, and telling myself to relax. It became easier as the days went by and I began to feel happier and more able to work. I was relieved and felt that perhaps I could "make it" in the convent.

My feeling of relief was short-lived however. I found myself fighting depression again. Most of the time, I managed to stave off depression by virtue of the fact that I had to get up early, go to chapel for prayers, breakfast and then to school. After school there was always some activity, classes to prepare, papers to correct, prayers and dinner. By the time night came, the fatigue of the day enabled me to sleep.

Vacation was a different matter altogether. With no activities to keep going, my mind became cluttered with depressing doubts. We were in the process of building a new convent. The older sisters were living in the original convent, and the younger sisters lived in the old boarding school quarters. A long corridor connecting the two buildings separated the boarding school from the convent. Five of us shared the top floor of a huge dormitory building, and five others shared the second floor. When Christmas vacation time rolled around, we brought up a phonograph from one of the classrooms and some records. It was relaxing to sleep late, listen to music, take naps, and talk freely-freedom we had not experienced since entering the convent.

This leisure, instead of providing a healthy respite, intensified my lack of inner quiet. I found myself seeking out my friends, to do things so I wouldn't have too much time alone.

Just prior to Christmas, we addressed Christmas cards to various people. The team leaders of the fall workshop were among the recipients. . I eagerly grasped the opportunity to write Paul a note.. The note I wrote to Paul showed my loneliness . I didn't realize it then, but surely Paul picked up on my state of mind.

I was tense and afraid to open his card when I saw the return address. It was a tender note. He confessed that he had also mulled over our experience and had hoped that our lives would have been different, so that we could have developed a relationship. However, things being the way they were he had developed a relationship with a woman he had known for a number of years, and he intended to marry her. He asked me not to be hurt by his decision and to remember the experience as one that he would always cherish and find meaningful.

After reading his note, I was stunned. First of all, I was pleased to think that Paul's feelings for me were deeper than I had imagined. His decision to marry had another effect on me – but his decision to marry alerted me to the fact that life was passing me by. He had taken his future into his own hands.

What was I going to do? "Where was I going?" as he had put it to me. I didn't know. I had not realized how intense this personal experience had been. Through the months, I had successfully put it out of my conscious mind. The effect of the note was to stir it up in me again. I wondered what it would have been like if I hadn't been a nun - if I had been able to cope with this relationship? Would I have been happier? It brought home a clear message: there were other Paul's in the world, i.e., men capable of loving me. Perhaps I could only be happy with this kind of intense one-to-one relationship.

A week later, we received news that Charles Davis was leaving the priesthood and intended to marry at the end of the month. Charles Davis was a British Catholic Theologian, a priest who was a hero in the American Catholic World. His book, Liturgy and Doctrine, explained the foundations of the current radical theological movement and his lucid moderate liberalism was evident in his monthly articles appearing in the Jesuit publication, **America**.

I was shaken by Davis' decision. His reasons for leaving the Church and the priesthood were familiar. I agreed almost completely with them. On January 8, I wrote in my diary:

This week, I heard of Charles Davis' decision to leave the priesthood and the church because of the rigidity that he had encountered. 'concern for the truth and for persons'. I felt terrible anguish of many Christian hearts at this moment. I thought of Pope Paul and Charles Davis' friends and of the many Christians who are now suffering for the Church and because of the structures in the Church. I thought of myself. What does God want in our day from our generation?

I didn't see Charles Davis as a *"renegade priest leaving the Church for a woman"* as others did. I regarded him as a symbol of all of us in the ranks who were struggling with the same problems, who were asking the same questions. I wondered if we would make the same decision.

Davis's announcement was followed in less than three weeks by that of Jacqueline Grennan that she was leaving the Sisterhood. Jacqueline Grennan was the president of Webster College and had received national publicity through articles in Life magazine for her forward looking, even radical ideas on education. She was a member of the President's Council for Economic Opportunity and an outspoken member of the American Sisterhood arguing for reform of the convents and the rules. She did not speak of marriage, nor did she announce that she would leave the Church. Her declaration was merely that she was unable to function well within the structures of the religious life, that she would maintain a close relationship with her community, the Sisters of Loretto, but that for her own sake, it was best that she leave.

I did not like Jacqueline Grennan. I had met her a year or so earlier. She had stayed overnight at Christ the King while attending a religious education conference held at the School. I was not sympathetic with her. Nevertheless, if I was going to leave, it was more likely that I would follow her lead rather than that of Charles Davis. Leaving the Church was inconceivable to me at that time and even admitting that I was interested in marriage was out of the question.

I laid all this confusion at the feet of my superior, Sister Mary Joy. I had been reluctant to discuss my concerns with her, though in some ways, Sister Mary Joy was a happy choice. She held me in high esteem both as a teacher and as a person. Furthermore, since we had been in the ranks together in Ozone Park and at Christ the King, she had witnessed Sister Joseph's hostility to me and wanted to "repair the damage." She thought of me as one of the Congregation's most gifted members who would render it great service as a superior and administrator. She feared that I would become so fed up that I might leave in disgust. Her positive feelings towards me made it easy for me to confide in her. Still, Sister Mary Joy was an anxious woman. Her need for approval was key to most of her behavior and led her to exaggerated attempts to attain consensus before making community decisions. Moreover, she tended to twist things, though not consciously or maliciously. She would repeat something she had been told, slightly twisted if need be to make it palatable to her listener.

Despite her good will and general warmth, I worried about exposing myself to her, but my need to talk was too great to hold off until Father's visit. I told her about my experiences with Paul and what it seemed to mean for me.

As I should have guessed, she became very involved in the details of the story.

"What did he say when you said...? What did he do...? Did he..?" I sensed her anxiety mixed with a voyeuristic curiosity. Did she want to know whether there had been any physical intimacy? I asked.

"Yes."

"No," I answered, realizing my mistake in speaking to her. "Nothing like that. Paul is a mature man who understood the possible traumatic consequences of that sort of behavior."

I was annoyed as she persisted in asking about seemingly irrelevant details . I then realized that she was attempting to experience vicariously by extracting my interaction with Paul. I was sorry I had said anything.

I soon was frustrated by another incident. Mother traveled to New York for a Superior's meeting and upon her return reported on what she had heard. She had had a long talk with Mother Benedict. They had discussed Mother Rosemary's, attitude towards me. She confided this conversation to me, unable to recognize that knowledge of it could only cause me more pain. I was ambivalent, wanting to know, but recognizing how difficult it would be for me to bear the knowledge.

I recorded my feelings in my diary on January 21st: Reflections on Mother Benedict's remarks to Mother:

The fact that Mother Rosemary told Mother Benedict (she must have) that I presented things as if I don't think they have any intelligence; I take nothing for granted. She felt I was accusing her of not doing what she should do.

Mother Benedict: "Yes, she has insight, but people feel she judges them, categorizes them and they can't grow any more. I guess they feel frozen in their categories."

I felt overwhelmed by a feeling of hopelessness that I am myself judged, placed in a category and I'm judged to be okay if only I agreed. Religious life seems to be the model life for the ordinary person who wants some voice, but not that much, some responsibility, some freedom. It seems totally unsuited to anyone who has an original idea. One can't step out of line, think differently, etc. It makes others too uncomfortable. This life is not made for people with ideas that might cause a radical change. It is too structured. Somehow, we can't seem to break out of them.

The same old story. I had that sense of weariness again, that sense of futility, of being misjudged, no matter what.

Deep down in my heart of hearts, I must have known at that time that eventually I would leave. It was, without a doubt, very much on my mind every day. Proof of it was that I wrote a long letter to my sister informing her of my confusion and deliberations about leaving. The letter was packed with details of "What life has been like," obviously my attempt to justify any future move.

I also decided to warn my mother about the possibility I might leave. Despite my mother's initial opposition to my becoming a nun, it was something she was resigned to it. She took comfort in the fact that I was settled. I wasn't sure how she would react. I called her one Saturday and asked her if she could come up for a weekend. I explained that I wanted to talk with her and that it seemed best if we had time together alone. She agreed, and came up at the end of February. There was a terrible snowstorm the evening of her flight and the plane had to land in Bangor, some 200 miles away. The airlines provided taxi service for the northbound passengers, but it was a full four hours before they arrived in Presque Isle, the plane's original destination. It was an extremely bright moonlit night, quite beautiful as we drove along watching the light dance on the freshly fallen snow.

Mom was tired and the drive to the Convent was another two hours. It must have been grueling for her, but I was so anxious about the whole situation that I kept her up to talk. I presented her with the constitutions and customs sheet, telling her to read them, and then proceeded to tell her story after story describing my nine years in religious life. I explained that I hadn't always been aware of how I was feeling but my discussion with Father Daly had enabled me to face some of these hidden feelings. It was hard to tell where all this would lead me but possibly I could leave.

I guess I really wanted to impress her with the fact that there were good reasons for my leaving convincing myself at the same time.

She sat there and quietly listened to me. "Rachel, why didn't you tell me? Why didn't you leave? You're an intelligent girl. How could you continue in this way?"

"I don't know, Mom. I thought something was the matter with me - that I was wrong because I could not accept things as they were, that I should try harder and adjust."

"You know, you can leave now. You can come with me when I leave. This isn't religion, this is nonsense."

"Listen Mom, I'm not sure that I want to go home. I think that I have a lot to offer the Congregation, and the Church, I could certainly help reform this congregation. It has already changed a great deal and will change greatly in the future. I'm respected by the sisters in the community and it's more than likely that I will have power in the future to make things better for other people. Maybe I should stay, I'm not convinced that I should leave."

Over the next two days, I talked more while she listened. My mother was a warm and loving person who made few demands. If anything, she was too passive in directing my life. She left on Sunday morning, assuring me that any time I wished to return, the door was open. Every single Saturday after that, she called to ask how I was and to repeat her assurance of love, interest and welcome to return home. I felt guilty that she went through such expense to call me for what I judged to be no *reason at all*, but her words gave me more confidence to make the decision to leave.

The winter passed without decision. Suddenly it was spring. I knew I had to make plans for the summer. The normal thing for me to do would have been to go back to St. John's for the summer and continue in the Asian Studies program. I knew that if I didn't stay in the convent, I would not continue at St. John's, so it seemed like a waste of time and money to go ahead. I decided to apply for a NDEA grant in history. That would be helpful in teaching and it wouldn't cost anything.

I talked it over with Father Daly, who not only agreed with me that it was a good idea, but suggested that being away from the Daughters of The Spirit for a time might give me a better perspective on things. I applied and was accepted at Dartmouth.

Looking back, I had already made the decision to leave, but I needed time to accept it.

I had another bout with depression before I left for school. It was just at the time that Father Terstroet, who was in the States for a special conference in Scriptural Interpretations, came to Maine for a special weekend of study. I was thrilled, and made an appointment to see him.

I wrote in my diary:

Yesterday, I had a wonderful meeting with Father Terstroet. He really gave me courage to go on because he felt that my ideas are right and worth fighting for. "God is molding you and forming you now so that you will understand the younger generation. You and I are co-creators. In the gospel, we see that the wheat is to grow with the thistle until the harvest, the grain must be crushed if it is to bear fruit. Father de Chardin in his time, was not appreciated. He said, "I will not leave the society" (of Jesus - Jesuits). God molds us through our passivities for the Church, for the Kingdom of God."

We always came back to the same thing - that suffering was a refining process out of which a better person emerged. I felt renewed.

The problem was that I constantly needed infusions of outside strength to keep going. I no longer had an inner belief in what I was doing. When you believe in yourself, when you believe in what you're doing, it's easy to weather all kinds of storms. But when you've lost that belief you have to search for external supports. The pattern of my life over the past couple of years had been to search for these external supports. If I read more theology, became more intellectually convinced, then I would believe. Or, if enough people assured me that in fact, yes, I was a good nun, and that I could both be myself and a good religious, then I would be assured. But these infusions lasted only temporarily until something threw me off balance again. So it was this time.

The superiors' retreat was scheduled for mid May and Mother again went to New York. We eagerly awaited her return because we lived cut off from the sisters. Besides, all of us were touched by the turmoil in the Church - Charles Davis' and Jacqueline Grennan's leaving had a profound effect many of us.. We all felt a little at sea. We awaited more news..

The religious habit was shorter, more modern. We had relaxed many of our silly confining rules. Family visits home were now permitted. We were allowed to have our pictures taken, were allowed to open gifts given to us. We were allowed to let our hair grow instead of routinely shaving it, and permitted to use color in our towels, linens and bedspreads.

The more we changed, the more I became aware that these were not the reasons why religious life was dated. It was something more fundamental. We spoke of it tentatively. We wondered about it in the secret twosomes and threesomes of our leisure gatherings. We dared not voice our doubts aloud, because were not prepared to defend our emerging conclusions.

In the fall, shortly after I had come to Maine, we had become embroiled with Mother Rosemary over a decision to build a new convent. We felt the time was not ripe for this large financial outlay. The sisters' continued presence in the public schools seemed doomed. We were no longer needed, at least we were not needed in the way we had been when, at the turn of the Century, a poor country priest had asked the sisters to come from France to teach his poor parishioners. There were no public schools to speak of then. There were very few well prepared local teachers. between.

At that time, the mission of the sister had been clear. But now what was our mission? Why were we still staffing the public schools when the State and local governments were replacing us with lay teachers.? The times had changed and we were being forced to change with them.

As the community, especially the younger sisters, argued these points, Mother Rosemary went ahead with plans to build a beautiful convent with sixteen private rooms, nine bathrooms and several large common rooms. It was to be built at an estimated cost of $100,000. We were appalled and we protested. We were told that our arguments had been heard, but that we had been overruled.

News of this decision left us wary of Mother Rosemary's sincerity. She often spoke of allowing the sisters to take more responsibility so as to develop more maturity. Yet, even though we felt we knew more than she did, our opinions had not been seriously considered.

Mother Mary Joy had other news for me. I had asked to go to New York with the sisters who were driving down for the summer and go on from there to Dartmouth. Sister Mary Joy had presented the request to Mother Rosemary for approval. The answer relayed to me through Mother Mary Joy was no. "Mother Rosemary said that you shouldn't go to New York because Superiors felt that the Sisters were upset enough without you going to upset them more."

How could I upset them? I wondered to myself.

"You know that Mother Provincial is afraid of you, Sister. You are a very persuasive person and furthermore, she doesn't know how to deal with your spontaneity."

My God, am I so irrational and difficult? I asked myself.

The comment sent me into a tail spin. Fortunately it was the end of the school year and we had a thousand things to do to prepare for graduation, to pack our things and to leave for the summer. I occupied myself with these things, trying to put the remark out of my mind, concentrating on my summer project. Maybe I would finally be motivated to end my enduring commitment

DARTMOUTH

I arrived in Hanover just after dusk on a warm Sunday evening. I felt very much "on stage", reasoning that nuns were few in number, so people would find me a curiosity. I had barely stepped out of the cab when a young man told me that there were two other sisters in the Institute. Was I looking for them?

"Oh my God," I thought to myself, just what I did not need. I did not relish the thought of having "nunny" nuns around me. Although once one of the strictest orders in the United States, the Daughters of the Spirit were now one of the most advanced in the theologically. I was accustomed to living with enlightened, sensitive and well educated sisters. Unless these nuns were extremely progressive, I knew I would find it difficult to be with them.

It was at least as bad as I had feared. Sister Michael, the older one, fit well the stereotype of the American nun. She expected laymen to offer her rides and do favors for her and was offended if this was not forthcoming. At 45, she gave little evidence of emotional maturity. She had a facile and simplistic explanation for changes in the Catholic Church and resisted any suggestions that things were in fact not as rosy as she painted them.

Sister Rose, my age, was an extremely shy and retiring young woman. Religious life offered a meaningful and satisfying existence enabling her to give to others without threatening the inner sanctum of her soul, placing no great demands on her emotions as would be the case in a personal relationship.

Sister Michael played the role of Mother Superior, knocking on my door at 5:30 a.m. to remind me to rush to Church in time to recite the

Divine office before Mass. I had not been going to daily Mass, nor had I appeared in Chapel each time she encouraged me to go along with her. Before I had left for Dartmouth, Father Daly and I agreed it would be best if I tried to relax and tried to be less compulsive about all my religious duties. I was faithful to the required daily prayers. I had a strong fear that I would reproach myself later if I failed. I did not want to feel I had brought it on by my own infidelity to prayer. Still, I did not want to keep a rigid schedule and especially not with Sister Michael. I decided not to explain anything to her and to let her cope with her own anxiety about my behavior. It was her problem. Rather than approach me for an explanation, she persisted in knocking on my door. It was her way of demonstrating her disapproval.

School got off to a rousing start. I breathed a sigh of relief when I discovered that neither of the two sisters was in my seminar. The institute was organized around one core course in American History attended by all the members. In addition, several smaller seminars were presented on specialized topics. I was assigned to "History and the Social Sciences- a look at the interdisciplinary approach between the two."

My seminar professor, Dr. Spitzer, was Jewish, in his mid-fifties, and spoke with a Bronx accent, successfully mingling the idiom of the street with an impressive erudition. He was clever and understandable. The students in the Seminar consisted of several men but just one other two woman. Early in the week we got into a discussion on the fear of communism in our society in the 1930's. Professor Spitzer talked about his membership in the communist party and the retaliation taken against him, resulting in his being black listed for many years from teaching in the New York State University system.

I listened intensely. I had spent my adolescent years reading about the Hiss Case, the McCarthy purges and the biographies of Whittaker Chambers, Elizabeth Bentley and others. From these I had formed a romantic picture of what life must have been like in the thirties, meeting in back rooms, discussing long into the night to find solutions to the country's social and economic dilemmas. I was sorry when class ended, and I was mulling over details as we broke for morning coffee. The half hour break was intended to remove the traditional barriers between faculty and students.

To my delight, I was standing in line next to Professor Spitzer. "Won't you sit down with me?" I asked.

He rolled his eyes and with a funny grin answered, "Oh no!" I didn't know what to make of it. Was he joking or serious? Did he mean, "Oh God, no, not you?"

"Well, I guess you don't have to if you don't want to," I replied with a smile, trying to hid my disappointment.

"Oh, I never do anything I don't want to do," he replied, and without pausing, pointed to a pair of chairs adding, "Let's sit down."

I was confused. Why the no, and then the yes. Not understanding, I decided to mask my confusion.

"You fascinate me and I'd like to get to know you better," I began in my unworldly way.

He tossed his head back and tensed up. "Why?"

"I don't know, I guess you regard the human race as fallible and yourself as part of that fallible race, and I appreciate that quality in you. So many professors exclude themselves from that category; besides, I enjoy your sense of humor."

"I don't want to you to get to know me too well. You have your faith, you keep it. I could disturb you. There are things in my life that you haven't experienced and it would be better if you didn't know about them."

Another mysterious statement. "Well, if that's the way you want it, and then tell me what you think of religious?"

"I don't know anything about religious life."

I was exasperated. He didn't want to talk about himself, and he had no opinion about religious life, "Well, everybody thinks something."

"You're the only religious I really know and when I look at you, I see only a very attractive woman, not a religious. I'm physically attracted to you. That's what I meant before about not getting to know me. I don't have a very high regard for chastity and I place a very high value on sex. If I got to know you, I'm not sure I could control myself and I feel that there's something in you which I'm not sure that you could control."

I remember thinking to myself that at that –like in the movies I should drop my cup and look aghast. I didn't know what I was thinking or what I was feeling.

I said with as much cool as I could manage, "Don't worry, I think I can control myself."

"As to the religious habit," he continued, "It gives you a spiritual quality, which is even more physically attractive."

I looked down at my coffee cup, wondering what to say. "Are you a believer?"

"No, I don't believe in anything. I do find myself placing more importance on moral values in our society, as I grow older, but certainly not on religion."

"How do you deal with the problem of after life?"

"I believe that I will live on in my books."

"And that is sufficient?"

He didn't answer. I did not really expect him to. Instead he began telling me about himself, his views on sex and morality. He had been an exchange professor for the State department and while in Cambodia and later in Japan, he had a mistress.

"It was very natural you see," he began, but we were interrupted.

All day long, I thought of that sentence, "I don't know if you can control that something in you." Today I would find that a very manipulative thing to say, making the other vulnerable by putting him in doubt about his ability to control himself. But at that time, I wasn't experienced enough to understand what was happening. His remark sent me into a long reexamination of my behavior. First, it had been Mike and then Paul, now this. Maybe I wanted him to find me attractive. Maybe I had unconsciously encouraged his attentions. I was worried about what his approach meant and wondered if I was to blame for this unseemly attention.

Since desiring or encouraging male attention was bad, I could not accept this aspect of myself. It was not consistent with being a good nun, so the only thing to do was to deny that it existed, or barring that, to deny any responsibility. I could not question myself in such frank terms, as "Was I being seductive or flirtatious?" I saw it only in terms of morality.

The next day at coffee break, Professor Spitzer motioned me into the next room.

I had an uneasy feeling about joining him but went anyway. He turned to me in all seriousness and said: "I have to apologize for my boldness yesterday. I guess I must have been drinking. I suppose I'm feeling very guilty about my past life and I wanted to tell you about it."

I laughed. "Well, you were drinking coffee so you were hardly drunk. Why are you saying this? Why are you apologizing? I don't think you are really sorry. I think you might be worried about what I really think of you."

"Well, I guess I want people to think well of me. But I may have given you the wrong impression. You see, I was alone in Cambodia, my wife was not with me."

"Are you close to your wife?"

"Yes," he answered thoughtfully. "In fact, our marriage is probably one of the most stable and satisfying marriages I know. Many of my friends and their wives are real drags. My wife and I are really compatible and our relationship is very satisfying, especially physically. I place a lot of importance on that aspect. It's more or less a measure of compatibility in other ways."

I didn't fully understand what he meant, but decided that thinking about it wouldn't help. I refrained from asking him to explain and dismissed the conversation from my mind.

In a funny kind of way, Professor Spitzer and I became friends.

My feelings toward him were suspended between fascination by him as an intellectual and fright of the emotion he stirred up in me.

The other person who influenced me that summer was Jim Gordon. A much younger man than Spitzer, Jim was teaching the core course in American History while he attempted to sort out things in his own life. He was drinking heavily that summer and rumor had it that he had a pretty bad marriage. He was fascinated by the idea of a modern woman locking herself in an institution. He was also fascinated that I was intellectually alert and quite competent as a student, cheery, bubbly and likeable. As I remember Jim had had no previous familiarity with nuns. He often remarked that he didn't find it strange that Sister Michael and Sister Rose had entered the convent. But why was I a nun? I was normal and happy.

The more Jim and others questioned me, the more I questioned myself about my motivation in becoming and remaining a nun. I wrote in my diary: *Can I live religious life in a positive way, without the drain of regret, looking back, wondering if marriage is more compatible with my personality, etc. Finding an adequate marriage partner would be a major problem. Would life with one man satisfy me? That's another question. This really has to be resolved though. I feel as if I'm living half in and half out at the present moment.*

I was beginning to see an alternative to my life. Trying hard to hide my mounting inner conflicts, I continued to engage in conversations that only served to intensify my inner struggle.

While at Dartmouth, the college sponsored a Fred Zinnemann film festival. ***The Nun's Story*** was one of his films selected for viewing – although it was seven years old. It was natural that classmates invited the 3 nuns to accompany them to view the film. As I watched the film, I became more and more tense. "Sister Luke" was harassed by her superiors and struggled with her vocation. After she returned to Belgium during WWII she was forced to submit to the Nazi authorities. I became so emotional during the film that I had to leave the theater.

A few days before the institute closed a group of us were invited for drinks at one of the married student's apartment. Jim and I sat next to each other and he began telling me how he enjoyed telling his friends about the "agnostic nun" he had met.

I was startled. "What does that mean?"

"Well, you openly search for the truth and at the same time you remain fully committed and dedicated."

I smiled. "Maybe the Jesuits are better off."

Everyone laughed and the conversation hung in the air.

Lucy, one of the few young women in the group, came over to me and whispered, "You know you're definitely Jim's favorite nun. He was telling me how impressed he was by you. He said, 'You know, she really challenged me in private. She's a very bright girl and with her interest in philosophy and religion she was the only one with the background to be the spokesman for the class, but she didn't take over. She was aggressive, but just enough. She just accepted her position, but always remained a woman. In private, she willingly questioned, but she defended in public the traditional Church position.'"

It was exciting and rewarding to have people say these things, but it scared me as well, because I knew the psychological cost of maintaining such a position. Later it was impossible to publicly defend the traditional church position..

The summer had been filled with conversation about religion and the ever present question: *"Why did you become a nun?"* The students generally had never thought of nuns as normal, but they found me exciting and knowledgeable. I had really changed their image of what a nun is like. I would say to myself: "Well this is certainly the right thing to do. I want to present the image of the modern woman who could have done anything, but who chose freely to do this. Only this kind of person who will make an impression. If nuns are weaklings, afraid of life, then religion will be seen as a refuge for these types."

Although I had enjoyed the summer, I looked forward to its end. I didn't think I had made any progress in coming to a decision and I felt anxious about the fall. I had a premonition - Something was going to happen soon. In retrospect, I probably just felt anxious about the decision I knew I had to make.

The night before we left, The institute held a banquet. Professor Spitzer and I sat next to each other.

We had a pleasant time. When dinner was over he turned to me and said, "I'll walk you back to the dorm."

"Okay," I answered, feeling flattered and happy that he had made the move and that I didn't have to make it.

We walked around for a bit.

"Are you anxious to get back to Maine?"

"Well, I really don't know how I feel. Yes and no, I guess. I was so physically and emotionally exhausted at the end of the year that I didn't think that I would ever want to go back. But now, I wish I could make some decision about religious life, to stay or to leave it. I went through such a period of conflict and that period isn't over really."

"Yes," he said, "I could feel the conflict. What caused it?"

"Well, it's whether I should stay in religious life or not. It's easy to say, you know, 'Stick up for your principles and fight for what you believe,' but it's hard to live a life without approval."

"Well, couldn't you find a way to serve the Church in a less structured situation? You could be free to develop yourself and your talents"

"I don't know. That's the point. I just don't know what to do. I don't know if the alternative is for me."

"Do you find it difficult to give up normal emotional satisfactions?"

"Do you mean marriage?"

"Yes, I guess so."

"Well, I think you can live a satisfactory life without sexual fulfillment if your other needs are taken care of. I mean if your life is fairly good in other ways: iIf you like your work, if you're convinced of what you're doing, then you can manage. The problem arises only if one's life is unhappy in all these other ways, then you begin to feel sexual loss."

"Well, I must confess that religious motivation is beyond me. I can't really understand it " he said.

"I've often wondered myself about the value of a religious life," I began. "During the summer I became aware of how easily the subject of conversation would turn to religion.   As a result, I can more easily understand how the religious nun is a sign of belief in an afterlife and a provocateur merely by her presence. It jolts people to think about the meaning of life. What I mostly wonder about is whether I can live it. I'm a very warm person. I mean I think that's a good thing, but it certainly brings its problems. Many sisters are like little girls who have never developed."

"Yes, often I find a pasty smile and there doesn't seem to be much underneath it, but with you there's a lot there."

We both laughed. He continued, "I think the Church needs people who are developed and warm to be a convincing witness to its truth."

"Whatever you do, besides developing yourself, get your degree, and establish yourself professionally. If you don't want to be a historian, then decide what it is you want to be and go after it. Whatever you do, don't give up religion."

"Oh, I wouldn't do that. I couldn't!"

"Sometimes people are driven to rejecting everything."

"I don't think I could, I'm much too involved emotionally."

We walked for a while in silence like two people who have known each other for a long time. My relationship to Professor Spitzer had that kind of quality almost from the beginning. We talked about his books, about the future and about the possibility of meeting again.

"You know, I think you should have had a daughter. You would have found that very satisfying."

"Funny you should say that. It's something that I have found hard to admit even to myself. But you're right, I would have liked a daughter."

We smiled, shook hands and said good-bye.

The next day I left. I had arranged to return to Maine with Aprile, a friend from high school days who was studying in Vermont. She was to pick me up in Connecticut in a week's time. On the bus to Connecticut panic set in. Though I had not given my conflict much conscious thought during the summer, now it became a pressing reality again.

Upon arriving in Connecticut, I encountered Mother Rosemary. I literally came across her in the hallway, both of us in a hurry. In the bustle and flurry of activity that accompanied the visits of the Provincial Superior, I hoped that my presence would go unnoticed. I didn't feel up to speaking with her. My heart sank as she motioned me to join her in an empty parlor.

"Sister, what have you decided?"

"I don't know. I really don't know where I am or what I'm going to do. I can't seem to say one way or another."

"Sister, you can't live like this forever. I think you should come to a decision. Let me know within the next few weeks."

I was frozen to the spot. I was frightened by her insistence, and I didn't like being pushed. I don't remember what I answered. I think I just filled up and we parted without further discussion.

I went back to Maine in an utter state of chaos.

Sister Aimee, the kitchen sister we had known since novitiate days, gave us a rich walnut covered layer cake to take with us as snack food along the way. I found myself gobbling it down in large chunks as I struggled to get a better grip on my mounting anxiety.

Aprile was wrapped up in her "boyfriend" problems and as I listened, I found my mind wandering.

"Two weeks!" It was an ultimatum. I felt sick from eating so much cake, or was it the indecision and anxiety?

What was I going to do?

The only solution was to stay. I surely could not make up mind in the next few weeks.

DECISION

I managed to defer my decision to leave by busying myself with school's opening. August passed into September, and it was potato harvest time again. The harvest recess usually lasted three to four weeks. Unlike the previous year, I was confident about my classes. Despite my depression I rallied my forces to prepare classes quickly. Once I accomplished this, I was left with a surplus of free time. I was beset by the same questions: "What should I do? What do I want to do? Should I stay? Should I leave?"

A fellow teacher loaned me several novels and I filled every free moment reading, hoping to forget my dilemma. It was the peak of autumn in Maine. The leaves had turned to various shades of red, orange and gold making the landscape into a rich tapestry. Climbing to the top of the hill, I would pass the Sisters' cemetery. It stood alone in the midst of pasture land, guarded by a wrought iron fence and a majestic pine grove. Occasionally, I walked through, looking at the names and dates, feeling myself a member in a long and beautiful procession of sainted women. How could I fail these pioneer sisters who had left France, coming to Maine to help teach the children of this once very poor rural isolated community?

I remembered the funeral of one of the sisters when I had been a young boarder of thirteen. The sisters had seemed so wonderful, so untouchable, so holy. I loved listening to the missionary sisters on leave from Africa, Haiti, Colombia, or Madagascar. I loved to their slide shows. It was an exotic world. I had wanted to be part of this larger than life order. As a sister in this order I would participate in the Great Christian mission of bringing love and solace to the world.

What had happened to this vision? I thought of Mother Mathilde and Mother Michael. If I were to leave my beloved Congregation, my beloved Sisters, how could they possibly understand? These women had loved me. They had nurtured me. How disappointed they would be! I wept for them and for myself.

I wished that Sister Mary Clare were still alive so I could discuss these matters with her. She had been my friend and advisor in high school. She had known me for a long time, but had died from cancer a few years before at age 42. I regretted my coolness toward her in her last years.

So many times in my growing years, I had walked this same dirt road. As boarders we often picnicked in the woods on the hill. The boarding school had been closed for some years now, a sign of the times. Were the priests and sisters who fled the confines of the ministry and the convents also a sign of the times? Was religious life doomed? Would it become extinct? I tried to push away these questions. My decision should be independent of the issue of the future of religious life. I did not want to camouflage my insecurities, my fears, and my failure by condemning the life. On this same hill eleven years ago, I had decided to enter the convent. Unconsciously I hoped that my faith would be renewed by visiting this sacred place. But no voice spoke to me. No inspiration came.

I hunkered down in the field to read: Camus, Hemingway, Steinbeck, Alain Robbe-Grillet, and Koestler. Instead of distracting me, each of these fed my thinking. In Arthur Koestler's <u>Darkness at Noon,</u> the author depicts his conflicts with the communist party - similar to my own conflicts with the religious order. I was confronted with the same kind of moral dilemma as the main character. I identified with him. The protagonist was instilled with a love for the common good, but also a belief that the individual good need not be suppressed for the good of the whole. It would find its true fruition only in the common good. But experience had taught him that often the collective judgment only represented collective weakness and did not, as communist orthodoxy suggested, overcome individual weakness. Moreover, this collective will, by placing itself in a superior position, was unrestrained.

It was a lesson that I too had learned, but training dies hard. I wondered if I could sacrifice the good of the Church for my own happiness. Did I lack the courage to continue because of my own weakness? Was my present harsh judgment of the religious structure merely an unconscious attempt on my part to justify myself? On the one hand, religious life seemed doomed, archaic and stifling; on the other, I felt that leaving the congregation would constitute running away from my Cross.

*　　*　　*　　*　　*

Surprisingly, we were granted permission to attend an education conference held in New York during the harvest recess. A group of us drove a full day to attend the conference. It was fun visiting friends and seeing some of my former students. I called Father Berry and arranged to see him. I spoke openly about my doubts and my uncertainties. I verged on tears as I spoke.

His calm and serenity were reassuring. He was untroubled by my doubts. "Leave, go to school. Feel free to leave," he advised. "Our lives are unpatterned. For a time you have spent your life in the religious order. Now God calls you to a new adventure. Feel lighthearted, daring."

I came away liberated. The world would not crumble if I should I leave the convent,. I could not feel lighthearted, or daring, but at least I was less anxious.

Back in Maine, my inner struggles began to reflect in my teaching. I was assigned to teach religion to students in their junior year, a year in which some abstract concepts were discussed. We came to the chapter entitled: "**Who is God?**" How was I to make a convincing case for his existence, I asked myself. I decided that the best approach would be to teach the chapter as honestly as I could, to present things as I saw them, controversial as that approach might be. I spent the better part of the preceding weekend preparing posters for my classroom to stimulate discussion.

"*God is Dead! Ha! Ha! Ha!*" was the sign that greeted each student as they came to my door on Monday morning. Quotes of Sartre, Camus, Kierkegaard, St. Paul, De Chardin and others lined the room. I'd collected pithy pro and con arguments; arguments they had never been exposed to before. They would not have to wait until they were twenty-six to ask themselves some of the key questions a believer must confront.

I knew this approach was revolutionary and threatening to the residents of this small Catholic town. But it meant a lot to me to be sincere and honest in presenting the "*truth*" as I saw it.

The reaction was much stronger than I had anticipated. The students -- even the faculty, filed through my classroom to see for themselves the display of shocking and scandalous statements against organized religion.

"Are you a Catholic, Sister?" some of the students kidded me half in jest. I smiled in response. We had lively discussions in religion classes those days. I considered it important to create an atmosphere of openness and questioning about beliefs that had been taken for granted. It was very successful!

Here again, the atmosphere created was merely an extension of my own uncertainties and the openness that I had created was in a way an attempt to justify my doubts and my step away from orthodoxy. How long could I continue this pretense? The thought that I was a living a lie began to trouble me.

"Sister Rachel Mary." The sound of my name sent me into long ponderous reflections. "Sister" ...Here I am; I represent the Church and its beliefs, beliefs I am no longer sure I can affirm. "Sister."

"Yes," I would finally answer. And so it went. Some days tears rolled down my cheeks at the mere thought of not being able to decide.

A few weeks later, Sister Theresa of Avila, wrote a brief letter informing all of us that she had decided to take a year's leave of absence from the community. I was shocked! Sister Theresa of Avila was a good friend but we had shared very little of our intimate feelings. I thought her unworldly. As the intellectual core of the liberal wing, she seemed the most unshakable of all of us. I needed to talk to someone, and I eagerly awaited Father Daly's visit. I became depressed and weary. The only thing to do now was to follow Sister Theresa of Avila's lead. I would request a year's leave of absence from the community. I could not bring myself to leave the congregation entirely. This way, I could live apart and decide during that year what I would do in the future. However I did recognize that leaving the congregation entirely and obtaining dispensation from my vows from Rome was too big a hurdle right now.

In October, 1967 I made the decision to request a leave of absence, almost eleven years after entering the convent. I felt relieved. Life was easier after that. I had to inform my superior, Father Daly my psychologist/priest therapist, my Provincial Superior, and write to Rome for permission to take a leave.

I first told Mother Mary Joy. *"But Sister, you mustn't leave the community. You are a bright, energetic and creative person. You will no doubt be a superior someday. If you leave the Congregation, what will become of it? We must struggle from the inside to change the community and make of it something meaningful for this generation."* It was a convincing argument, but I no longer had the energy to meet her challenge. For the first time I was totally unmoved.

I spoke to the provincial superior and to my mother. I knew what I must do. So, I sat down to write the long and painful letters to the Provincial Superior and to the Superior General.

November 11, 1967

Dear Mother Rosemary,
    As I wrote to you earlier this week, I had already made a decision and finished a long letter to you when Father Daly arrived. My emotions were mixed, happy to be able to talk

236

things over, but exhausted at the thought of
having to "hash out" the problem all over again.
I am very happy now that he did come "in the nick
of time, not that it has changed my decision but
I feel much better about it. And the reasons are
clearer.

I have certainly given much thought to my
decision since I saw you in August. I would like
to have a leave of absence from the community in
January. I hope I can clearly explain what I
think and feel, and the reasons why I decided to
take this step

When I saw you in August, I, for some
reason - probably emotional upset- misunderstood
you and Mother Benedict as saying to me "Make a
decision before the end of the week". I believe
Mother Mary Joy told you of this because she told
me you said you had not meant this. My emotional
reaction to this brief conversation was the
feeling of being pushed to say definitely YES or
NO-to stop delaying a basic decision of personal
commitment; that it was not religious life
changing that would solve the problem. I did say
this to some friends when I went to New York in
September and Mother Benedict wrote me about her
confusion over my expressing gratitude for the
"freedom from pressure to stay" on the one hand
and feeling on the other that neither of you
really cared what decision I made, just as long
as I made one. Yes, I am grateful for the
freedom and I sincerely meant this, and do mean
it. Yet, at this Connecticut encounter, my
delayed reaction to the whole thing was to feel
that you did not care. Not because you did not
want to care but because I don't think you could
care anymore. I felt that you were very tired,
and that it is too much to expect for it to be
otherwise. There is only so much emotional pull
a person can take and I really think that for
your own sake, you can't afford to "emote" over
everyone. That's what I felt and expressed. I

am sorry now that I said this, though it is hard
to live in isolation and not to say to people you
are close to how you feel. I see that it has led
to more misunderstanding.-God knows we've already
had too much of that. Perhaps I should have
written to you and told you I felt this way- but
I honestly believed you when you expressed on
several occasions that you were too pressured to
answer the sisters' letters and that you couldn't
personally handle their problems – that the
sisters should as much as possible speak to their
superiors -that your job was to deal with the
superiors.

I also expressed the feeling that I have
that many people would breathe more easily if I
left. Yes I feel this way. I don't consider
myself as extraordinarily ___(word not clear),
nor "powerful", not "talented" nor "creative ",
Perhaps this is because I express what I think
and most people, as I am finding out, don't. At
any rate, I feel that you think of me in terms of
complaining about the existing structures of
religious life.
**Note: The beginning of this next paragraph
was cut off when the original was bound in an
earlier draft.**

saying that you do not think this, but I
feel that this is your attitude towards me –
right or wrong, conforming to reality to reality
or not, that's what I feel. Perhaps I have not
asked you about it so specifically before because
I'm afraid you'll say yes; it is your attitude.
I don't know. It is hard to explain the basis of
feelings, even to oneself.

Despite these unavoidable
misunderstandings, I cannot say no to religious
life; however I cannot bring myself to commit
myself without reserve. I explored with Father
Daly the reasons why I think I feel this way.

My ten years in the community have been
lived in "confusing" circumstances, beginning
with the postulate, novitiate, juniorate, college

and through Ozone Park and Christ the King.
Father feels that these years of repressed
hostility have taken deep roots because of the
intense emotional life I lead, and that this has
not had sufficient release, consequently, I am
not freed from these restraints and cannot bring
myself to commit myself to what I fear
emotionally - The religious life has become
oppressive in my mind, because of the built-up of
tension held in for so long. He has said that I
can't expect to desire what has been a
suffocating experience for me.

I wonder too if my experience with the boy
in college and the consultant in the T-group, a
professor this summer, these being the most
prominent indicate within myself an unconscious
desire and need for these attractions and
attentions. This summer I experienced something
a little different. One of my professors told me
he was physically attracted to me and he did not
value chastity and he wouldn't want to get too
close to me for fear he could not control himself
since he did not usually exercise control in
these matters. I was stunned at first and a bit
frightened. I explained that I was quite self-
controlled and had no intention of becoming his
mistress. He apologized the next day and at the
end of the summer said that this had been his
first real meeting with a person whose "behavior"
was religiously motivated. And that it had caused
him to re-evaluate his own life position
regarding God, morality and religion generally.
Regardless of the outcome, I was left with the
question: would a man normally approach a woman
in this manner, especially a religious woman if
he did not feel a receptivity in her
beforehand?...a receptivity in this case that I
was not aware of? In other words, is there in me
an unconscious attraction for and/or need of this
kind of male attention? Despite the fact that I
have not been physically disturbed by these

experiences, and none have "involved" me in any outward manifestation of affection, I wonder why these things happen to me. It's not the usual experience of sisters.

Father's reaction was that my forthright nature might appear brazen and appeal to men generally -My outgoing nature and natural warmth could also be a reason. Of course the man's previous experience, philosophy etc., could account for the approach. He does feel however that I should "keep this door open" to explore further.

I am not terribly pulled by marriage. I don't think I have ever really desired children and though I enjoy male companionship I can't really picture myself as wife and mother. I honestly think I would find marriage limiting – but am I being honest with myself?

At the end of a few lengthy sessions, Father attempted to summarize what he got out of what I said, and to give me a few points to reflect on. It's at this point that Father likened it to being on the edge of the swimming pool and unable to jump in.

Perhaps I would need more help to find the block. Right now I know one thing, I cannot continue in this state until June. I spoke to Mother Benedict when she came in August- I'm sure she told you of this. I decided right after this talk to finish out the year and ask for exclaustration in June. However as time passed I found myself in a terrible state of depression, very tense and irritable. I realized then that it was with good reason that Mother Benedict had asked me if I could last the year. Though School has been better than last year in many ways, I find it harder to be "in it", and to be patient because of my own inner conflict. I find myself scolding for no reason and shocked myself when I told an elder sister not to talk to me, that I was in a bad mood. That is not me.

School is a pressure in another way. As the year progresses, we will be getting more involved in planning for curriculum renewal – and the workshop this coming summer. I am already on the planning council and it would be difficult to stay on and pull out at the last minute. This week we found out about the working committees and I was placed chairman of the Social Studies Group (Sr. Georgio was assigned elsewhere).

Leaving on exclaustration in January seems the best solution at this time. To leave then however, means breaking our contract which requires a thirty-day written notice.- If this means thirty teaching days, I would have to serve notice by November thirtieth. There is also a possibility that Mr. Houghton might feel it would be better to leave during the Christmas break so that the students would have time to hear about it and adjust. I think it will be shocking experience for them as well as for the lay teachers. There is no interterm recess in January. I would like to ask him what he thinks. I am presuming it is my duty to inform-unless you think otherwise- also, that there will be no sister to replace me.

Someone suggested asking for my obedience to New York where the teaching day would not be such a drain. I can't deny that teaching here is the hardest it's ever been- in fact the first real hard teaching I've had to do. Yet, the community atmosphere is good. The sisters on the whole are optimistic about the future of religious life, of our congregation and of our province. They read and we have good discussions. There is a real concern I feel for the Church and our part in its apostolate. We have problems as a community -no community hasn't- but I doubt if I could find elsewhere the openness and forgiving charity as I do here. On our brief visit to New York in September, I found the sisters generally tense and the conflict that I thought we had passed through two or three years ago - Let's call it the

Liberal/Conservative struggle - still a problem. It would merely be replacing one pressure by another. Ultimately all it could do would be to create an atmosphere anyway and the decision would still have to be made by me. Father agreed with me.

As far as time out is concerned is concerned, I'm not sure how exclaustration works and the length of time one can have, however, I'd like longer than a year so that if I should go to school in September, and decide to return, I could finish out the year.

My mother is prepared for the eventuality since last February, so I'm sure I could live with her in Boston.

In the midst of all this, I have thought over and prayed over almost constantly whether I am called to/ want to/ and can live the religious life. Meditating on St. Paul's epistles inspire in me the desire to commit myself to the apostolate such as is possible in a community of religious women. I am aware, not fully I am sure, of the higher caliber of people I've been living with these past years. I know I cannot find such wonderful Christian women in so great a number as I have found here. Still I cannot bring myself to make the commitment.

I spoke to Father Daly about the fear I have of remaining in a state of indecision, he felt exclaustration might solve my problem by enabling me to look at religious life from another perspective and say definitely "this is what I want" - or on the other hand, find the lay state that I want. However, in the event that I cannot decide I would probably need the help of psychiatrist. If it should come to this, I'm sure I can contact Father for the names of some respected psychiatrists in the Boston area.

I have tried to be as honest with you as I am with myself. There are no other hidden motives, forces, drives etc., that I am aware of. I am sorry for the suffering I may have caused you. Despite my seemingly overly critical

attitude, I do feel that the Province has
benefitted immensely from the insight you have
given the sisters and the projects initiated.
You are a good woman Mother. I m sorry I haven't
gotten to know you better.
        Sincerely,

        Sister Rachel Mary of Jesus

December 14, 1967

Reverend Mother Francois du Christ
Superior general

Reverend and Dear Mother,
I freely and willingly request an Indult of
exclaustration and release insofar as is
possible, from my three perpetual vows of
Poverty, Chastity and Obedience which I made on
the second of February, 1959. I have carefully
considered this and have consulted with a priest-
psychologist regularly since August 1966.

I have found religious life stifling and
upsetting during most of my years in the
community. For a long time, I tried to be the
person demanded by others, by the novitiate
model, by each of my superiors; I tied to fit the
type, to be a good religious. It seemed as if I
never measured up. As I did more reading and
studying what religious should be, I began to
realize that it wasn't all me that didn't fit,
but that many things in the religious life were
not human and tolerable. I hoped for change, and
the chapter of 1964 renewed this hope. The
results however showed that a renewal would be
long in coming – it would mean a change in
mentality on the part of many sisters and
superiors. I told myself I understood this, and
I thought I accepted it.

In the 1965-1966 school year, I felt very
tense and pressured – At that time, I experienced
many doubts concerning the Faith and this added
to my unrest. In June, 1966, I received a change
of house. The change came when I was already re-
considering my vocation. It was at this time
that I decided to expose my fears that I was not
suited for religious life. I began visits with
the priest-psychologist. I soon found that many

of my reactions to superiors' desire to make me
humble by humiliations and the like had become
buried feelings of hostility. These had been
piling up. As a result, I felt that I would
collapse psychologically if I stayed in religious
life. Father helped me to see that my problems
with faith were tied up emotionally with my
problems with authority. Little by little, much
of this pressure has been lifted, but I still
can't say that I really can psychologically live
this life forever; nor am I convinced that I
can't. I'm asking for time out to get into an
atmosphere where I would feel more free to come
to a decision.

I entered the community at seventeen after
six years of boarding school. I realize now that
a real choice for religious life was never really
made before, though I thought I made it many
times. I had never really considered marriage as
a possibility.

It was suggested that I go away to school
this summer to see if the time away would help
create a sufficient "distance" to re-evaluate.
It did not. When I returned, I found myself
upset to be unable to come to a decision. It has
made me tense and irritable.

I know I could get an obedience to another
house if I wanted but the community is lovely,
the sisters very charitable and understanding.
The houses where I could go are in the New York
area where some sisters are still opposing the
'new thinking", where I feel the atmosphere of
the houses themselves are tense. Instead of
helping me, I think it would only intensify my
own tenseness.

I hope that the time away will give me
the strength and distance I need to think more
clearly – to find it within myself to choose the
religious life once and for all – if such be
what I feel God is asking of me.

I love the sisters of the Congregation and

I am taking this step with much hesitation -still
I feel I must.   I thank you Reverend Mother for
your prayers as I am one of those "sisters in
trouble" for whom you pray.
        Sincerely
        Sister Rachel Mary of Jesus

It was a painful experience with misunderstandings on both sides.
But my mind was made up. I went through the steps mechanically -
pressing forward, despite my lingering doubts.   I tried to continue my
normal routine while waiting for the responses to my letters.

Our new convent was ready, so our Thanksgiving weekend was
filled with packing and moving. Occasionally, I broke away from the group
to wander the long corridors of the old convent in an attempt to recreate
my past, to understand my roots and my future. I already felt cut off from
all the things I had loved - from my students, from my sisters, from the
child like good times we had together. I sat in the chapel and remembered
the days I had spent there as a youngster trying to decide whether or not to
enter the convent. I felt afraid for myself, for the Church. I cried to relieve
the tension.

In late November, I made an appointment to speak with the
superintendent of schools to inform him of my decision and to request a
secular replacement. I volunteered to stay to the end of the semester (end
of January) but he felt that Christmas was a more natural break, and felt
that it would be too much emotional strain for me to stay much beyond
that point. Sister Giorgio had guessed my decision. This made it easier by
allowing me to discuss it somewhat. As Christmas week approached, I told
Sister Mary Joy that I wanted to tell the sisters myself. There were several
elderly who had known me from the days when I had come to the
Daughters of the Spirit as a young innocent boarder of eleven years. I did
not want them to hear of my decision in a general announcement. So I
chose to tell each one individually. Each was a painful farewell.

During my last week in the convent, Mother Mary Ambrose, my
superior in my Juniorate year, who frequently humiliated me, traveled to
Maine. I met her by chance in the hallway of the convent. We stepped into
a side room. Turning toward me she said *"By asking your forgiveness will you
change your mind and stay on in the Congregation?"* No. *Too late,* I replied. She
seemed disappointed by my response. I was surprised by her apology and
reaction.

Mother Mary Joy and I shopped for clothes. I would leave as I had
entered, possessing only the clothes on my back. I had no interest with
fashion. I did not remember my size. I chose a coat and dress two sizes
too big and much too long - a fact I was to learn from my mother weeks

later. I hardly cared what I looked like. I had not thought much about life after the convent. I just wanted to leave.

On the long trip to the airport, we all chatted animatedly, trying to mask our gloom. For a fleeting moment, I wanted to go back, to say it was a mistake. I loved the Church. I loved the Congregation. What was I doing? Inside, I felt panicky. I boarded the plane with a heavy heart, fighting back the tears. I was doing what I had to do. I was ending an era in my life. I was doing it for peace of mind. But why didn't I feel joyous, relieved, free?

I closed my eyes as the plane took off. I was leaving the convent. How had I come to this point from the enthusiastic, joyful, lively, eager postulant of ten and a half years before? I had failed somehow. I thought of the mementos of those years that I had found carefully folded on my clothes shelf. There, almost untouched, was the slip of paper on which was written my religious name, Sister Rachel Mary of Jesus, as well as my identification number, 15575. I had received both on my vow day and kept the slip sacredly among my few possessions.

I was finally leaving! It was very hard for me to absorb. I thought of Hammarskjold's reflection on the Himalayan climbers:

"While thinking of those who had succeeded I could not forget those who had failed. They had been many and their glory written into the history of the mountain is that they went to the limits of the humanly possible and were defeated only by circumstances beyond human mastery."

Was it true? Had I done the humanly possible? I hoped I had...

AFTERTHOUGHTS

I left the convent on December 30, 1967, flying to Boston, where my mother and sister had relocated.

After only two days of nonstop crying, I was fairly confident that I had made the right decision.

I found a job with the Harvard School of Public Health's Department of Psychiatric Epidemiology, which led to a full time summer job with the team in Nova Scotia.

In June 1968, while driving to Nova Scotia, I completely wrecked my car in a freak accident. After extricating myself, I glanced at the wrecked car and thought to myself, as a great sense of relief swept over me, "At least, I don't have to report this to my superior!"

I realized how much the restrictions of convent life had weighed on me. Instead of thinking how lucky I was to be unhurt, I thought of not having to report the damage to my superior.

The summer job was a success. If I agreed to work in Nova Scotia for a year. Dr. Leighton guaranteed admission into a new PhD program in the School of Public Health. Feeling that I was already too old to delay graduate school, (I was 28!), I entered the PhD program at Brandeis in Anthropology that fall.

After three years of study – completing the course work and the qualifying exams, I decided not to pursue the two years of field work in Haiti.

In the meantime, I had met a young professor and decided instead to marry him. Now out of graduate school, I sought a job.

Through my contacts at the Harvard School of Public Health I was offered a job as a research assistant to the psychiatrist at The Catholic Guild for All the Blind (now renamed the Carroll Center for the Blind) in Newton, Massachusetts. In 1976, I was appointed executive director of the agency as it teetered on the edge of bankruptcy.

The agency survived and even thrived. I've had a very satisfying career helping to salvage an important institution, an institution which provides valuable services to persons who are newly blinded.

All the while my husband and I raised two wonderful sons who give us great pleasure and pride. We have had a happy 41-year marriage despite the differences in our religious backgrounds. He is now a retired professor of mathematics, and computer science.

My almost eleven years in the convent informed my life, and testing me so severely that I never again questioned my ability to survive any trauma and tribulation, any test of my character. The convents are no longer the rigid militaristic institutions they were when I entered on August 2, 1957.

In a way I was lucky that it was such a wrenching experience; if instead of Maine, I had been sent to Africa where the sisters had much more freedom- where a friend founded a college and another founded clinics in the bush - I might not have left the convent. I was stifled by the oppressive authoritarian structure. My family understood far better than I that I was not suited for a life of total obedience and submission- it was just too contrary to my natural personality.

During 1968 — a year of turmoil in the world-- many left. I was amazed to discover years later that the number of Daughters of the Spirit worldwide had fallen from 5,000 to 2,500. The ex-sisters and the remaining sisters stayed on good terms and organized reunions at the site of our former Novitiate. We also met former and current sisters at high school reunions. At a reunion at Christ the King, Mother Joseph, former principal and superior of that convent approached me to ask forgiveness. *"Well, it all seems so long ago now and forgotten"*, I said. *"Yes, of course I forgive you"*.

This book was mostly written between 1968-1971, while I was in graduate school. It began as a cathartic effort to relieve the emotional burden I felt upon leaving the convent.

At that time I wrote the following:

I believe that for the most part religious orders have seen their heyday and will never again reach the levels of popularity they did during certain centuries of church history. The Western world has grown too cold, too cynical and too self-indulged.

I believe Religious orders killed themselves by not responding to the needs and demands of the time. They were too busy preserving the past to deal with the present and plan for the future.

Where are the sister-lawyers who could serve as advocates for the poor?

Where are the sister-doctors to operate third world clinics or urban inner city clinics?

Where are the compassionate, incorruptible nurse-sisters to run the needed homes for the elderly?

Where are the sister-nurses and sister-teachers to work with teenage mothers who having never been mothered themselves are now unable to cope with their children?

Where are the sister-psychologists to run the drug and alcohol treatment centers?

Every day the world is scandalized by some new revelation of abuse from its members.

I do not want this book to be a shock to religious sisters and the Church's faithful body of believers. I truly believe I am a better person because of my almost eleven years in religious life.

The sisters that I lived with and met in those years were truly exceptional women,-more generous, more self-sacrificing, more able to derive satisfaction and joy from "little things" more so than the majority of lay persons. The sisters were detached from the profound materialism that engulfs society today.'

To readers who say I did not portray the sisters in this way, then I have failed

.

APPENDIX A –Sisters in order of appearance

Sister Mary Clare, my high school teacher who "sponsored" my entry into the order of nuns. She was the principal of the academy during my first year of teaching. Page 10

Mother Marie Alexandre, the Mistress of Postulants who was elected to the governing council in Rome. Page 16

Mother Michael, the Mistress of Novices who became the Provincial Superior while I was a novice Page 19

Mother Mary Kathleen, the second Mistress of novices who replaced Mother Michael when the latter was named Provincial Superior. Page 19

Sister Dorothy, Sister Fiorella two older candidates, already nurses, who entered with our group in 1957

Mother Mary Ambrose, the Rome-trained theologian who became the Superior of the Juniorate when it is initiated after the General Chapter of 1957. Page 67

Sister Constance Mary, Sister Fiorella's name in religion. Page 73

Sister Caitlen, from New York (O'Shea) who entered on August 2, 1957 with my group of postulants. Page77

Sister Louis Mary, from New York, entered on August 2, 1957 with my group of postulants and later taught with me at the Academy. Page77

Sister Elena, from New York, entered on August 2, 1957 with my group of postulants and was later assigned to the College Community. Page77

Sister Florence Jane, from New York, entered on August 2, 1957 with my group of postulants and later taught with me at the Academy. Page78

Sister Herman, sister who was in charge of the kitchen in the college community. Page 85

Mother Marie Mathilde, the volatile Superior of the College Community. Page 84

APPENDIX B- ORIGINAL CUSTOMS LIST

Scanned copy of the Customs given to me at the four o'clock instruction

WISDOM'S 'little' CUSTOMS

FIDELITY is the outgrowth of LOVE. "La fine fleur de l'Amour" (Marmion)

Virgin, Most Faithful, pray for us.
"Très pur Coeur de Marie, je me confie en Vous!"

THE CHAPEL

1. Do I always answer the bell promptly and take my line for chapel noiselessly ?
2. Do I always go into the chapel in grey, with my sleeves down ?
3. Do I hold my Rosary when entering ? (asking Mary to enter with me)
4. Do I always take Holy Water when entering ?
5. Do I make a slight inclination when passing in front of the Superior's place ?
6. Do I genuflect together with the others ?
7. Do I keep any books I may be bringing into chapel in my sleeves ?
8. Do I lift my skirt a little when about to kneel ?
9. If I arrive late do I remain in back until the Veni Sancte etc. is said ?
10. When late, do I report to the Mistress or Sister in charge ?
11. Do I always kneel and make an act of adoration when I arrive at my place in chapel ?
12. Do I always cover my hands with my sleeves, whenever possible ?
13. Do I pick up my cloak (if wearing it) when sitting down, and pull it down when standing ?
14. If I am obliged to leave, do I ask permission ?(except for regular charges)
15. Do I always bow to the Tabernacle when I pass in front of it ?
16. Do I always go into chapel prepared ?
17. Do I sit at the right time, if I feel the need, during the rosary ?
18. Do I stand at the right time, if I have been sitting during the rosary ?
19. Do I sit and stand in a manner befitting the Divine Presence ?
20. Do I kneel correctly , not leaning on my arms nor slouching ?
21. Do I avoid turning around to look when someone leaves or enters ?
22. Do I ask permission to open and close windows ?
23. Do I pass the paten correctly ?
24. Are all my books covered?...with the right type of paper ?
25. Do I avoid loud yawning and any other impoliteness or indelicacy ?
26. Do I avoid making useless noise ?...turning unnecessary pages ?

OFFICE AND PRAYERS

1. Do I answer all vocal prayers ?
2. Do I say my prayers aloud but not shouting ? "Pray your prayers, don't say them"
3. Do I say my prayers piously and distinctly ?
4. Do I do my best to keep the tone neither raising nor lowering it myself ?
5. Do I always hold up my book when praying or reading ?
6. Do I always put something under my finger when using a book ?
7. Do I follow all my prayers in the prescribed book ? (for 5 years)
8. Am I careful not to change the wording of the prayers ?
9. Do I pause for two counts at the mediant of the psalms ?
10. Do I endeavor to maintain a proper speed ?
11. Do I bow and incline at all the places indicated ?
12. Do I make all the necessary signs of the cross, finger to lips, hand on heart etc.,
    that are necessary ?
13. Am I faithful to bowing reverently during the Gloria Patri ...to Spiritu Sancto?
14. When it is my turn to say prayers, do I prepare carefully...checking on special
    intentions, list of the dead, special feasts, examens, meditations etc. ?
15. Do I always read an Examen on Mary on Saturdays ?
16. Do I make use of the card giving the directives for saying the prayers ?
17. Do I ask a penance if I have said the prayers badly and given cause for distract-ion ?
18. Am I persuaded that the fervor of the Community Prayers depends largely
    on the care and preparation I take in saying the prayers ?

THE NOVITIATE

1. Do I bless myself with holy water when entering?
2. Do I always arrive on time....when late do I kiss the floor?
3. Do I bow when passing the crucifix?
4. Am I attentive when the Veni Sancte is said...and other prayers?
5. Do I listen attentively to the instructions?
6. Do I cover my feet when sitting?
7. Do I keep my hands in my sleeves when not writing or sewing?
8. Do I take down the thoughts that strike me most...at least one at each instruction?
9. Do I always have my lessons prepared?
10. Do I always stand when addressed?
11. Do I answer loudly enough?
12. Do I always prepare the place for the Mistress?
13. Do I endeavor to see God in the Person giving the Instruction?
14. When general or personal remarks are made do I kneel, say thank-you, and kiss the
15. Do I avoid looking out of windows and useless curiosity?   floor?
16. Do I avoid useless conversation before and after instructions and idle remarks during instructions?
17. Do I regard the Novitiate as a sanctuary?
18. Do I always have sewing when I am supposed to?
19. Do I refrain from doing anything else during instructions?
20. Do I ask permission to change my place when it is necessary?
21. Do I thank Father and the Mistresses for the Instructions?
22. Do I avoid unnecessary noise in the novitiate....moving chairs quietly...sitting and standing noiselessly?
23. Do I always leave everything in order?

THE DORMITORY

1. Do I take Holy Water morning and night?
2. Do I get up at the first signal of the bell?
3. Do I put on underskirt first thing on rising?.....stockings also?
4. Do I say my morning offering (on my knees)?.....and the Angelus?
5. Do I kiss my holy habit when putting it on and taking it off?
6. Do I empty my basin before making my bed?
7. Am I faithful to making my bed as I was taught?
8. Do I strip my bed twice a week....and turn the mattress?
9. Do I put my rosary in my pocket (or leave it off) while making my bed?
10. Do I keep my night table in order?.....my basin, glass, combs and brushes clean?
11. Do I carry a towel with me to get water?
12. Do I wipe up any water I may accidently spill?
13. Do I ask permission to go to the dormitory during the day?
14. Do I ask permission for sewing, writing (ink) etc., in my cell?
15. Do I fold the curtains in the pleats?
16. Do I avoid putting pins in my curtains; sewing on tapes if necessary?
17. Do I always wear underskirt, night-point and bonnet in the dormitory?
18. Do I wash and dress modestly?
19. Do I say a Hail Mary and an Act of Contrition first thing at night, before removing even a pin?
20. Do I try to fold my spread with another, whenever possible...and remove pin?
21. Do I put night-point on before taking off kerchief?
22. Do I put clothes on the chair (and hanger) correctly?
23. Do I always let down the sleeves of my Holy Habit?
24. If I take water for the next morning, is it cold?
25. Am I always in bed on time? Do I report faithfully if I am not?
26. Do I take underskirt off, last thing at night?
27. Am I faithful to keeping Grand Silence....to the spirit of Grand Silence?
28. Do I report immediately the next morning if I have broken Grand Silence?
29. As much as possible, do I avoid sitting on my bed?
30. Do I avoid leaving things in my cell or on the night table during the day?

THE REFECTORY

"Whether you eat or whether you drink, do all for the glory of God!"

1. Do I bless myself with Holy Water when entering the refectory ?
2. Do I bow when I pass the crucifix ?..... the Mistresses ?
√ 3. Do I say my prayers attentively ?
√ 4. Do I   follow my prayers in my prayer book ?
√ 5. Do I stop circulating when the Gloria Patri and Benedicite are said ?
6. Do I avoid circulating when others are performing their practices ?
7. After graces, do I bow to the Crucifix before bowing to the Mistresses ?
8. Do I present myself to my Superior when I am late (graces finished) and kiss the floor?
9. Do I listen attentively to the reading ?
10. Do I go simply to La Chère Soeur , with my sleeves down and on my knees, ask for a knife if I have forgotten my own.....and then kiss the floor ?
11. Do I place my stool and open and close my drawer quietly ?
12. Do I prepare my reading, making use of the directives given ?
13. Do I read loudly and distinctly ?
14. Do I stop when the Martyrology or work of Fr.de Montfort is read ?
15. Do I observe silence at all times except when recreation is given ?
16. When I receive a remark for my reading or make some noticeable error, do I kiss the floor?
√ 17. Do I observe modesty of the eyes at table?
18. Do I place my napkin wrong side up ? Do I fold it correctly?
19. Do I wait until La Chère Soeur has served herself before starting service?
20. Do I take at least two pieces of bread at meals ?
√ 21. Do I make a spiritual communion at each meal ?
22. Do I try to take what is nearest to me on the plate, not choosing or picking ?
23. Do I serve myself reasonably ?
24. Do I perform some mortifications at each meal ?
25. Do I avoid putting my knife to my mouth ?
26. Do I eat slowly and in a polite manner, being attentive to all rules of politeness given ?
27. Do I wipe my lips before and after drinking ?
28. Do I chew my food with my mouth closed ?
29. Do I avoid drinking with food in my mouth ?
30. Do I hold my knife and fork properly ?
31. Do I refrain from touching my neighbor's cup, spoon,etc., to signify what I want?
32. Do I pass the dishes across the table .... and hold the plate for myself ?
33. Do I help finish dishes? Am I attentive to the needs of my sisters ?
34. Do I pick up crumbs at meals ..... at collation ?
√ 35. Do I avoid stretching in front of another to get something ?
36. Do I ask for bread , water etc., by signs ?
37. Do I avoid coughing and blowing my nose at table ?
38. Do I facilitate service by piling up dishes etc.?
39. Do I wait for the Superior to finish folding her napkin before folding mine?
40. Do I put dishes on hot plates ?   (except breakfast & fast nights)
41. Do I pick the dishes up to pass them, not sliding them along?
42. Do I use a reasonable amount of water to wash my fork and spoon ?
43. Do I refrain from putting my elbows on the table and stretching my legs under the table?
44. Do I sit up straight?
45. Do I faithfully avoid keeping food in my drawer?
46. Do I eat bread with my meals ...even with dessert (except fruit in morning)?
47. Do I avoid sliding food off the serving plate ?

COLLATION:

1. Do I take my collation at the proper place ?..... in silence ?
2. Do I help finish the dishes if leftovers are served ?
√ 3. Do I pick up my crumbs and leave my place clean ?
4. Do I try to face the crucifix while eating?
5. Do I serve myself reasonably (2 pieces of bread if possible)?
6. Do I perform some acts of mortification at collation,especially on Saturdays and penance days?
7. Do I avoid all dissipation ?

Am I faithful to the performance of my charges in the refectory and at the dishes?
Am I generous in offering my services...in doing dishes? Do I always wear an apron?

THE CLASS

1. Do I always come on time for class ?
2. Do I do the lessons assigned ?
3. Am I careful not to interrupt the Mistress or Sister by hasty questions or answers?
4. Do I answer in a loud , clear voice?
5. Do I avoid listening to remarks given privately to another ?
6. Do I refrain from answering a question addressed to another?
7. Do I keep my desk in order...also the Community desk and shelves ?
8. Do I refrain from writing in text-books ?
9. Do I keep all my books covered....with clean covers ?
10. Do I avoid having too many library books out ?
11. Do I place books back in the library correctly ?
12. Do I mark the library account card....and follow faithfully all other library rules?
13. Do I avoid taking things out of another's desk without permission ?
14. Do I avoid leaving things lying around the study-room...on my desk or chair ?
15. Do I avoid speaking to my sisters during study time without permission ?
16. Am I careful not to waste Scotch Tape,paper, etc. ,using all in a spirit of poverty?
17. Do I keep my desk in line with the others ?...and place my chair straight when
18. Do I avoid looking at anything on the desk of others ?   leaving?
19. Do I always ask permission to leave the classroom ?
20. Do I always present myself to the Mistress when I am late ?

MENAGE

1. Do I report promptly to my ménage ?
2. Do I begin by a prayer ?
3. Do I follow all instructions that have been given me regarding my ménage ?
4. Do I strive to do my work very well and keep my ménage spotlessly clean ?
5. Do I skate well ?....sweep, mop and dust thoroughly ?....every day ?
6. Do I pick up things lying around ?
7. Do I seethings to be done .... and then do thm ?
8. Do I clean my mops , brooms, skates etc., every day ? ... in the right place ?
9. Do I keep my box in order ?..... and the ménage closet ? ..service sink etc.?
10. Do I fold my apron neatly in the box ?
11. Do I ask permission to take a clean apron ?
12. Do I give myself wholeheartedly to "grand ménage"?
13. Am I faithful to all responsibilities accompanying my charge...windows, doors etc?

SEWING

1. Do I apply myself to sewing and mending as a duty of my state of life ?
2. Do I keep my sewing neatly in a box ?
3. Do I keep my needle case (small one after profession) and thimble in my under pocket?
4. Do I ask permission to undo work that has been badly done ?..... and ask a penance
   when a considerable amount has to be undone?
5. Am I careful to follow all directions?
6. Do I always wear my thimble ?
7. Do I always take needles out of my work when I am finished sewing ?
8. Do I place my name tape on my work ?
9. Do I do Community work at all times except evening recreations and Thursday and
10. Am I careful not to waste thread, mending cotton etc.?   Saturday afternoons?
11. Do I keep my stockings and personal clothing mended and in good condition ?
12. Do I endeavor to do my part in Community mending....coiffes,kerchiefs,cornettes etc.

ACCUSATIONS

1. Am I attentive to my turn for accusations?
2. Do I use the right formula and follow the directives given ?
3. Do I word them correctly,accusing no one nor excusing myself ?
4. If I am not sure, do I have them checked by a Mistress ?
5. Do I accuse myself of about 3 and never more than 4 faults ?
6. Do I word my accusation humbly and simply ?
7. Do I listen attentively to the advice given me and believe it to be the word of God?

D.S.

RECREATION

1. Do I offer my recreation to Mary asking her to sanctify it ?
2. Am I as prompt in reporting to recreation as to other exercises ?
3. Do I refrain from talking until I have reached the place of recreation?
4. Am I faithful in observing regular places even during recreation ?
5. Do I wait for the group to report from dishes, refectory etc.?
6. Do I wait until we are three to talk ? (Novitiate)
7. Do I prepare a place for the Mistress? Do I always include her in the conversation?
8. Do I pause when a Mistress arrives, to greet her good angel ?
9. Do I prepare places for those who are at dishes and obliged to arrive late ?
10. Do I take as companions those Providence has provided for me ?
11. Do I speak only to those I am with on a walk ?
12. Do I avoid being always with the same Sisters ?
13. Do I greet everyone with the salutation,"I greet your good angel"?
14. On walks, am I careful to give good example....to walk in line ?....not to talk
    and laugh in a rough and common manner ?
15. Do I refrain from breaking branches and picking flowers etc. ?
16. Do I conduct myself with religious modesty when playing games ?
17. Do I avoid all uncharitable conversations ?
18. Do I avoid using all incorrect and slang language ?
19. Do I refrain from using familiar language ?
20. Do I avoid all familiarity such as touching another, holding hands or pulling
    another by the Holy Habit ?
21. Do I avoid speaking of myself and of my family immoderately ?
22. Do I avoid passing around letters and clippings etc. without permission ?
23. Do I avoid discussing indiscreet subjects such as health and direction etc.?
24. Do I give in to the opinions of my sisters in indifferent things ?
25. Am I careful not to interrupt others ?
26. Do I refrain from monopolizing the conversation ? Do I contribute my share ?
27. Do I endeavor to maintain a cheerful, bright atmosphere ?
28. Am I a good listener ?
29. Do I speak and laugh in a moderate tone ?
30. Do I accept a joke at my expense ?
31. Do I listen attentively to the remarks ?
32. Am I faithful in making 2 remarks a week ....2 maxims a year ?
33. Do I wait until permission is given to talk after remarks are given ?
34. Do I politely listen when the Mistress (later on, the Superior) is speaking to the group ?
35. Do I leave for my bath at the proper time ?
36. Do I say my night prayer beforehand, on the day of my bath ...at prescribed time ?
37. Do I leave the place of recreation only with permission ?
38. Do I report on my return ?
39. Do I frequently call to mind the presence of God during recreation ?
40. Do I at least try to speak French on Wednesdays and Saturdays(for a time at least)?
41. Am I faithful to Community sewing ? Do I do my part ?
42. Do I keep busy with work during recreation even at 4 o'clock and 10 o'clock ?
43. Do I leave the room in order after recreation is over ?
44. Do I stop talking at the first stroke of the bell ?
45. Do I say the noon and night prayers with fervor and devotion, arriving on time
    for the night prayer in chapel ?

SILENCE and REGULAR PLACES

1. Am I faithful to use the greeting,"Our Lord Jesus Christ be praised " during silence time ?
2. Do I speak in a subdued tone in time of silence ?
3. Do I use as few words as possible when speaking during the time of silence ?
4. Do I avoid breaking silence by signs, writing notes etc.,unnecessarily ?
5. Do I stop speaking at the first sound of the bell ?
6. Do I refrain from taking recreation before it is given ?
7. Do I speak in a lady-like tone ?
8. Do I refrain from passing a remark when some one else is speaking ?
9. Do I ask permission before talking in class ? (Novitiate)

SILENCE and REGULAR PLACES cont'd

10. Do I report when I break silence ?
11. Do I faithfully and scrupulously observe Grand Silence and report if I break it?
12. Do I avoid breaking silence of action ?.
13. Do I perform the penance if I miss ?
14. Do I open and close doors noiselessly ? ..... refectory drawer ?
15. Do I lift my chair when moving it in the refectory ?..... other furniture ?
16. Do I observe silence in moving about .... in walking...on stairs etc.?
17. Do I avoid banging the benches in chapel with my Rosary ?
18. Do I keep perfect silence in all regular or silence places (dormitories, halls, stairs, refectory, pantry, etc.)
19. Do I observe the rules of religious modesty and recollection in walking , sitting standing, etc. ?
20. Am I convinced that I will make no progress in the interior life if I am not faithful to the rule of silence ?

LAUNDRY - VESTRY - COIFFING

1. Do I wash the sleeves of my tunic before sending it to the wash .(Novitiate)
2. Do I turn my tunic inside out before sending it to the wash ?
3. Do I tie my stockings together before sending them to the wash ?
4. Do I turn apron pockets inside out and brush the dirt from lining ?
5. Do I tie apron strings individually ?
6. Do I take out all pins from clothing before putting them to the wash ?
7. Do I untie the tapes of my coiffe and roll it as prescribed when putting it to wash?
8. Am I delicate in putting my clothes to the wash, washing out all stains that might be offensive ?
9. Do I avoid sending too much clothes to the laundry..... washing out my own stock- and underwear, if need be, during the week ?
10. Do I put each piece of clothing in the respective laundry bag, in the manner req-
11. Do I always arrive at coiffing on time and report if I do not ?   uested ?
12. Do I take the kerchief and coiffe that are given me...without showing preference?
13. Do I kiss my cornette and coiffe before putting them on ?
14. Am I faithful to putting pins in my cornette and coiffe in the manner prescribed ?
15. Do I take the clothes I need for Sunday off my shelf on Saturday afternoon ?
16. Do I ask permission to coiffe myself at other than prescribed times ?
17. Do I refrain from letting others fix my coiffe, kerchief etc., without permission?
18. Do I polish my shoes every week and clean my walking shoes & boots occasionally?
19. Do I polish the shoes of the Mistresses and Sisters ?
20. Are all my clothes marked neatly and legibly ?
21. Do all my stockings have tapes ?
22. Do I ask permission to change pockets and underskirt when necessary ?
23. Are all my clothes in good condition ?
24. Do I mend my clothing when it begins to wear ?
25. Are my shelves neat ?...... and marked with my name ?
26. Do I mark my name on the reserve coiffe on my shelf ?

PARLOR

1. Do I ask permission to go to parlor? ....to receive and accept gifts ?
2. Before parlor, do I prepare my room ?..... Do I clean it up after parlor is over ?
3. Do I say a Hail Mary and Veni Sancte before going to parlor ?
4. Do I receive my parents with respect and affection? Do I show gartitude for the visi·
5. Do I introduce my parents to the Mistresses? Do I avoid using "La Chère Soeur" when speaking of my Mistress ?
6. Do I bring my family to chapel for a visit? Do I keep within the limits of grounds?
7. Do I avoid opening packages in parlor ? Do I politely refuse offers of food etc.?
8. Do I avoid speaking of things that should not be spoken of ?....posing for pictures?
9. Do I walk modestly, behaving like a true novice, modest and simple....hands in sleeves
10. Do I leave promptly at the bell or at the prescribed time ?
11. Do I see my Superior and give an account of my parlor...and hand in gifts received?
12. Do I always make up my parayers if I have missed any because of parlor ?

RELATIONS WITH MISTRESSES

Anything said should be applied to relations with Superiors in the Houses.

1. Do I treat with respect anything that is for the use of the Mistress ?
2. Do I incline respectfully whenever I pass a Mistress ? (Ave Christi)
3. DO I hold open the door and let the Mistress pass first?..do I offer to carry things?
4. Do I stand when a Mistress enters a room ? ....When she addresses me ?
5. Do I respect the place of the Mistress ?
6. Do I look for occasions to render services to the Mistresses ?
7. Am I thoughtful and delicate in rendering those services ?
8. Do I present the Mistress her cape before chapel?...and hang it up after chapel?
9. Do I make sure that there is a chair and footbench prepared for the Mistress at recreation, prayers etc.?
10. Do I greet the Mistress at recreation ?..and always include her in the conversation?
11. Do I present myself to the Mistress when I arrive late ?..and say where I come from?
12. Do I thank the Mistress for any remark she may see fit to make ?
13. Do I apologise, religiously and on my knees, when I am at fault...have been rude etc.
14. Do I always thank the Mistress for any general remark or public announcement she may see fit to make ?
15. Do I avoid all words of criticism or censure with regard to my Mistresses ?
16. Do I avoid going to see the Mistress in my work apron...sleeves rolled up etc.?
17. Do I always politely add, Ma Chère Soeur, when addressing a Mistress ?
18. Do I always speak of my First Mistress as La Chère Soeur ?

PERMISSIONS

Everything done with permission is done with a blessing .

1. Do I ask all my permissions religiously and on my knees ?
2. Do I lift my white apron and skirt a little before kneeling ?
3. Do I put my hands in my sleeves and assume a respectful attitude ?
4. Do I ask permission to go to the dormitory outside of prescribed times ?
5. Do I ask permission to change my coiffe....to fix another's coiffe ?
6. Do I ask permission to change kerchief?.... to turn it ?
7. Do I ask permission to wear baguettes ?
8. Do I ask permission to take a new bar of soap..toothpaste...etc.?
9. Do I ask permission to finish my bed?....Do I kiss the floor afterwards?
10. Do I ask permission to write in ink or sew in my cell ?
11. Do I ask permission to wash my table napkin ?.... or change it ?
12. Do I ask permission to leave for my bath at the prescribed time?
13. Do I ask permission to go to the pharmacy ?
14. Do I ask La Chère Soeur permission to make little mortifications ?
15. Do I ask my list of permissions at Direction?
16. Do I ask necessary dispensations ?
17. Do I ask permission to exchange charges with other sisters ?
18. Do I ask permission to give or receive anything ?....To lend or borrow ?
19. Do I ask permission to show pictures, clippings, poems etc.?
20. Do I ask permission to put holy pictures in my letters ?
21. Do I ask La Chère Soeur permission to write extra letters ?   days?
22. Do I ask permission to mend my clothes ? to mend stockings on other than prescribed
23. Do I ask permission to speak with the Sisters of the Community...postulants?
24. Do I ask permission before reading a book.... magazine etc.?
25. Do I ask permission to write or do anything else during spiritual reading ?
26. Do I ask permission to sing during recreation ?
27. Do I ask permission to leave the room ?
28. Do I ask my necessary permissions before Grand Silence ?
29. If I am obliged to presume a permission, do I always render an account ?
30. Do I avoid asking permission in corridors , regular places etc.,
31. Am I in the disposition to accept the Superior's answer to my permission as the Will of God for me ?
32. Do I ask permission of the Sister replacing the Superior just as faithfully as I would if the Superior were present ? (not on my knees, however)

Afterthoughts

ABOUT THE AUTHOR

Rachel Ethier Rosenbaum was born in Van Buren Maine, a town on the Canadian border on May 26, 1940 .She was the President of the Carroll Center for the Blind, Newton, MA from 1976-2009. After retiring, she became the executive director of CANnect. CANnect is a consortium of providers of accessible online courses for the blind. www.cannect.org. CANnect aims to be an aggregator, the One Stop Shopping (Like Orbitz, Travelocity, Kayak) for persons who are blind or visually impaired and their teachers and families to locate accessible and usable online courses and other resources.

Rachel lives in Newton, Massachusetts with Peter, her husband of 41 years. They have two children David lives in Raleigh North Carolina and Joel in Seattle. They recently welcomed their 3rd grandchild into the family.